CREATIVITY AND INNOVATION
IN ORGANIZATIONAL TEAMS

CREATIVITY AND INNOVATION IN ORGANIZATIONAL TEAMS

Edited by

Leigh L. Thompson
*Kellogg School of Management,
Northwestern University*

Hoon-Seok Choi
Sungkyunkwan University

LEA LAWRENCE ERLBAUM ASSOCIATES, PUBLISHERS
2006 Mahwah, New Jersey   London

Lawrence Erlbaum Associates, Inc., Publishers
10 Industrial Avenue
Mahwah, New Jersey 07430
www.erlbaum.com

Cover design by Kathryn Houghtaling Lacey

Library of Congress Cataloging-in-Publication Data

Creativity and innovation in organizational teams/[edited by] Leigh L. Thompson,
Hoon-Seok Choi.
    p.   cm. — (Organization and management)
"Chapters of this book were presented at a conference held at the Kellogg School of
Management in June, 2003"—Preface.
Includes bibliographical references and index.
ISBN 0-8058-4968-8 (alk. paper)
    1. Teams in the workplace—Congresses.   2. Organizational behavior—Congresses.
3. Creative thinking—Social aspects—Congresses.   I. Thompson, Leigh L.   II. Choi,
Hoon-Seok.   III. Kellogg School of Management.   IV. LEA's organization and management
series.

HD66.C74   2005
658.4'022—dc22
                                                                        2004063595
                                                                        CIP

Books published by Lawrence Erlbaum Associates are printed on acid-free paper,
and their bindings are chosen for strength and durability.

Printed in the United States of America
10   9   8   7   6   5   4   3   2   1

Contents

v

II TEAM AND GROUP DYNAMICS OF BRAINSTORMING

III ORGANIZATIONAL INFLUENCES OF CREATIVITY AND INNOVATION

Series Foreword

Approaches to the study of creativity in organizations seemed to have blossomed, with the problem being tackled by multiple disciplines at multiple levels of analyses. Thompson and Choi's collection of chapters represents this diversity of interests in creativity and an attempt to bring them together. The collection, for instance, addresses the microsociology of creativity, psychological safety in innovative teams, and creative templates in negotiations. We trust you will find the volume as stimulating as we did. We are pleased to welcome Thompson and Choi's book to the series.

Arthur P. Brief
Tulane University

James Walsh
University of Michigan

LEA'S ORGANIZATION AND MANAGEMENT SERIES

Series Editors
Arthur Brief
Tulane University
James P. Walsh
University of Michigan

Associate Series Editor
Sara L. Rynes
University of Iowa

Ashforth (Au.): *Role Transitions in Organizational Life: An Identity-Based Perspective*

Bartunek (Au.): *Organizational and Educational Change: The Life and Role of a Change Agent Group*

Beach (Ed.): *Image Theory: Theoretical and Empirical Foundations*

Brett/Drasgow (Eds.): *The Psychology of Work: Theoretically Based Empirical Research*

Darley/Messick/Tyler (Eds.): *Social Influences on Ethical Behavior in Organizations*

Denison (Ed.): *Managing Organizational Change in Transition Economies*

Early/Gibson (Aus.): *New Perspectives on Transnational Work Teams*

Elsback (Au.): *Organizational Perception Management*

Garud/Karnoe (Eds.): *Path Dependence and Creation*

Jacoby (Au.): *Employing Bureaucracy: Managers, Unions, and the Transformation of Work in the 20th Century*, Revised Edition

Kossek/Lambert (Eds.): *Work and Life Integration: Organizational, Cultural, and Individual Perspectives*

Lampel/Shamsie/Lant (Eds.): *The Business of Culture: Strategic Respective on Entertainment and Media*

About the Editors

Leigh L. Thompson is the J. Jay Gerber Distinguished Professor of Dispute Resolution & Organizations in the Kellogg School of Management at Northwestern University. Her research focuses on negotiation, team creativity, and learning. In 1991, Dr. Thompson received the multiyear Presidential Young Investigator award from the National Science Foundation for her research on negotiation and conflict resolution, and she has received several National Science Foundation grants for her research. In 1994–1995, Dr. Thompson was a Fellow at the Center for Advanced Study in the Behavioral Sciences in Stanford, California. At Kellogg, she is the director of the Kellogg Team and Group Research Center. She is the director of the Leading High Impact Teams executive program at Kellogg and the director of the Behavioral Laboratory at Kellogg.

Leigh Thompson has published over 90 research articles and chapters. She has authored four books: *The Mind and Heart of the Negotiator* (3rd ed.), *Shared Cognition in Organizations* (with John Levine and David Messick), *Making the Team* (2nd ed.), and *The Social Psychology of Organizational Behavior: Key Readings*. She is a member of the editorial boards of *Organizational Behavior and Human Decision Processes, Journal of Personality and Social Psychology, Journal of Experimental Social Psychology, Journal of Behavioral Decision Making*, and *International Journal of Conflict Management*.

B.A., 1982, Communication Studies, Northwestern University; M.A., 1984, Education, University of California, Santa Barbara; Ph.D., 1988, Psychology, Northwestern University.

Hoon-Seok Choi is Associate Professor in the Department of Psychology at Sungkyunkwan University in Seoul, Korea. From 2003 to 2004 he was Assistant Professor of Organizational Behavior and Human Resource Management at the University of Ottawa's School of Business, and from 2001 to 2003 he was the Kellogg Team and Group Research Center (KTAG) Post-Doctoral Fellow at the Kellogg School of Management, where he taught MBA courses on teamwork. His research focuses on group composition, group development, and team creativity. While at Kellogg, he supervised the Kellogg Team Consultant Training Program and participated in a range of team-building workshops for managers and executives.

He has presented his research across the United States and Korea and is a member of the American Psychological Association, the Academy of Management, and the Society for Personality and Social Psychology.

B.A., 1992, Psychology, Sungkyunkwan University, Seoul, Korea; M.A., 1994, Psychology, Sungkyunkwan University; Ph.D., 2001, Psychology, University of Pittsburgh.

Contributors

Deborah Ancona
Massachusetts Institute of Technology

Henrik Bresman
Massachusetts Institute of Technology

Hoon-Seok Choi
Sungkyunkwan University

Amy C. Edmondson
Harvard University

Doris Fay
University of Aston

Cameron M. Ford
University of Central Florida

David R. Gerkens
Texas A&M University

Jacob Goldenberg
Hebrew University of Jerusalem

Andrew B. Hargadon
University of California, Davis

Eyal Maoz
Hebrew University of Jerusalem

Josephine P. Mogelof
Harvard University

Toshihiko Nakui
University of Texas at Arlington

Bernard A. Nijstad
University of Amsterdam

Dina Nir
Hebrew University of Jerusalem

Paul B. Paulus
University of Texas at Arlington

Vicky L. Putman
University of Texas at Arlington

Eric F. Rietzschel
University of Amsterdam

Claudia A. Sacramento
University of Aston

Eric L. Santanen
Bucknell University

Jami J. Shah
Arizona State University

Steven M. Smith
Texas A&M University

Wolfgang Stroebe
University of Utrecht

Leigh L. Thompson
Kellogg School of Management

Noe Vargas-Hernandez
Arizona State University

Michael A. West
University of Aston

Preface

The chapters of this book were presented at a conference held at the Kellogg School of Management in June 2003, titled, "Creativity and Innovation in Groups and Organizations." The conference presenters included behavioral scientists from psychology and organizational behavior. We had one simple rule for the conference—no one could talk about research that was already published. Rather, the goal was to discuss the latest, newest ideas and investigations.

The Kellogg Team and Group Research Center (KTAG) supported the conference. In addition, the Kellogg School of Management cosponsored the event. We are grateful for the generous support of the KTAG center and the Kellogg school on this project and the subsequent development of this book.

Assistance with the coordination of the conference and preparation of this volume was provided initially by Rachel Claff, who ran the conference beautifully. Subsequent administrative and editorial assistance was spearheaded by Sean McMillan, Cecelia Yu, and Aarthi Kuppuswamy, who worked with all the authors and reviewers on a breakneck production schedule.

This book is the first planned in a series of topical themes related to groups and teams. Every 2 years, the KTAG center at Kellogg hires a postdoctoral fellow in the area of groups and teams. The conference (and corresponding book) is a testament to their achievements at Kellogg and beyond. This book is lovingly dedicated to the past, present, and future KTAG postdoctoral fellows: Nancy Rothbard, Ken Savitsky, Hoon-Seok Choi, Kristin Behfar, and Sujn Lee. It is truly their intellect, energy, and generosity that make endeavors like this possible.

—Leigh L. Thompson
Hoon-Seok Choi

Introduction

The idea for a conference on creativity and innovation in organizations resulted from a collision of three events. First, we came to the conclusion that there are at least three definable *camps* of scholarship on creativity and innovation that may not be aware of each other. These camps represent research on group brainstorming, research on cognitive processes underlying creative thinking, and organizational processes and structures that facilitate or debilitate creativity and innovation. We wanted to introduce the young leaders of these different research traditions and see if they wanted to date. (They did!)

Second, the business climate has never been so keen on creativity. With over 30 books on creativity released in 2003 alone, companies and organizations are crying out for knowledge about how to build a better mousetrap. We were pompous enough to believe that we could assemble the people who could provide the answers.

Finally, the two of us wanted to memorialize the tremendous intellectual stimulation we had exchanged for KTAG's research and teaching.

The scholars who have written chapters in this book are diverse with respect to their training and backgrounds: some grew up in psychology departments, others in sociology departments, some even in computer science departments, and some (heaven forbid) have even done a tour of duty in the real world. Although the chapter authors are intellectually diverse, they are strikingly similar in terms of being at the apex of their careers—nearly uniformly young, dynamic, and producing cutting-edge research.

The volume is divided into three major parts: One focuses on individual-level cognitive processes (Part I), another on teams and group dynamics (Part II), and a third on organizational, macrolevel processes (Part III). The organization of this volume reflects a long-standing notion that creativity in the world of work is a joint outcome of three interdependent forces—individual thinking, group processes, and organizational environment.

Part I explores basic cognitive mechanisms that underlie creative thinking. Smith, Gerkens, Shah, and Vargas-Hernandez (chap. 1) discuss the cognitive foundations of creativity. They argue that attempts to understand creativity mandate investigations of basic principles and mechanisms of human cognition. In so doing, Smith and his co-authors discuss how basic cognitive processes such as memory, concepts and categorization, analogy, mental imagery, and meta-cognition affect people's ability to produce creative ideas. In addition, they explain cognitive underpinnings of several phenomena common to creative endeavors, such as fixation, incubation, the use of metaphor, and combination of ideas. Taking one step further, they propose a cognitive model of group creativity and discuss how the creative cognition approach can help better understand the creative process of groups. Using incubation as an example, Smith and his co-authors introduce intriguing findings from their ground-breaking research on creative cognition.

Santanen (chap. 2) proposes a cognitive network model of creativity that explains how and why creative solutions form in the human mind. Building on previous research in cognitive psychology and studies of creativity, he offers eight propositions, each of which is distinctively linked to creative solution generation. He also provides provocative findings illustrating the benefits of what he calls a *directed brainstorming*. Using a subtle, but powerful experimental manipulation, he explains how two seemingly contradictory processes—stimulating individuals to follow relatively long chains of spreading activation, versus exposing individuals to disparate mental frames in rapid succession—enhances creative problem solving.

Goldenberg, Nir, and Maoz (chap. 3) import their ground-breaking concept of *creativity templates* to the study of creative idea generation in negotiation context. Creativity templates represent a systematic approach to inventive thinking. Goldenberg et al. provide several compelling examples of how companies have used creativity templates to envision, develop, and bring to market new products. They describe four basic templates: attribute dependency, multiplication, replacement, and displacement. They work through careful applications of each template in the generation of new ideas for conflict resolution. They also describe the results of a study of how managers map the creativity templates onto actual negotiation outcomes.

Part II is devoted to understanding how groups and teams in organizational settings produce creative ideas and implement innovations. Paulus, Nakui, and Putman (chap. 4) provide a compelling, top–down view of what works and what does not work for brainstorming groups. They contrast the illusion of group productivity with the empirical research on the ineffectiveness of brainstorming groups. They propose three new rules for brainstorming: stay focused on the task (i.e., do not tell stories and do not explain ideas), keep the brainstorming going, and return to previous categories. They find dramatic support for the effectiveness of these techniques over and above groups that follow Osborn's initial four rules. As arguably the quintessential leader of brainstorming research, Paulus and his coauthors carefully separate practitioner-based recommendations from empirically proven recommendations.

Choi and Thompson (chap. 5) take up the question of whether it behooves organizations and their teams to tolerate and even encourage team reorganizations. After analyzing potential consequences of membership change in teams, they put forth a counterintuitive stimulation hypothesis and argue that changes in team membership stimulate team creativity. Choi and Thompson pinpoint three dynamics that happen when the team's borders are open rather than closed—teams become more task-focused, newcomers diversify the team's knowledge-base, and the presence of newcomers elicits social processes that are conducive to creativity. Choi and Thompson introduce empirical evidence for their proposition and urge researchers as well as practitioners to pay more attention to the brighter side of team reorganization.

Edmondson and Mogelof (chap. 6) explain how the presence of psychological safety in a team provides a critical foundation for creativity. Psychological safety encompasses the taken-for-granted beliefs that others will respond positively when a person takes a risk. Because the creative process involves divergent thinking, it is a risk. Edmondson and Mogelof investigated several project teams and measured psychological safety at key points in time during a project. More important, individual differences in terms of two of the Big Five personality factors—neuroticism and openness to experience—were associated with greater psychological safety in teams.

West, Sacramento, and Fay (chap. 7) distinguish creativity and innovation and discuss the paradoxical effects of external demands during the entire process of innovation in teams. They advance a proposition that high external demands, engendered by uncertainty, time pressure, and competition, inhibit creativity during early stages, but facilitate innovation at later stages via innovation implementation. West et al. carefully lay out the theoretical underpinnings of this proposition by illuminating how external demands interact with group task characteristics, diversity in group knowledge and skills, and the nature of group processes. Based firmly on his empirical research on team innovation for the past several decades, West and his co-authors make a number of specific and practical recommendations to promote creativity and innovation in work teams.

Nijstad, Rietzschel, and Stroebe (chap. 8) summarize group idea generation research and propose a combination of contributions framework for
analyzing group creativity. In this framework, they identify two important
factors that determine the overall effectiveness of groups: the resources
that group members bring to the group and the processes involved in the
way these resources are combined to yield group outcomes. Using this
framework, Nijstad and his co-authors discuss four specific principles gov-
erning the ability of groups to generate creative ideas. They first define the
potential creativity of groups based on the resources available and potential
contribution of group members. They then discuss how the creative potential of groups are facilitated or hindered by the way group members share,
process, and select ideas.

Part III contains three chapters that discuss the role of social, organizational context in which creative endeavors take place. Ancona and Bresman
(chap. 9) build on their ground-breaking investigations of the dynamics of
X-teams to build a theory of how innovative organizational actors beg, borrow, and steal outside the boundaries of their own team to import innovation. They carefully distinguish the process of creative idea generation from
the organizational tightrope of winning support for ideas and ultimately receiving organizational buy-in. They argue that the most innovative teams
have a marked disrespect for traditional teams and even organizational
boundaries, and that this fluidity drives the innovative process. They identify five key components of X-teams with respect to the innovative process:
external activity, extensive (network) ties, expandable tiers (managing up
and out), flexible membership, and coordination among ties.

Hargadon (chap. 10) argues that creativity involves two complementary,
but seemingly opposing, processes: bridging and building. Bridging, according to Hargadon, requires that two previously distinct worlds or domains be brought together via pattern recognition or making a new connection. To this end, Hargadon provides compelling case examples from
physics to rock n' roll. The building process, according to Hargadon, requires that new patterns be built involving both understanding and action
within those social groups that serve as the arbiters of the creative output.
Hargadon bases his theory on the microsociology of creativity.

Ford (chap. 11) makes a point that opportunities are not simply recognized, but created. He adopts an evolutionary view of creativity and delin-
eates the dynamic interplay between creative associations and social networks
in creating new entrepreneurial opportunities. Ford introduces a variety of
case examples and provides insightful analyses of how creative products or
services are being introduced to the marketplace. As an attempt to integrate
various factors that affect the creation of entrepreneurial opportunities, he
advances seven propositions, each of which opens up an important avenue of
research in entrepreneurship as well as organizational creativity.

Part I

COGNITIVE PROCESSES
OF CREATIVE THINKING

Chapter 1

Empirical Studies of Creative Cognition in Idea Generation

Steven M. Smith
David R. Gerkens
Texas A&M University

Jami J. Shah
Noe Vargas-Hernandez
Arizona State University

Creativity and innovation are seen as critically important in many applied domains of endeavor, such as business, science, engineering, and the arts. However, *creativity* is difficult to define, and creative products are not universally judged as such by all experts. Moreover, a consensual blueprint or formula for producing creative products does not exist, nor is a deterministic method for producing creative products likely to emerge in the near future. Worse yet, creativity is different for different people—it varies from one domain to another, from one society to another, and from one historical period to another. In short, creativity is something we desperately need, but we do not know how to get it, and we are not really sure what it is. How can one possibly find anything universal to say about this slippery subject?

There are many approaches to understanding creativity, there are many methods for researching creativity, and there are many aspects of creativity that are studied. For example, the historiometric approach examines historical trends in creative innovation, whereas a personality approach tries to find the traits that give a person a creative disposition. Research methods for studying creativity range from psychometric methods to pop psychology and economic analyses. Aspects of creativity include attitudes about creativity, group creativity techniques, and product development. Thus, there is tremendous variation in what people have said and studied about creativity.

Presented at the Kellogg Team and Group Research Center's Conference on Creativity and Innovation in Organizations, James L. Allen Center, Northwestern University, June 27–28, 2003.

One constancy about creativity, however, is that it always involves people, specifically, ideas, products of the intellect. Creative products do not simply happen; they are generated by human minds. Thus, one universal about all creative products is that they emerge from the minds of people. This constancy, the centrality of the human mind to all creative activities in any context, has guided our own research in creativity. The study of the mind is referred to as *cognitive psychology*, so our approach to studying creativity is called the *creative cognition approach* (e.g., Finke, Ward, & Smith, 1992; Smith, Ward, & Finke, 1995; Ward, Smith, & Finke, 1999). At the heart of the creative cognition approach is the notion that creative ideas are products of the mind; as such, they are subject to the same principles and mechanisms that are involved in all aspects of cognition.

Because creative cognition, like noncreative cognition, involves causal mechanisms, the experimental method is usually used in research so that inferences about cause and effect can be drawn from analyses of the results. Case studies, surveys, questionnaires, and correlational studies can provide descriptive and even predictive relationships among variables, but only the experimental method can logically address issues of cause and effect. Causal relationships must be known to understand the processes in the mind that produce creative ideas. Only when we understand the cognitive processes that produce creative ideas will we know how to train people to think more creatively. Furthermore, an understanding of the roles of cognitive mechanisms in creative thinking can also clarify how to maximize the benefits of groups or teams of people, as well as what limitations can prevent optimal progress in creative groups.

Although the artificial nature of laboratory conditions makes it possible to control many factors, the down side of experimental laboratory research can be a lack of ecological validity. That is, because laboratories are so careful to control extraneous factors, the resultant conditions may be quite artificial, unlike any real-world situation one might ever encounter. Of course the down side of more naturalistic field studies of creative thinking is that such studies are typically slow and expensive in terms of human capital, numerous real-world factors routinely interact, and control of extraneous factors is more difficult. Our approach to this issue has been *alignment of methods*—a plan that takes advantage of a combination of both field research and laboratory studies of creativity. The idea of aligning research methods across levels of complexity is to conduct a small set of parallel experiments in both naturalistic and laboratory settings, manipulating similar factors, and measuring similar dependent measures. If the results of the experiments done at different levels of complexity show the same findings, then one may have more confidence that results of subsequent laboratory studies will likewise generalize to more ecologically valid situations.

In this chapter, we discuss research related to a number of cognitive components of creativity, and we relate those cognitive mechanisms to various components of group idea-generation techniques. Using incubation effects as an example, we then discuss research that aligns questions tested in simple laboratory tasks with questions posed in more realistic idea generation settings. Given that research methods align, we identify future directions for similar research questions.

CREATIVE COGNITION

The underlying premises of the creative cognition approach are twofold: The production of creative ideas can be described in terms of the cognitive mechanisms that give rise to those ideas, and cognition has inherently creative aspects. The first premise—that creativity depends on the workings of the mind—offers a different focus than do other approaches, such as the psychometric approach, which looks at common patterns of behavior among individuals; the case study approach, which examines in depth the experiences of highly creative individuals; or pragmatic approaches, which focus on methods for producing creative products. Each of these approaches to the study of creativity brings several insights and advantages for understanding various aspects of creativity. The psychometric approach, probably the most common in psychological studies of creativity, studies abilities and cognitive styles that distinguish creative people from noncreative ones. One important insight of this approach is that it treats creativity as a multidimensional set of abilities, rather than endorsing the notion of a single creative ability or process. A limitation of this approach, however, is that the individual differences that are observed are correlational measures, rather than experimentally controlled variables. Therefore, questions concerned with cause and effect in creative thinking cannot be adequately addressed, as they can in the creative cognition approach, which is experimentally oriented. Case studies are particularly valuable because of their ecological validity, representing, as they do, cases of recognized creative achievement. Causes of the creative products, inventions, and discoveries, however, cannot be known from case studies because such cases are inherently rich in terms of the number of factors that come into play in these creative achievements. Pragmatic approaches to creativity, such as the "creative templates" approach (Goldenberg, Nir, & Maoz, chap. 3, this volume), focus not on psychological issues, but on methods for creating valuable new products independently of the creators. That is, independently of the creator's personality, abilities, or emotional states, a novel and valuable product can be generated if the pragmatic approach is followed. Clearly, a creative cognition approach focuses on psychological states and processes, rather than on the final product. Although practical templates can be used to guide people to many creative products, it is also clear that much creativity has arisen in the absence of such pragmatic approaches, and that most creativity has resulted from human minds. Furthermore, the personal consequences of creative thinking, such as intrinsic rewards, motivational consequences, or flow states, cannot be investigated with such pragmatic approaches.

Although we focus on the first of these two premises in the present chapter, the second one is worth mentioning as well. Classic conceptions of the mind see cognition as passive, and reacting to stimuli encountered in the environment, reliably playing back sequences of past experiences when memories are retrieved. It is now clear, however, that much cognition is constructive, generative, and productive. This more generative view of cognition applies to perception, comprehension of language, memory, mental imagery, and the use of concepts and mental categories. For example, the simple fact that one's perception of reversible figures such as a Necker Cube can be switched from one interpretation to another without any change in the actual figure shows that perception of objects involves active generative processes and cannot be explained with simple passive perceptual processes. Likewise, the fact that ambiguous sentences (e.g., *Last night I shot an elephant in my pajamas*) can have multiple meanings indicates that comprehension requires the active participation of the listener. The existence of false memories shows that memories of the past cannot be passively replayed, but rather they must be actively generated. This active generation, in which perceptions, memories, and comprehension are created from inferences and bits of knowledge, is necessary for nearly every aspect of cognition.

The creative cognition approach seeks to understand creativity with the methods and concepts of cognitive science. No one cognitive process can be identified as *the* creative process. Rather, creative thinking includes particular combinations of the same cognitive processes involved in noncreative activities. The creative cognition approach has its origins in the associationist tradition, which focused on the learning of multiple-stage problems; in Gestalt psychology, which emphasized insight as a holistic phenomenon similar to perception; and computational modeling, which tried to capture the operations and informational states involved in complex thinking. The associationist tradition bought into a simple work ethic in which work is compensated with products and success. The associationist work ethic can be seen in contemporary researchers who believe that creative ideas are generated in discrete increments. The Gestalt perspective, however, differed from that of the associationists. In particular, Gestalters focused on the importance of insight—a special process involved in creative thinking that involves rapid restructuring and its role in creative discovery.

The creative cognition approach to understanding creativity assumes that the same cognitive structures and processes involved in noncreative cognition can explain creative thinking as well. This approach might be interpreted as stating that creative thinking is not an ordinary activity and that noncreative cognition is well understood. Of course neither supposition is accurate. Creative thinking clearly involves many aspects of ordinary cognition, and much noncreative thinking remains to be understood. Creative cognition supports our understanding of both creativity and human cognition.

Ideally, the creative cognition approach informs us about ways of optimizing creativity. A personality approach can tell us how to identify which people are more creative, but does not inform us much about the process of creative thinking. The creative cognition approach, in contrast, concentrates on the cognitive processes that enable creativity. Once these processes are understood, it will extend and refine our ability to apply those processes to more real-world activities. Whereas a personality approach has little to say about how to train creative thinking, the creative cognition approach does focus on processes that can be affected by training.

A number of cognitive processes and operations are relevant to creative thinking, including memory mechanisms such as those involved in memory blocking and recovery, as well as false or created memories. Cognitive processes and knowledge structures involved in concepts and categorization, and those involved in analogy and mental models, provide the basis for creative thought in a variety of imaginative tasks. The roles of verbal and nonverbal modalities, such as mental imagery, are often intrinsically important to the exploration of creative ideas. In addition, higher order processes, such as those involved in reasoning and metacognition, are crucial for creative cognition.

COGNITIVE COMPONENTS OF CREATIVITY

Although a complete treatment of creative cognition is beyond the scope of the present chapter, we briefly review some of the key cognitive mechanisms and structures that underlie creative thinking. An understanding of these components of creative cognition is necessary for understanding creative thinking as a system of mechanisms and structures, just as the functioning of an organism, a weather system, or a vehicle might be better grasped if its components are understood. The interested reader can find more thorough coverage of creative cognition elsewhere (e.g., Finke, Ward, & Smith, 1992; Smith, 1995a; Smith, Ward, & Finke, 1995; Ward, Smith, & Finke, 1999; Ward, Smith, & Vaid, 1997).

Memory Mechanisms

There are many memory mechanisms that play important roles in creative cognition, including working-memory capacity, interference or blocking, recovered memories, created memories, and cryptomnesia or unconscious plagiarism. *Working memory* refers to the temporary storage area in which conscious thought operates—often referred to as *short-term memory*. This type of memory has a limited capacity, and it is the capacity of working memory that varies as a function of factors such as age, personality, and intellectual ability. For example, a better working-memory capacity may better enable an individual's ability to consider multiple concepts all at once, an essential step in many creative thinking exercises. For example, in brainstorming, it may be useful to supply participants with note-taking materials to augment their limited working-memory capacities; otherwise they may forget their ideas before they get a turn to voice the ideas in the brainstorming session. Memory *interference*, also known as memory *blocking*, is a mechanism that prevents memories from successfully entering consciousness as a function of retrieval failure. Memory blocking and *fixation* in creative problem solving have been attributed to the same underlying cognitive mechanism (e.g., Dodds, & Smith, 1999; Smith, 1994, 1995b; Smith & Blankenship, 1989, 1991). For example, creative ideas may be displaced by interference from other ideas that are noncreative, but that are more recent or more frequently encountered than are the creative ideas. Memories that are blocked from conscious awareness can be recovered, and the mechanism for *memory recovery* has been studied as the same as that which causes *incubation* and *insight* in creative problem solving (e.g., Dodds, Ward, & Smith, 2004; Smith, 1994, 1995a; Smith & Dodds, 1999; Smith & Vela, 1991). So, for example, the same cognitive mechanisms that unexpectedly resolve one's tip-of-the-tongue (TOT) experiences may also underlie the sudden insights that resolve impasses in one's creative thinking. *Created memories*, sometimes referred to as *false memories*, arise from the same mechanisms that lead to creative idea generation; both are composed of material drawn from a combination of past experiences plus factual or conceptual knowledge, all cobbled together according to a schema or related knowledge structure (e.g., Smith et al., 2000). For example, you might falsely recall that you ate fried chicken 3 months ago on Sunday if that meal fits your schema for your Sunday dinner, and/or if you had fried chicken recently and misremembered it as having happened on a different occasion. Similarly, your creative imagination might produce ideas for fried chicken restaurants that are influenced by your schema for such establishments and/or by your recent experiences in such restaurants. Finally, *cryptomnesia*, also known as *unconscious plagiarism*, results from the combination of a successful form of unconscious memory (called *implicit memory*) along with a failure of conscious memory (called *explicit memory*). Unconscious plagiarism obstructs creative thinking because old ideas are brought to mind via implicit memory, but they are thought of as new ideas when one fails to consciously attribute the true source of such ideas (e.g., Smith, Ward, & Schumacher, 1993). For example, a composer might write a song without recognizing the origin of the rhythms or melodies that inspired the song.

Concepts and Categorization

A *concept* is an abstract knowledge structure, much like a *category*, that specifies general rules or principles that determine whether specific items are examples of that concept or category. Even the most novel and creative ideas usually arise from our existing concepts, and new ideas tend to reflect the structure of already known concepts. For example, camera phones resemble both cameras and cell phones. Combining concepts, such as a camera and a telephone, is one way to extend the boundaries of traditional ideas because new creative qualities can emerge from combinations of concepts, even when those novel properties do not exist as features of any of the component concepts.

Analogy

The use of *analogy* is the basis of many important novel ideas, inventions, and discoveries. Although the cognitive basis of many forms of reasoning has been studied, the use of analogical reasoning in the production of new ideas has been most central to creative thinking methods. Analogies constitute complex type of similarity, and the best analogies are generally those that are more abstract and conceptual. There are at least two aspects of analogies that are fundamentally important for creative cognition—what can be termed *retrieval* and *mapping*. Retrieval of analogies occurs when an object or system at hand (the *topic domain*) reminds one of a similar object or system that is already known (the *vehicle domain*). For example, in working on traffic problems, a civil engineer might retrieve from memory the flow of fish in a school or the ants in a colony. Simple propositions and more complex relations that already exist in one's vehicle domain can then be *mapped* onto the topic domain as a means of inductive inference—a way to expand our knowledge and ideas. For example, to consider solutions to traffic problems caused by unexpected accidents, one might see how ants deal with unexpected impediments in their paths. Mental models resemble analogies, but they can contain more complex relations within which one can often run mental simulations in the service of hypothetical reasoning. In one's mental model for a traffic system, for example, one might be able to visualize vehicles moving, stopping, and turning as a function of various changes in the system, such as accidents or various weather conditions.

Mental Imagery and Verbal Versus Nonverbal Modalities

Mental imagery is a powerful tool for many forms of cognition, and it refers to the consciously directed activity in which visual-like mental representations can be generated, manipulated, and transformed at will. For example, in the course of inventing or designing a new probe that will maneuver the Martian terrain while probing for certain substances, one may need to visualize the rover in various situations that could occur. Although many mental activities can be verbalized, which is the basis for the *think-aloud* introspective methods used in protocol analysis, there are some activities, such as rotating complex objects within a mental space, that are not verbalizable. Mental imagery is computationally expensive and takes up a portion of working memory called the *visuospatial sketchpad.* Mental images may seem complex, but they do not contain as much information as do perceptual images, which are far more short-lived and less deliberately manipulable than are mental images. Mental images have often been cited as inspirational insights that led to important discoveries and innovations, such as the structure of the chemical benzene or the discovery of the polymerase chain reaction (PCR) that replicates DNA from tiny amounts. Mental imagery is the basis for *preinventive forms* (e.g., Finke et al., 1992) that can be explored and developed into creative products.

Metacognition

Metacognition is thinking about thinking. It takes three forms: metacognitive monitoring, metacognitive control, and metacognitive knowledge. To the degree that we are aware of our own thoughts, memories, and comprehension, we are capable of *metacognitive monitoring,* or observing our own thought processes. For example, even when you cannot immediately recall a name, a fact, or the answer to a question, you still might feel certain that you have the knowledge and that you might be able to produce it later. *Metacognitive control* refers to intentional direction of one's actions, which is necessary for activities such as decision making or error correction. *Metacognitive knowledge* is simply one's understanding (or misunderstanding as the case may be) of how one's mind functions. Metacognition plays many important roles in creative cognition, and it is important for planning, persistence, intuition, and insight. For example, knowing when to persist at a difficult problem, versus knowing when one should put the problem aside, can be critically important for the ultimate success of creative thinking.

Creative Cognition Phenomena and Theories

Beyond the cognitive operations that underlie creative cognition, there are several phenomena that are common to creative endeavors and that have been explained in terms of their cognitive underpinnings. One of these phenomena is *fixation* in problem solving and creative thinking, a pattern of persistent failures on problems that defy common solutions. In many of our studies (e.g., Smith, 1994, 1995a; Smith & Dodds, 1999; Smith &

Blankenship, 1989, 1991), we have linked fixation with memory blocks under the hypothesis that both phenomena are caused by the same underlying mechanisms. Another common phenomenon is termed *incubation*, a situation in which it is easier to reach a solution or an insight into a problem by deferring one's efforts, rather than by persisting with unproductive plans. Incubation effects have been attributed to recovery from fixation or, alternatively, to unconscious incrementing of the activation of solutions (e.g., Smith, 1994). The use of *metaphor* in creativity is another phenomenon of interest in creative cognition. Metaphor is used commonly in creative thinking methods and has been studied in research groups working on scientific discoveries. Yet another phenomenon common to creative thinking is the use of *combinations of ideas*, a practice that is encouraged in brainstorming group activities. Combinations of concepts is thought to result at times in emergent effects that go beyond the features of the individual components. Although this is by no means an exhaustive list of phenomena that occur in creative thinking, it is nonetheless a compelling set of situations that commonly occur in the course of creative activities.

Several theories of creative thinking are based in cognitive psychological mechanisms and theoretical constructs. These theories are not intended as all-encompassing descriptions of the entire creative process, nor are they intended as support for a computationally specifiable system that deterministically produces creative products, just as an addition algorithm can reliably manufacture correct numerical sums. For example, one of these theories focuses on the importance of *remote association*, the discovery of unusual ideas rather than common ones. Further, to retrieve remote associations from one's memory rather than common ones, it may be that lower arousal and diffuse attention are better than are focused attention and high arousal. Another theory of creativity, the *geneplore* theory (e.g., Finke et al., 1992), breaks down creative cognitive processes into two types: generative and exploratory. Generative processes include memory retrieval, association, and analogical transfer, whereas exploratory processes include attribute finding, conceptual interpretation, and hypothesis-testing. The geneplore theory is a heuristic theory, intended as descriptive of a creative process that sees alternately generative phases in which preinventive structures are set in place, and exploratory phases in which temporarily adopted structures are explored and manipulated.

A Cognitive Model of Group Creativity

The cognitive system of an individual can be seen as an analogue for a creativity group. When individuals think in creative ways, the components of their cognitive systems are functioning in a certain way. These components of cognition have specific roles and functions, and they contribute to both creative and noncreative thinking. If the individuals in a group play the roles of these cognitive components, then the group can function like a mind, except that the group can potentially have greater creative power than an individual mind. The added potential that a group can have is that there are more resources on which to draw in the group, including added knowledge, skills, effort, and time. A potential drawback of this sort of group, relative to an individual mind, is the possibility that individuals in a group might not communicate as fluidly as do the components of an individual's mind. Furthermore, a group, like a mind, can fall into patterns of noncreative output, such as fixation or conformity. Having the potential to be creative does not guarantee creative outcomes.

Here is a crude overview of the components of the mind and how they interact. Sense organs, such as eyes and ears, give us information about the world around us. Our long-term memory system stores vast amounts of information and can perform complex calculations. Our response systems carry out all of our physical functions. Working memory, like the creativity group session, is that central place where so much is happening. Working memory interprets sensory input, stores and retrieves information in long-term memory, solves problems, makes decisions, and exerts conscious control over those parts of our bodies that are not being automatically taken care of (see Fig. 1.1).

This model of the mind portrays a dynamic system composed of structures and processes. The structures include sensory systems, working mem-

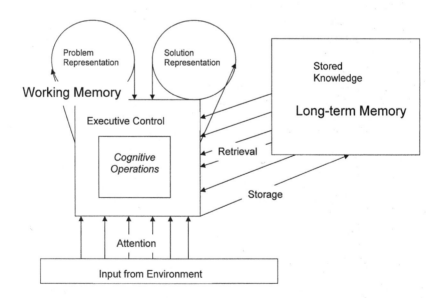

FIG. 1.1. Functioning of a creative cognitive system.

ory, long-term memory, and response systems. These systems are referred to as *cognitive structures* because they are fixed and rigid; that is, they have capacities and limitations that cannot be exceeded. The cognitive processes in the model, shown as arrows, include pattern recognition, attention, rehearsal, storage, retrieval, incidental learning, and intentional and automatic responding. These processes allow information in one structure to affect another structure. They provide the means for an almost infinite flexibility in human thought.

The four major cognitive structures have special functions. Sensory systems operate rapidly to record the vast avalanche of stimuli that bombard our senses every moment, but the recordings last only briefly before the next bombardment of stimuli occurs. Response systems can be thought of as the machinery that carries out our intentions and habits, resulting in observable behavior. Long-term memory contains an enduring repository of personally experienced events, factual knowledge, and knowledge of how to do things. Working memory is the structure where conscious awareness occurs. Working memory holds information for less than a minute unless the information is refreshed, and it only holds about seven ideas at a time, yet this structure is the heart of much of our creative thinking.

Working memory has one component that can record, remember, and create visual images, and another that allows us to maintain an awareness of words or other types of spoken information. These two mechanisms allow us to remain consciously aware of visual and verbal information. They serve as slaves to the *executive control system*, the cognitive structure in working memory that comprehends meanings, forms ideas, makes decisions, and, in general, guides our conscious thinking. In our group analogy, the executive controller is the leader or facilitator of the group; the rest of the group members serve the leader's needs as he or she goes about the business of the group.

When the human cognitive system is in use, working memory is the center of the operation. Sensory systems supply working memory with information about the outside world, and long-term memory supplies information that you have previously learned. Some responses are deliberately controlled by the executive system, whereas other responses are automatically activated by long-term memory, without one's conscious awareness. This is the big picture about how the human mind functions from the perspective of cognitive psychology. Using this proven system for generating creative ideas as a model for a creative group or team does not necessarily suggest that there is a one-to-one correspondence between components of the cognitive system and group members. Rather, what is important is that the members of a creative team carry out the functions of the creative cognitive system.

The functions suggested by this Cognitive Model of Group Creativity include executive control, attention to input from the environment, representation of the problem, representation of the current solution plan, storage of knowledge, and retrieval of knowledge. Such an orientation to creative activities focuses on the various factors that impact most on the construction of creative ideas, and it also suggests places where the creative process can break down. An example of such a breakdown is too narrow a focus of attention to the environment and too narrow a range of ideas retrieved from long-term knowledge. A broader distribution of attention and retrieval yields more remote combinations, which are good sources for creative ideas. Another example is the representation of the problem and the adequacy of the current solution space for generating a solution.

The Cognitive Model of Group Creativity described here is compatible with the work of other psychologists who have discussed the connection between individual creativity and the creativity of groups of individuals, such as Paulus (2000) and Nijstad et al. (2002). For example, these authors studied the effects of such variables as working memory capacity in group versus individual idea production. Related work also includes a body of writing on shared cognition in groups of individuals, such as Levine, Resnick, and Higgins (1993) and Thompson, Levine, and Messick (1999).

Alignment-of-Levels Research

How can we optimize the creative output of individuals and groups of people? One reason that this question is so difficult to answer is that creative output in naturalistic settings can be influenced by so many different interacting factors. Can the causes of observations in such complex situations be known? Furthermore, are the findings of our laboratory experiments on creative cognition ecologically valid? That is, is it valid for us to generalize from well-controlled and simplified laboratory conditions to more naturalistic contexts in which many factors can interact? We describe a methodological approach for studying creativity in applied contexts. The approach, which we refer to as *Alignment of Methods Across Levels*, provides a plan for studying causal mechanisms of creative outcomes in real-life contexts.

Components of Creative Idea Generation Methods

One goal of applied research in creative cognition is to provide empirical tests of the efficacy of various components of the creative idea generation methods often used in applied settings. In engineering design, a number of critically important components of idea generation techniques have been identified (e.g., Kulkarni, 2000). Although the list is far from complete, the key components of idea generation methods in engineering design include the use of provocative stimuli, an emphasis on the quantity of ideas generated more than the quality of ideas, encouragement of flexible representations of problems, shifting frame of reference, incubation or time off from the problem, and exposure to examples, which can cause needless conformity effects that restrict the range of creative thinking. We have experimentally tested the effects of these key components of ideation methods.

Provocative stimuli are primitive ideas that are related to the problem at hand, but that are not well developed. Such stimuli are intended to provoke designers to consider various trains of thought that they might not otherwise think about. In some creative idea generation methods, such as the C-Sketch method (e.g., Shah, 1998), group members' initial quick sketches were shared by other participants. A second key component we tested was the *emphasis on quantity* (vs. quality) of the ideas generated by group members. An emphasis on quantity is expected not only to increase the number of creative ideas generated by a group, but also to liberate members from self-criticism that can obstruct creative thought. A third key component that we examined was the *encouragement of flexible representations* of problems, rather than continuing with one's initial representation of a problem. For example, the modality of a problem representation (i.e., whether it is visual vs. verbal) constitutes an aspect of its cognitive representation. Next, the effects of *shifting frames of reference* in a problem were examined; more shifts are expected to allow different perspectives, and therefore more divergent solutions to problems. *Incubation,* or time away from the problem once progress has reached an impasse, is another key component of many idea generation methods. Finally, exposure to examples can cause *conformity effects* in idea generation, such that ideas tend to conform to the features seen in the examples (e.g., Jansson & Smith, 1991; Smith, Ward, & Schumacher, 1993).

Consideration of these components of creative idea generation can have implications for the creative productivity of groups of people. For example, flexible representations of problems are useful when individuals think creatively. For an individual, the way to encourage flexible representations is to encourage multiple perspectives, such as prompting the individual with multiple contexts. For a group, the way to form flexible representations is to take advantage of the multiple viewpoints of the individuals. For example, it should be important for individuals to record their initial reactions to problems first before group exposure to initial ideas leads to conformity in the group's thinking. The initial reactions may provide the multiple points of view necessary to build a flexible representation of the problem.

Experimental Tasks, Manipulations, and Metrics

The more naturalistic and complex design task used was a problem in which designers were asked to create a device to transport a ping-pong ball. The device was to be powered by a spring, and the key requirement of the device was to go as far a distance as possible. Designers were allowed to use a spring, PVC tubing, copper tubing, steel wire, wood, cardboard, styrofoam, aluminum sheet, bolts, and nails. Examples of the ideas generated by subjects in these tasks are shown in Figs. 1.2A and 1.2B.

This rather complex design problem was then compared with simpler laboratory tasks, such as generation of members of open-ended categories (e.g., *things that float*), divergent thinking tasks (e.g., *list all possible alternative uses of a 2-liter soda bottle*), and creative idea generation (e.g., *devise novel tools that sentient aliens might use*). In every case, including these laboratory tasks and the more complex design tasks, the same four measures of productivity

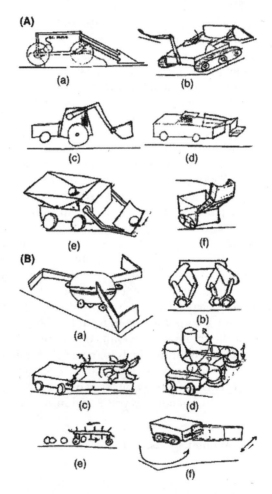

FIG. 1.2.   (A) High novelty set and (B) low novelty set (Shah, Vargas-Hernandez, & Smith, 2002).

were utilized. Those measures were the *quantity* or number of ideas generated by individuals, the *variety* of the ideas generated, the *novelty* of the ideas, and the *quality* of ideas. Thus, although there was quite a bit of variability among the design and laboratory tasks, the same metrics were observed in all studies so that the results would be more comparable across levels of complexity.

Two experiments were conducted to examine the effects of incubation, one involving a laboratory task that examined divergent thinking and the other involving an engineering design problem that a team of engineering students worked on as part of a design class. The two experiments were far apart in many ways, including the tasks used (a realistic design assignment vs. a simple idea generation task), the team versus individual contributions to the creative products, the time scale (1 hour vs. weeks of work), and the level of expertise of the participants. Nonetheless, both experiments interjected breaks in the task (vs. no break), allowing for incubation, and both measured the effects of that incubation manipulation on the number of ideas generated, the variety of those ideas, the novelty of the ideas, and the judged quality of the ideas.

The results of the two incubation experiments are shown in Tables 1.1 and 1.2. Although the overall numbers of ideas, their variety, and their quality were different for the two experiments, it can be seen that incubation (as compared with continuous work without the break) improved creative output in both experiments on all measures.

The parallel effects of incubation on ideation metrics in both laboratory and design contexts shows that the studies are *aligned*. That is, what was observed in one experimental domain was also observed in another. This alignability of studies provides evidence that future laboratory experiments

TABLE 1.1
Laboratory Experiment: Mean Divergent Thinking Scores
as a Function of Incubation Versus Continuous Work Conditions

Condition	Quantity	Variety	Quality	Novelty
Control Group	1.51	1.20	1.47	2.82
Incubation Group	1.93	1.60	2.37	3.73

TABLE 1.2
Design Experiment: Mean Ideation Effectiveness Scores
as a Function of Incubation Versus Continuous Work Conditions

Condition	Quantity	Variety	Quality	Novelty
Control Group	4.86	2.81	6.15	4.71
Incubation Group	5.11	6.24	7.31	6.76

should give results that are ecologically valid and relevant to applied contexts. It is also important to note that the same effects were observed whether the creative products were generated by a group or by individuals. Although there are clearly effects of groups versus individuals on creative work, this alignability nonetheless shows that studies conducted with individuals can have relevance for creativity in groups and teams.

SUMMARY AND FUTURE DIRECTIONS

The important features of the research in the present chapter include the focus on cognition in creative endeavors, an emphasis of empirical studies to test the mechanisms of creative cognition, and the need for alignment across levels of complexity and ecological validity. Our initial studies showed remarkably good alignment across levels, thereby supporting the efficacy and generality of results of simple laboratory studies of creative cognition. We are now conducting further studies of alignability that involve other components of group ideation techniques. These components include the use of provocative stimuli, emphasis on quality versus quantity, flexible representations of problems and solutions, frame-of-reference shifting, and exposure to biasing examples. This same focus on cognition and empirical methods should generalize to other domains of creativity and innovation as well.

The future of research in creative cognition is likely to be in three directions. One of these directions is likely a continuation of investigations of the underlying cognitive processes that support creative idea generation and idea development, including the neural substrates of such processes. For example, fundamental questions about the processes that underlie insight, or that underlie remote association, remain unanswered. Second, a continuation of the analogy between individual cognitive processes and group creativity processes is needed. How can our understanding of individual cognition be used to address the interactions of groups or teams that are devoted to creativity? Finally, and perhaps most pragmatically, research is likely to be aimed at the development of artificial systems that can augment human cognitive abilities, and therefore should enhance creativity. For example, a software system that mitigates the burdens of working memory capacity or duration could conceivably support creative thinking. Likewise, a software system that could quickly provide relevant factual knowledge, or one that could suggest appropriate combinations of the user's ideas, could also augment creative thinking. Understanding creative cognition is necessary if we are to invent ways to support and augment our creative cognitive processes.

ACKNOWLEDGMENT

The authors would like to acknowledge the support received through NSF Grant DMI-0115447 for this work.

REFERENCES

Dodds, R. A., & Smith, S. M. (1999). Fixation. In M. A. Runco & S. R. Pritzker (Eds.), *Encyclopedia of creativity* (pp. 725–728). San Diego, CA: Academic Press.

Dodds, R. A., Ward, T. B., & Smith, S. M. (2004). A review of the experimental literature on incubation in problem solving and creativity. In M. A. Runco (Ed.), *Creativity research handbook* (Vol. 3). Cresskill, NJ: Hampton.

Finke, R. A., Ward, T. B., & Smith, S. M. (1992). *Creative cognition: Theory, research, and applications.* Cambridge, MA: MIT Press.

Jansson, D. G., & Smith, S. M. (1991). Design fixation. *Design Studies, 12,* 3–11.

Kulkarni, S. V. (2000). *A framework for the experimental evaluation of idea generation techniques.* Unpublished master's thesis, Arizona State University, Tempe.

Kulkarni, S. V., & Shah, J. J. (1999). *Survey for evidence of components of creativity* (Tech. Rep. No. ASU/DAL/IG/99-7). Tempe: Arizona State University, Design Automation Lab.

Levine, J. M., Resnick, L. B., & Higgins, E. T. (1993). Social foundations of cognition. *Annual Review of Psychology, 44,* 585–612.

Nijstad, B. A., Stroebe, W., & Lodewijkx, H. F. M. (2002). Cognitive stimulation and interference in groups: Exposure effects in an idea generation task. *Journal of Experimental Social Psychology, 38*(6), 535–544.

Paulus, P. (2000). Groups, teams, and creativity: The creative potential of idea-generating groups. *Applied Psychology, 49*(2), 237–262.

Shah, J. (1998). *Experimental investigation of collaborative techniques for progressive idea generation.* Proceedings of ASME DTM Conference, Atlanta, GA.

Shah, J. J., Vargas-Hernandez, N., & Smith, S. M. (2002). Metrics for measuring ideation effectiveness. *Design Studies, 24*(2), 111–134.

Smith, S. M. (1994). Getting into and out of mental ruts: A theory of fixation, incubation, and insight. In R. Sternberg & J. Davidson (Eds.), *The nature of insight* (pp. 121–149). Cambridge, MA: MIT Press.

Smith, S. M. (1995a). Creative cognition: Demystifying creativity. In C. N. Hedley, P. Antonacci, & M. Rabinowitz (Eds.), *The mind at work in the classroom: Literacy & thinking* (pp. 31–46). Hillsdale, NJ: Lawrence Erlbaum Associates.

Smith, S. M. (1995b). Fixation, incubation, and insight in memory, problem solving, and creativity. In S. M. Smith, T. B. Ward, & R. A. Finke (Eds.), *The creative cognition approach* (pp. 135–155). Cambridge: MIT Press.

Smith, S. M. (2003). The constraining effects of initial ideas. In P. Paulus & B. Nijstad (Eds.), *Group creativity: Innovation through collaboration* (pp. 15–31). Oxford, England: Oxford University Press.

Smith, S. M., & Blankenship, S. E. (1989). Incubation effects. *Bulletin of the Psychonomic Society, 27,* 311–314.

Smith, S. M., & Blankenship, S. E. (1991). Incubation and the persistence of fixation in problem solving. *American Journal of Psychology, 104,* 61–87.

Smith, S. M., & Dodds, R. A. (1999). Incubation. In M. A. Runco & S. R. Pritzker (Eds.), *Encyclopedia of creativity* (pp. 39–43). San Diego, CA: Academic Press.

Smith, S. M., & Vela, E. (1991). Incubated reminiscence effects. *Memory & Cognition, 19*(2), 168–176.

Smith, S. M., Ward, T. B., & Finke, R. A. (1995). *The creative cognition approach.* Cambridge, MA: MIT Press.

Smith, S. M., Ward, T. B., & Schumacher, J. S. (1993). Constraining effects of examples in a creative generation task. *Memory & Cognition, 21,* 837–845.

Smith, S. M., Ward, T. B., Tindell, D. R., Sifonis, C. M., & Wilkenfeld, M. J. (2000). Effects of category structure on created memories. *Memory and Cognition, 28,* 386–395.

Thompson, L. L., Levine, J. M., & Messick, D. M. (Eds.). (1999). *LEA's organization and management series.* Mahwah, NJ: Lawrence Erlbaum Associates.

Ward, T. B., Smith, S. M., & Finke, R. A. (1999). Creative cognition. In R. Sternberg (Ed.), *Handbook of creativity* (pp. 189–212). New York: Cambridge University Press.

Ward, T. B., Smith, S. M., & Vaid, J. (1997). *Creative thought: An investigation of conceptual structures and processes.* Washington, DC: American Psychological Association Books.

Chapter 2

Opening the Black Box of Creativity: Causal Effects in Creative Solution Generation

Eric L. Santanen
Bucknell University

Organizations must be continuously creative to survive and thrive. Globalization, changes in the workforces, and more informed customers each drive enormous changes in the marketplace. The rate of obsolescence seems only to grow faster, necessitating increasingly frequent technological and procedural changes. Government regulations, environmental concerns, economic trends, and a renewed focus on privacy and ethical practices create further complexities that need to be addressed. The organization that is unable to generate creative solutions to address these and other pressures will eventually face extinction.

Because of the importance of the topic, much has been written about how to improve creativity. Nearly a century of research has explored a variety of approaches, yet the causes of creativity can still seem elusive. Organizational managers might feel daunted by the sheer volume of readings available. The Four Ps of Creativity (Rhodes, 1961) is a useful way to organize and understand the existing creativity literature in terms of author perspectives. It notes that various authors have framed creativity as an attribute of:

- Product—some ideas, solutions, and designs are more creative than others.
- Person—some individuals are more creative than others.
- Press—some physical and social environments produce more creativity than others.

- Process—some thinking techniques produce more creativity than others.

Many investigations into these four perspectives result in prescriptions for enhancing creativity (discussed later) that produce significant, measurable improvements in creativity. The continuing success of these prescriptions implies that some principles of cause and effect must be at work, yet many investigations leave a host of unanswered questions. Studies of creativity as an attribute of the product do not tell us how to create even more creative products. Studies of creativity as an attribute of the person do not tell us how to make a given person even more creative. Studies of creativity as an attribute of processes do not tell us how to design processes that produce even greater levels of creativity. A causal model of creativity—a model that explains how and why creative solutions form in the human mind—might help us understand how to make people more creative and might help us determine which parts of the various creativity prescriptions are the most effective and why. With a simple and clear understanding of that which causes creativity, we may be able to design processes and environments that could make people and the products they produce even more creative than has been possible in the past.

This chapter offers a cognitive model of the mechanisms that cause creative solutions to emerge from the human mind. Creative solutions are those that work and that fall outside the set of known solutions. Rather than seeking to answer the questions "Is this person creative?", "Is this product creative?", or "Will this particular environment foster creativity?", the model addresses this question: "What causes creative solutions to form in the human mind?" Building on the logic of the model, this chapter proposes several techniques for leveraging the cognitive mechanisms of creativity to help people or groups of people generate creative solutions to their problems.

Although there has been a great deal of research indicating that creativity is enhanced as a result of using groups composed of people with varying levels of expertise, selecting group members with nonoverlapping backgrounds, or composing groups according to some aspect of cognitive style, this research looks at a more fundamental approach to enhancing the results of creative efforts. The Cognitive Network Model of creativity suggests techniques that are well suited to leveraging creativity within existing groups of people when circumstances or resources dictate that it may not be feasible to exchange group members. In an organizational setting, meeting planners may not always know in advance the exact roster of participants and therefore may be unable to carefully compose groups according to specific personal traits. It may also be the case that meeting planners are simply unaware of or do not have access to tools designed to reveal individual differences in cognitive preferences or abilities that may be useful for problem solving or creative ideation.

The remainder of this chapter then presents the results of an experiment that compares several brainstorming techniques and argues that the findings offer some empirical support for the new model.

PROCESS MODELS OF CREATIVITY

A number of authors have proposed process models of creativity. These models are also referred to as *stage models*. These models of the creative process can be grouped into three primary categories: descriptive, prescriptive, and cognitive modes.

Descriptive stage models typically consist of step-by-step mechanical sequences of mental activities that are involved with the creative process. Based on a study of inventors, Rossman (1931) produced a sequence of stages involved in the creative process. These stages include (a) observation of a need or difficulty; (b) analysis of the need (problem formulation and definition); (c) survey of available information; (d) formulation of possible solutions; (e) critical examination of the advantages and disadvantages of the possible solutions; (f) formulation of new ideas; and finally (g) testing and elaboration of the most promising solution. Similarly, Simon (1960) suggested a three-stage approach to problem solving comprised of intelligence, design, and choice. Intelligence involves activities that develop useful problem definition through recognition and analysis of some problem, design refers to the generation of solutions to that problem, and choice represents the selection and implementation of a solution.

Prescriptive stage models carry the descriptive models a step further: They aim to enhance human problem-solving performance by formalizing a protocol that helps ensure none of the previously identified stages are skipped during problem-solving efforts. The models that have been developed are as varied as the sequence of stages that have been identified. For example, Amabile (1983) presented a model of the creative process that involves a specific sequence of stages and a set of factors that influence these stages. The process begins with the presentation of the task or problem to be solved. In the second stage, preparations for response generation are made. These preparations include either learning about or activating the requisite knowledge. In the third stage, responses are generated by searching the available knowledge pathways. These responses are then evaluated against specific domain knowledge. Finally, the last stage evaluates the progress of the previous stages toward the ultimate goal. If the original goal has been attained, the process terminates. If the goal is not attained and no reasonable responses generated, the process also terminates. If there is some progress toward the goal, however, the process returns to the first stage. Thus, work on any given task or problem may involve a long series of loops through the process until success is achieved. Other noteworthy examples of prescriptive models include Goswami (1996), Isaksen and Parnes (1985), Van Gundy (1987), and Woodman, Sawyer, and Griffin (1993).

Descriptive and prescriptive stage models represent an important step forward in the understanding of creativity and have given rise to a list of useful techniques for improving creativity. At the same time, however, many of these models tend to treat creativity as a "black box" process as few details are provided that might offer insights to cognitive explanations of creativity or how it may be further improved.

Cognitive stage models of creativity shed additional light on the process of creativity by offering various insights into actual cognitive processes that underlie creative thinking. A variety of cognitive models of the creative process have been proposed. Two influential cognitive stage models are those of Mednick (1962) and Koestler (1964). Mednick focused on the associative aspect of the creative process, indicating that creativity is the process of forming mental elements into new combinations that either meet specified requirements or are in some way useful. He further indicated the more mutually remote the elements of the new combination, the more creative the resulting process or product. Koestler's process of bisociation is similar to Mednick's ideas of association. Bisociation suggests that creativity flows from the association of two typically incompatible frames of reference within some new context. Thus, the creative product is characterized as one that is both unexpected and perfectly logical within each frame of reference. For example, in a study of eminent achievement among artists, writers, physical scientists, and social scientists, Koestler found that new ideas or new understandings often derive from the spontaneous fusion of two or more schemata.

Cognitive factors related to creativity have been investigated from a variety of perspectives. Driving this diversity in perspective is the equally large number of phenomena of interest concerning creativity. For example, when investigating creativity, many researchers have used the brainstorming paradigm popularized by Osborn (1957). Using brainstorming as a springboard, many researchers have developed interesting and insightful cognitive models of the creative process.

Nagasundaram and Dennis (1993) presented a cognitive approach to solution generation and creative problem solving. They argued that in certain environments brainstorming is best viewed as an individual, cognitive phenomenon (rather than a social phenomenon), and is therefore subject to the limitation of the human information-processing system. This model of cognitive stimulation maps various stimulus attributes (diversity, cardinality, and temporal distance) of previously generated ideas that are presented to individuals participating in electronic brainstorming to response attributes (innovativeness and productivity) of new ideas generated by the participants as a result of exposure to the previous ideas. In the context of this model, stimulus diversity is viewed in terms of the idea that triggers the subsequent response generated by the participant. Diversity can vary along several dimensions, such as the semantic domain of the idea; the contributor of the idea; the idea that stimulated the generation of the new idea; and the number of characters contained in the previous idea. According to this model, then, diversity in the stimuli that brainstorming participants receive will increase both the innovativeness and productivity (quantity) of responses produced. An analysis of the linkages within the model reveals that greater emphasis is placed on explaining productivity as opposed to explaining creativity.

Interested in learning more about group interactions during verbal brainstorming, Brown, Tumeo, Larey, and Paulus (1998) developed a simulation model of cognitive interactions during verbal brainstorming. This model employs a matrix of probabilities that represent the likelihood that a brainstormer will either produce his or her next idea from within a currently activated category (from long-term memory) or will switch to a new category from which his or her next idea will originate. The matrix model sheds a great deal of light on the role of attention and category switching on the quantity of ideas produced during a brainstorming session as the behavior of the model closely approximates that of verbally interactive brainstorming groups. The model demonstrates the principles behind divergent and convergent cognitive styles (Mednick, 1962) by varying inter- and intracategory transitional probabilities, and provides ready explanations for how exposure to the ideas of others should have positive impacts on the productivity of group brainstormers. Perhaps most interesting, the model uses the principles of attention to the ideas of others and category switching to explain why verbally interactive brainstorming groups tend to converge on a small subset of ideas rather than fully exploring the full range of possibilities (cf. Gettys, Pliske, Manning, & Casey, 1987).

More recently, Paulus (2000) presented a model that illustrates the impact of social and cognitive factors on creativity in verbally interactive, idea-generating groups. He posited that cognitive factors such as production blocking, task-irrelevant behavior, and cognitive load will lead to lower creativity for interacting groups. Conversely, cognitive factors such as novel associations, priming, attention to the ideas of others, presence of conflict, heterogeneity of participants, divergent style, and incubation of ideas should lead to increased creativity for interactive groups.

The various stage models presented earlier help conceptualize the creative process. These models illustrate that creative solutions do not automatically occur whenever problem solvers are faced with a difficult problem. Rather, creative solutions are the result of sustained and complex mental effort over time. These models have helped us learn a great deal about the creative process and even begin to hint at the possibility of a discrete cognitive mechanism associated with the creative process.

Because the Cognitive Network Model of creativity rests on a set of foundations that derive from problem solving, cognitive psychology, and creativity, the underlying assumptions of the model are not dissimilar from those of other models. Where the Cognitive Network Model diverges from existing models is in the underlying phenomenon of interest and the associated predictions made by the model. Whereas various existing models may include social and organizational influences, the Cognitive Network Model attempts to exclude these impacts. Many existing models of creativity also make specific predictions about resulting constructs such as quantity of ideas or solutions, flexibility or fluency of ideas, and overall productivity levels, while the Cognitive Network Model of creativity deals exclusively with the construct of creativity. These and other differences are made more clear shortly. Furthermore, the Cognitive Network Model of creativity as presented in this study illustrates how important it is for researchers to be increasingly precise and clear about tools or technology that are used, the configuration of these tools, and the instructions given to participants when evaluating the results of brainstorming and creativity studies.

A COGNITIVE NETWORK MODEL OF CREATIVITY

The Cognitive Network Model of creativity results from the synthesis of principles and research findings drawn from the fields of creativity, cognitive psychology, and problem solving. The model is presented in two steps. First, a brief overview of the foundations on which the model rests is presented. Second, the causal linkages embodied by the model are described.

Foundations of the Model

The most fundamental assumption of the Cognitive Network Model of creativity is that human knowledge is stored in memory as highly associative bundles of concepts referred to as *frames*[1] (Minsky, 1975). For example, the

---

[1]Although there are many cognitive structures proposed to exist in human memory (including schemata, scripts, concepts, categories, and frames), their specific differences are not important to this model. What is important is that items stored in long-term memory are not atomic in nature, but rather stored as complex bundles of related items. The term *frame* is simply chosen for consistency.

frame representing *picnic* might include basket, out-of-doors eating, red-checkered tablecloth, green grass, trees, sunshine, and ants. The model further posits that the contents bundled together in a frame serve as associative links to other frames that include similar or related concepts (Neisser, 1966). For example, the frame for *picnic* might have an associative link to the frame for *lumber* through the concept *tree*, which is bundled in both frames. The conceptual interconnections among frames in human memory form a vastly complex network, which represents the entirety of an individual's knowledge and experience.

The model further assumes that the associative links between frames vary in strength (Collins & Loftus, 1975). Some concepts may be strongly linked (*picnic–basket*), whereas others may be more weakly linked (*picnic–shade*). Some are close to each other on the knowledge network (*picnic–ants–ant spray*), whereas others are more distant from one another in the knowledge network (*picnic–tree–lumber–lumber mill–industrial accidents*). Frames are said to be less related to one another when they are connected by relatively weak links or long pathways consisting of many hops from frame to frame. Frames are said to be more closely related when they are connected by stronger associative links or when they are close to one another on the knowledge network. Thus, our knowledge networks are composed of countless frames that are interconnected via both strong and weak associations that form our long-term memory of knowledge and past events.

Working memory is the temporary workspace for frames to which an individual is paying attention (Baddeley, 1990). The transference of frames from long-term memory to working memory is called *activation*. By following the links that connect activated frames to those that reside in long-term memory, these additional frames become primed, such that they can become activated more easily than they would have otherwise due to their associations with currently activated frames (Collins & Loftus, 1975).

This network structure of strongly and weakly linked frames may be one of the sources of functional fixedness (e.g., see Dunker, 1945) that serves to limit creativity for people attempting to solve new problems. Consideration of a new problem tends to activate frames for similar situations from long-term memory, so people may tend to retrieve frames related to old solutions and attempt to adapt them to the new set of circumstances—a practice sometimes referred to as *satisficing* (Cyert & March, 1963). Activation of existing frames in working memory spreads out along the strongest links to other closely related frames (e.g., thinking about *cat* may lead you to think about your pet and then to a friend's pet). The end result of following these strong links serves to reinforce known patterns of thinking and can result in the "stuck in a rut" syndrome of not being able to find a creative solution.

One simple way to overcome the repetitious thought patterns that can easily occur while problem solving is by delivering some form of external stimuli to the problem solvers as they work. External stimuli automatically activate frames in the knowledge network (Anderson, 1990). If the stimuli activate different frames than the problem does, then the problem solvers may break free from their rut and explore different sections of their web of knowledge. Much research has shown that creative solutions typically result from the combination of frames from previously disparate areas of knowledge networks within the context of the problem at hand (Mobley, Doares, & Mumford, 1992). Many creativity techniques involve bombarding the participants with stimuli that are not obviously relevant to the task (e.g., "How is your problem like a horse?").

Martindale (1995) argued that creative ideas are *always* new combinations of old ones—a poet does not make up new words, he argued, but rather puts old words together in new ways. Combinations of more distant frames may yield solutions of greater creativity than combinations of more proximally located frames (Mednick, 1962).

The entire process of forming new associations, however, comes with its own set of constraints. The pool of resources available for working memory is limited in both capacity and persistence. Much research has shown that people are only able to manage five to nine activated frames at a time (Miller, 1956), and unless they are actively rehearsed will begin to fade within 20 seconds (Brown, 1958). Because of these mechanisms of the mind, people may tend to rely heavily on their past experiences, reusing routine patterns of activation as bounded by the limits of working memory. As a result, it is highly likely that developing creative solutions to problems is challenging without some form of intervention.

Causal Relationships of the Cognitive Network Model of Creativity

If the assumptions about the nature of memory and knowledge hold, then the causal propositions illustrated in Fig. 2.1 should also hold. These eight propositions aim to explain the mechanisms responsible for the production of creative solutions to problems.

The Cognitive Network Model of creativity posits that creative solutions are caused by the formation of associations (new links or frames) in working memory of previously unrelated frames in the knowledge network (Koestler, 1964). As an example of this combination process, Rothenberg (1986) found that greater creativity results when artists are given stimuli consisting of two superimposed images than when stimuli contain the same two images presented side by side or as a composite (nonsuperimposed) image. Thus, conditions that increase the likelihood of new associations among previously unrelated frames should also increase the production of creative solutions (Arrow A). The likelihood of forming new associations

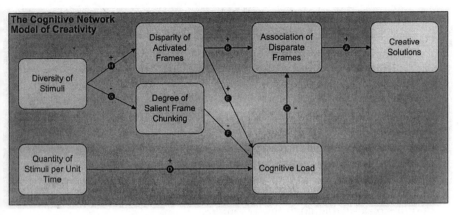

FIG. 2.1.   The propositions of the Cognitive Network Model of creativity. Each box–arrow–box combination represents a causal proposition. The direction of the arrow indicates the direction of causation. The mathematical operator on each arrow indicates whether a positive or inverse relationship exists between the constructs in the boxes it joins.

between previously unrelated frames increases as the disparity among the frames in working memory increases (Mobley et al., 1992; Arrow B). Consider that when any two frames are located in close proximity to one another in a knowledge network, it is highly likely that there may already exist a number of different relationships between these frames (e.g., consider the concepts *red, green, yellow,* and *blue*). Due to their similar meanings (they are all colors), these frames are separated by relatively small associative distances (Collins & Loftus, 1975), therefore limiting our potential to form new associations among them.

Simply increasing the disparity among the frames present in working memory, however, may not be sufficient to ensure that creative solutions will be produced. When cognitive load is high, we may simply lack the processing resources to extensively search our memory or develop new associations between distant salient frames. Thus, cognitive load interferes with the ability to create new associations among frames currently in working memory (Brown, 1958; Arrow C), suggesting a highly plausible explanation for satisficing. Furthermore, cognitive load will increase as the number of stimuli to which problem solvers are exposed per unit of time increases (Anderson, 1990; Miller, 1956; Arrow D) and as the disparity among the currently active frames increases (Anderson, 1990; Miller, 1956; Arrow E).

There are, however, some potential sources of economy that may help offset the limits of working memory. For example, Belleza and Young (1989) demonstrated that when frames are simultaneously active in working memory, they may become chunked into larger frames that an individual can wield as a single frame, thus reducing the current level of cognitive load. As a simple example, chunking enables us to group the string of digits 1, 4, 9, 2, 1, 7, 7, 6 into two significant dates in history: 1492 and 1776 (Lackman, Lackman, & Butterfield, 1979). In this manner, chunking allows us to reclaim some of our cognitive resources by consolidating the contents of working memory (Arrow F). Conversely, active frames that are highly diverse are not as likely to chunk as readily as frames that are more closely related (Belleza & Young, 1989; Arrow G). Finally, as the diversity of stimuli increases, so too does the disparity among the active frames (Anderson, 1990; Arrow H) as each new stimulus has the potential to act as a new entry point into one's knowledge network from which new frames may be activated. Thus, increasing the stimulus diversity increases the potential of making new associations among active frames while consuming greater amounts of available cognitive resources.

Therefore, the Cognitive Network Model of creativity represents a plausible answer to the question "What is a basic cognitive mechanism responsible for producing creative solutions to a problem?", one that is grounded in cognitive psychology, problem solving, and creativity research (for a more rigorous derivation of this model, please see Santanen, Briggs, & de Vreede, 2002). Readers with an especially keen interest in cognitive modeling approaches to creativity are also referred to chapter 1 (this volume).

EVALUATING THE COGNITIVE NETWORK MODEL OF CREATIVITY

Several experiments have been designed and carried out to evaluate the Cognitive Network Model of creativity at a high level (a precursor to future efforts to validate each individual link in the model). The following subsections describe two of these experiments in detail.

Four Variations on Solution-Generation Prompts

The model was evaluated in a laboratory setting and made use of networked computer workstations that were randomly arranged into groups of four people each through group support systems[2] software. Next, the Electronic Brainstorming (EBS) tool of the group support system was configured to mirror a traditional pencil-and-paper brainstorming session, where each participant had his or her own electronic sheet of paper on which to record his or her solutions. After each individual solution was typed and submitted, the EBS tool would automatically exchange that participant's elec-

---

[2]This study was conducted using the Electronic Brainstorming tool from GroupSystems for Windows Work Group Edition Version 2.1.

tronic sheet with another sheet from within the group. Having one more electronic discussion sheet than there are group members ensures that every group member will always be able to exchange their sheet for a new one, rather than simply getting back their same sheet. Having multiple discussion sheets is also a mechanism for limiting both information and cognitive overload because it segments the discussion of the group rather than presenting the entire contents of the group interaction in a single display area. After submitting a solution, each group member gets in return a different electronic discussion sheet that contains one or more solutions previously submitted by the remaining group members.

Benefits bestowed by EBS tools include parallel communication, group memory, and anonymity (Nunamaker, Dennis, Valacich, & Vogel, 1991). Parallel communication is especially potent because it allows all group members to contribute their solutions simultaneously, rather than wait to take their turn to speak as would normally occur in the social setting of oral brainstorming. The EBS provides a group memory as it automatically creates a log of all solutions that have been contributed by the group members. This memory allows individuals the opportunity to review previous solutions, stop to think, and then rejoin the discussion. Finally, anonymity decouples the solution from its particular source. These benefits have been shown to dramatically reduce the major sources of productivity losses in verbally interactive groups such as evaluation apprehension, production blocking (Diehl & Stroebe, 1987), and cognitive inertia (Lamm & Trommsdorff, 1973).

The most salient argument favoring the use of groups, however, is that the model predicts better results with groups than with individuals. Consider that if cognitive networks of knowledge result from exposure to stimuli, then because no two individuals have exactly the same experiences, knowledge networks should be different for every individual. Therefore, presentation of the same stimuli to different people should result in different patterns of spreading activation from person to person. Thus, the total knowledge applied to any given problem situation is greater in a group setting than in an individual setting, providing a strong case for group collaboration when solving complex problems, particularly during idea generation exercises (Osborn, 1957; Rickards, 1974). Similarly, it has been argued that solving ill-structured problems requires ideas from different people with different experiences to identify as many significant solution factors as possible (Rickards, 1988).

In a departure from much of the idea generation literature, Osborn's brainstorming rules were not employed for this study. Although a long history has demonstrated that following these rules provides specific benefits for groups (Parnes & Meadows, 1959), it is important to remember that these prescriptions were developed for verbally interactive groups. In contrast, the present study utilizes electronic brainstorming, calling into question the appropriateness of Osborn's rules. For example, consider each of these four rules in light of electronic brainstorming: (a) Criticism is ruled out, (b) freewheeling is welcome, (c) quantity is wanted, and (d) combination and improvement are sought.

Contrary to Osborn's first rule, several studies (Connolly, Jessup, & Valacich, 1990; Nunamaker et al., 1991) have demonstrated that critical (as opposed to supportive) feedback during an electronic brainstorming session, when coupled with anonymity, leads to significant benefits when compared with situations where this criticism is not offered. Second, if the only interaction that a group has derives from building on the ideas of others, combining and improving ideas can potentially lead to the production of a narrow set of similar ideas at the expense of a more diverse set of ideas. For example, many studies have highlighted the convergent tendencies (groupthink) of verbally interactive groups (Brown et al., 1998; Connolly, Routhieaux, & Schneider, 1993; Gettys et al., 1987). Osborn acknowledged that interacting groups often "fall into a rut" by concentrating and elaborating on a single problem dimension rather than exploring the entire problem space. Osborn's third principle is that quantity is wanted. This premise is based on the assumption that a certain percentage of any pool of solutions is likely to be considered better than the others. Therefore, as the size of the overall solution pool increases, so too should the number of good solutions. Although there is evidence supporting this premise (Diehl & Stroebe, 1987; Gallupe et al., 1992; Taylor, Berry, & Block, 1958), Briggs, Reinig, Shepherd, Yen, and Nunamaker (1997) cautioned that the model "Quality follows Quantity" may be incomplete, finding that idea quantity explained only 18% of the variance found in idea quality.[3] Thus, some evidence suggests that quantity alone may be insufficient for predicting and explaining constructs related to idea quality or creativity. Finally, with regard to freewheeling, Briggs et al. (1997) also found that idea quantity had a correlation of 0.93 with the number of useless ideas (those that make little or no difference on any problem symptom). Thus, freewheeling has a large potential to generate noise within the group. Because the purpose of experimental treatments (described later) is to focus the deliberation of the group, freewheeling may actually be counterproductive to creative problem solving.

In light of the previous discussion concerning Osborn's brainstorming rules, it appears that they might not apply to all group brainstorming situations. In particular, they do not seem appropriate to an EBS environment.

---

[3]Although it is possible that some undocumented attribute concerning the manner in which the Briggs et al. study was conducted was responsible for the low correlations between idea quantity and quality measures, this chapter presents evidence that is consistent with the findings of Briggs et al.

Given the significant differences that exist between verbal and EBS environments, Osborn's rules were replaced with directed brainstorming prompts that were delivered to the group members by a facilitator at specific timed intervals. The technique of directed brainstorming presents group members with a controlled set of stimuli that are specifically designed to activate multiple starting frames from which to explore the generation of new solutions to the problem tasks. Each new stimuli-activated frame might provide ready access to different areas of the knowledge network, thus avoiding the narrow activation patterns that can occur when problem solvers are given only a single problem statement as stimulus (Dennis et al., 1997). According to the model, multiple stimuli should help participants more easily find areas of their knowledge networks where they can create new associations between disparate frames, resulting in the generation of more creative solutions.

The experiment was designed to manipulate the model by presenting a specific set of stimuli to problem solvers as they generated solutions. Two problem-solving scenarios were used for this experiment: (a) a crisis response scenario for providing drinkable water to the victims of a typhoon, and (b) an organizational improvement scenario for a hypothetical school of business suffering from 19 interrelated symptoms. Each scenario was broken down into five problem-related topics (labeled A through E for illustrative purposes), as suggested by Davis (1986). Nearly any number of problem-related topics can be determined by someone such as a meeting facilitator or stakeholder, but for purposes of comparison within this study, five topics were chosen. Next, a series of 20 prompts were created—4 prompts from each of the five problem-related topics (see Table 2.1 for the prompts used for the school of business task).

These prompts were delivered to the four-member groups of problem solvers by a facilitator at a rate of one prompt every 2 minutes. Thus, the stimuli deliberately direct the attention of problem solvers to different facets of the solution space.

By varying the ordering of the prompts, three experimental conditions were created: solo, duet, and quartet. The solo variation presented problem solvers with the highest level of variety by arranging the prompts such that each prompt addressed a different topic than the one that preceded it. Topic changes occurred every 2 minutes and followed the pattern A-B-C-D-E-A-B-C-D-E-A-B-C-D-E-A-B-C-D-E. At the opposite end of the spectrum was the quartet variation, which presented problem solvers with the lowest level of variety by arranging the prompts in blocks of four, such that problem solvers received four different prompts for one topic and then four different prompts for the next topic. Thus, topic changes occurred every 8 minutes and followed the pattern AAAA-BBBB-CCCC-DDDD-EEEE. Finally, the duet variation introduced an intermediate level of variety by presenting prompts in pairs before changing to the next topic.

TABLE 2.1
Twenty Prompts Provided to Problem Solvers by the Facilitator

Topic	Directed Brainstorming Prompt
A	Suggest a solution that will solve the problems faced by the school of business.
A	Suggest another solution that will solve the problems.
A	Suggest a solution that will solve these problems that is different than any you see so far.
A	Suggest one more solution that will solve the problems of the school of business.
B	Suggest an inexpensive solution that will solve the problems in the school of business.
B	Suggest another solution that won't cost a lot to implement.
B	Suggest a solution that is cheap to implement that is different than any you have seen so far.
B	Suggest one more solution that is not costly and will solve the problems in the school of business.
C	Suggest a solution to the problems in the school of business that can be easily implemented.
C	Suggest another simple solution.
C	Suggest a solution that is easy to do that is different than any you see on your screen.
C	Suggest another simple solution that will solve the problems in the school of business.
D	Suggest a solution that can be implemented quickly.
D	Suggest another fast solution to the problems in the school of business.
D	Suggest a fast solution to these problems that is different than any you have seen so far.
D	Suggest one more solution that will quickly solve the problems faced by the school of business.
E	Suggest a solution that satisfies all of the different perspectives involved.
E	Suggest another solution that will be acceptable to each of the groups in the business school.
E	Suggest a different solution that will make everyone in the business school happy.
E	Suggest one more solution that takes each of the different groups into account.

Thus, topic changes occurred every 4 minutes and followed the pattern AA-BB-CC-DD-EE-AA-BB-CC-DD-EE. The final experimental condition, termed *free brainstorming*, served as a control; groups worked on their own without any form of facilitator prompting. Participants using free brainstorming were instructed to respond to the solutions of others in one of three ways:

- Expand on the solution, adding details.
- Argue with the solution.
- Suggest a completely new solution.

Subjects in all treatments brainstormed for a period of 40 minutes.

Expert judges with an average of 15 years of professional experience in the domain of the problem evaluated the brainstorming solutions contributed by participants and assigned each a creativity score (Amabile, 1983). Each solution was judged by at least two independent judges; interrater reliability scores exceeded 0.80 for both tasks.

As predicted, the results indicate that varying the presentation order of the same set of prompts led to significant differences ($p < .001$) in the concentrations of creative solutions generated by the groups across the various treatments.[4] The concentrations of solutions that were deemed creative for the solo- and quartet-directed brainstorming patterns were, on average, two and a half times greater than were the corresponding concentrations of creative solutions resulting from the duet condition. These findings are both statistically significant and consistent across each of the various creativity threshold levels for both tasks. Subjects who experienced the duet pattern of facilitation did not produce solutions of greater creativity than did subjects working without any prompting at all, nor were there any significant differences in the concentrations of creative solutions between the solo and quartet treatments. Interestingly, these results stand in direct contradiction to the notion of *quality equals quantity*: The three directed brainstorming treatments yielded highly similar quantities of unique solutions, yet the number of creative solutions across the treatments was significantly different. Finally, the control group that received no prompting during their brainstorming session resulted in the greatest amount of task-relevant discussion (such as asking one another questions about the problem or a previous solution).

Furthermore, content analysis showed that the nature of the creative solutions produced by the solo- and quartet-prompting patterns was different. The 50 solutions judged most creative in the quartet-prompting pattern tended to be narrowly focused (convergent) on one specific symptom at a time. An example of a narrowly focused solution resulting from the quartet treatment is: "Compensate the professors by providing them with housing that can be used as a tax benefit for the school." This solution specifically addresses the symptom of poor faculty compensation. Conversely, the 50 solutions judged most creative for the solo-prompting pattern were much more broad in scope (divergent) because many of them addressed several of the interrelated symptoms simultaneously. For example, the solution "Have social events that will allow teachers and students to get to know each

---

[4]The concentration of creative solutions was determined by dividing the number of solutions that exceeded a creativity threshold value (solutions were scored on a 5-point scale, 5 being *most creative*) by the total number of unique solutions produced by each respective group. Comparisons were made for creativity threshold values between 2.5 and 4.75, adjusted in 0.25 increments. However, due to the uniformity in the quantity of unique solutions generated by each group across the treatments, the outcomes remained unchanged when this same analysis is repeated simply using the quantity of creative solutions.

other outside of the school environment" is too broadly focused to neatly map to any single, known symptom for the school of business task.

The Cognitive Network Model suggests plausible explanations for these results. The quartet variation is likely to have produced a broad range of creative solutions because the probing pattern allowed for substantial spreading activation before a change of topics to explore solutions in a different part of the knowledge network. By staying on topic for four consecutive prompts, participants were required to move beyond the simple and obvious solutions that immediately came to mind when the first frame was activated by the first prompt. Problem solvers could then explore longer associative pathways, resulting in an increased likelihood of forming new associations among the activated frames.

For the solo variation, the more rapid topic switching resulted in more frequent juxtapositions of frames from diverse areas of the knowledge network, but the frequent topic switches led people to follow shorter associative paths, so the creative solutions did not stray as far from the topics of the prompts. By activating frames in rapid succession from disparate parts of the knowledge network, there is a higher likelihood of finding new associations among the resulting activated frames, thereby increasing the likelihood of generating creative solutions.

The duet pattern, which presented two consecutive prompts from the same topic, offered neither benefit of increased topic switching nor the benefit of traversing longer associative paths. Due to the prompting pattern, the frames that simultaneously occupied working memory in the duet variation were likely to have derived from more proximal locations in the knowledge network, thus providing less opportunity of forming new associative relationships ultimately providing no creative benefit.

Three Solution-Generation Techniques

Recently, Hender, Dean, Rodgers, and Nunamaker (2002) also investigated creative problem solving using the Cognitive Network Model of creativity. They constructed several experiments that explored the impacts of stimuli diversity on the resulting creativity level of the solutions to a problem-solving task. Their investigation involved the comparison of three creative solution-generation techniques: brainstorming, analogies, and assumptions reversals. In brainstorming, the only source of stimuli is the emerging pool contributed by the problem solvers as they work. Therefore, it is also the most basic of the three techniques.

The assumption reversals take a more structured approach to solution generation than does brainstorming. In this technique, people state their assumptions about the problem (e.g., "I assume the customers want us to maintain quality and keep prices low") and then brainstorm ideas that would be appropriate if the assumption were reversed (e.g., "What would we do if the customers wanted us to cut quality and raise prices?"). Because assumptions stem from traditional associations (strongly linked frames) about a problem, reversing them to introduce nontraditional, problem-related assumptions (weakly linked frames) might increase creativity by forcing the thinker to activate frames not traditionally associated with the problem.

The analogies technique uses stimuli that are designed to activate frames that are unrelated to the problem and then attempt to force new relationships (or associations) between the problem and the newly activated frames. This technique is essentially what Van Gundy (1988) termed the *forced relationships* technique. In this technique, people receive prompts like, "How is your problem like a duck in a sports car?" or "In what ways is your problem like a piece of polished granite?"

Based on the Cognitive Network Model, Hender et al. predicted that solutions generated using the analogies technique would be more creative (due to the use of unrelated stimuli) than solutions generated with either the assumptions reversals (which uses related stimuli) or more traditional brainstorming techniques (which uses no external stimuli). Their findings were consistent with predictions they derived from the Cognitive Network Model of creativity.

Distinguishing the Cognitive Network Model of Creativity From Existing Models of Creativity

The Cognitive Network Model of creativity and its predictions differ in several important ways from the models reviewed earlier in this chapter. For example, the matrix model presented by Brown et al. (1998) focuses on explaining cognitive factors related to the productivity of verbally interactive groups of brainstormers over a period of time and successfully models various individual cognitive traits such as preferences or tendencies for convergent versus divergent streams of ideas. The Cognitive Network Model, however, predicts specific circumstances under which creativity is likely to emerge and shows that manipulations of stimuli provided to problem solvers can result in pools of creative solutions that can be either convergent or divergent in nature. Thus, rather than viewing convergent and divergent styles as a specific antecedent to brainstorming activity, this study has shown that these styles can be easily manipulated and each style is capable of resulting in creative solutions in ill-structured problems.

The model of social and cognitive factors related to creativity in idea-generating groups presented by Paulus (2000) contains specific social and cognitive factors that are proposed to contribute to creativity in groups. Although the Paulus model does indicate that constructs such as novel association, priming, and attention are important to creative performance, the

Cognitive Network Model of creativity has demonstrated that there are at least two ways to create novel associations that ultimately lead to creative solutions. The first is to encourage participants to follow relatively long chains of spreading activation (the quartet facilitation pattern), whereas the second way is to activate frames from disparate areas of a knowledge network in rapid succession (the solo facilitation pattern). This study has demonstrated that both methods are effective means to improve creativity.

The model of cognitive stimulation in idea generation presented by Nagasundaram and Dennis (1993) endeavors to explain both productivity and innovativeness through the use of such factors as diversity, cardinality, and temporal distance. Although diversity of stimuli is hypothesized to positively influence creativity, the present study based on the Cognitive Network Model of creativity has shown that creativity can be manipulated while holding diversity of stimuli constant. For example, all three facilitated treatments employed the same set of directed brainstorming prompts, effectively controlling for the diversity of stimuli.

Another interesting model that has origins similar to the Cognitive Network Model of creativity is the Search for Ideas in Associative Memory (SIAM; Nijstad, Stroebe, & Lodewijkx, 2002). Although this model is derived from many of the same principles as is the Cognitive Network Model of creativity, SIAM is used to make predictions concerning the impact of semantically homogenous or diverse stimuli on the resulting levels of productivity of verbally interactive brainstorming groups. Findings based on SIAM indicate that providing diverse stimuli increases the breadth of idea production (ideas span many semantic categories), whereas providing homogenous stimuli increases the depth of production (ideas span few semantic categories). Although these findings are consistent with the findings obtained from the present study of the Cognitive Network Model of creativity, SIAM makes no predictions concerning the creativity of the resulting ideas. Additionally, SIAM predicts that switching from one semantic category to another as people are generating ideas is a form of cognitive interference that leads to productivity losses (a negative consequence). In an interesting contrast, the CNM predicts that each category switch is an opportunity for a creative solution to occur (a positive consequence).

Thus, the underpinnings of the Cognitive Network Model of creativity may be similar to the foundations of other models used to investigate brainstorming activities, yet the results obtained in this study cannot be explained by any of the brainstorming models described earlier in this chapter. This is largely a result of the differences in the phenomena of interest from each of these studies. Some authors have investigated productivity by measuring the quantity of unique ideas obtained during the study. Other authors have investigated quality or feasibility of ideas and then likened this qualitative measure to creativity. It is not immediately clear that quality, feasibility, and creativity can be directly equated to one another because each involves or invokes different constructs. For example, in the present study, one solution for the crisis response scenario was "Send millions of Energizer bunnies across the ocean with water bottles tied to their backs." This solution scored very highly for creativity (4.5 on a 5-point scale), yet received a score of only 1.0 (on a 5-point scale) for feasibility. Although this scoring is not surprising, it clearly illustrates that feasibility and creativity tap different underlying constructs, at least in the eyes of our field domain experts. Many researchers have long assumed that the quantity of ideas or solutions resulting from a brainstorming session is an appropriate surrogate for the quality of those same ideas. The results obtained by Briggs et al. (1997) and those presented in this study call that assumption into question. In the present study, three different treatments presented the same set of stimuli to groups engaged in electronic brainstorming. The average number of unique solutions resulting from each of those treatments was highly similar, yet the corresponding levels of creativity were significantly different.

Finally, one of the most salient contributions from this work highlights the importance for reporting even the most minute of procedural details concerning brainstorming activities. The experiment presented in this chapter introduced a subtle manipulation to solution-generation efforts, yet revealed powerful, distinct, and robust differences in outcome across two unstructured problem-solving tasks. This suggests that simply using the term *brainstorming* as a methodological description is far too ambiguous. Important details such as whether oral, written, or electronic brainstorming was used, the procedures followed by the participants, the specific configuration of the electronic brainstorming hardware and software, the presence or absence of a facilitator, the specific role played by that facilitator, and even the specific instructions given to the participants each play a vital role in the ability to compare and reconcile various brainstorming studies.

PRACTICAL IMPLICATIONS AND FUTURE DIRECTIONS

Empirical evidence suggests that the Cognitive Network Model of creativity may be a useful way to understand the causes of creativity. It may eventually help us understand the effects of the myriad of creative problem-solving techniques that currently exist. Furthermore, the Cognitive Network Model of creativity may also enable practitioners to better use existing creativity techniques. The model may also help researchers and practitioners alike to create new and improved methods for generating creative solutions to the problems they face. For example, consider some of the results of this study and the possible techniques that can be derived to benefit teams and organizations.

The first result that stands out is the high degree of discussion among the participants in the free brainstorming group (those who received no facilitation). Many of the contributions from these groups were from members seeking clarification, additional details, or some other form of task-relevant interaction as opposed to actionable solutions. This suggests that this type of brainstorming session may be well suited to situations where the problem is not well understood or defined clearly enough. Thus, the discussion type of interactions may well be important to help a group build consensus or shared understanding about a particularly difficult or complex problem.

Second, the solo-facilitation treatment resulted in highly creative solutions that were also sharply focused on a single dimension or symptom of the problem at hand. This finding indicates that the solo-facilitation pattern may be particularly useful in situations where it is important to focus the efforts of the problem solvers on some critical aspect of the given problem, or when creative solutions are needed to address problems that have small groups or homogenous groups of stakeholders.

Third, the quartet-facilitation treatment led to solutions of comparable creativity levels to that of the solo treatment, but were broadly focused and dealt simultaneously with many aspects of the problem at hand. This, in turn, indicates that quartet-like facilitation may be well suited in situations where there exists a large or heterogeneous constituency that needs to be considered.

Finally, these results suggest that there may even be some benefit to combining free brainstorming with either solo- or quartet-like facilitation when organizational circumstances dictate that problem discovery or consensus building is needed prior to focusing the efforts of the problem solvers on the specifics of the task at hand.

Although the CNM has revealed several interesting findings, there exist some caveats that need to be addressed in future research. For example, the individual propositions embodied by the model are in need of more sharply focused validation. In the present form of the model, it is difficult to gain specific insights concerning the diversity of stimuli construct because it is proposed to both increase the potential for creative solutions by increasing the disparity among activated frames and decrease the potential for creative solutions by increasing cognitive load. Thus, both positive and negative impacts are expected to result from manipulation of the same construct. It is currently unknown which of these impacts has greater significance to the model and to creative solution production. It is expected that the model will continue to evolve in the future as further insights are revealed. In its present form, the model has proved useful in learning about the production of creative solutions. It is hoped that the Cognitive Network Model of creativity will serve as impetus for research and organizational communities to be even more creative about new ways to improve creative problem-solving efforts.

REFERENCES

Amabile, T. M. (1983). The social psychology of creativity: A componential conceptualization. *Journal of Personality and Social Psychology, 45*, 357–376.

Anderson, J. R. (1990). *Language, memory, and thought.* Hillsdale, NJ: Lawrence Erlbaum Associates.

Baddeley, A. D. (1990). *Human memory: Theory and practice.* Needham Heights, MA: Allyn & Bacon.

Belleza, F. S., & Young, D. R. (1989). Chunking of repeated events in memory. *Journal of Experimental Psychology, 15*, 990–997.

Briggs, R. O., Reinig, B. A., Shepherd, M. M., Yen, J., & Nunamaker, J. F., Jr. (1997). Quality as a function of quantity in electronic brainstorming. In J. F. Nunamaker, Jr., & R. H. Sprague, Jr. (Eds.), *Proceedings of the 30th Hawaii International Conference on Systems Sciences* (pp. 94–103). Los Alamitos, CA: IEEE Computer Society Press.

Brown, J. A. (1958). Some tests of the decay theory of immediate memory. *Quarterly Journal of Experimental Psychology, 10*, 12–21.

Brown, V., Tumeo, M., Larey, T. S., & Paulus, P. B. (1998). Modeling cognitive interactions during group brainstorming. *Small Group Research, 29*, 495–526.

Collins, A. M., & Loftus, E. F. (1975). A spreading activation theory of semantic processing. *Psychological Review, 82*, 407–428.

Connolly, T., Jessup, L. M., & Valacich, J. S. (1990). Effects of anonymity and evaluative tone on idea generation in computer-mediated groups. *Management Science, 36*, 689–703.

Connolly, T., Routhieaux, R. L., & Schneider, S. K. (1993). On the effectiveness of group brainstorming: Test of one underlying cognitive mechanism. *Small Group Research, 24*, 490–503.

Cyert, R. M., & March, J. G. (1963). *A behavioral study of the firm.* Englewood Cliffs, NJ: Prentice-Hall.

Davis, G. A. (1986). *Creativity is forever.* Dubuque, IA: Kendall/Hunt.

Dennis, A. R., Valacich, J. S., Carte, T. A., Garfield, M. J., Haley, B. J., & Aronson, J. E. (1997). Research report: The effectiveness of multiple dialogues in electronic brainstorming. *Information Systems Research, 8*, 203–211.

Diehl, M., & Stroebe, W. (1987). Productivity loss in brainstorming groups: Toward the solution of a riddle. *Journal of Personality and Social Psychology, 53*, 497–509.

Dunker, K. (1945). On problem solving [Special issue]. *Psychological Monographs, 270*(58).

Gallupe, R. B., Dennis, A. R., Cooper, W. H., Valacich, J. S., Bastianutti, L. M., & Nunamaker, J. F., Jr. (1992). Electronic brainstorming and group size. *Academy of Management Journal, 35*, 350–369.

Gettys, C. F., Pliske, R. M., Manning, C., & Casey, J. T. (1987). An evaluation of human act generation performance. *Organizational Behaviour and Human Decision Processes, 39*, 23–51.

Goswami, A. (1996). Creativity and the quantum: A unified theory of creativity. *Creativity Research Journal, 9*, 47–61.

Hender, J. M., Dean, D. L., Rodgers, T. L., & Nunamaker, J. (2002). An examination of the impact of stimuli type and GSS structure on creativity: Brainstorming versus non-brainstorming techniques in a GSS environment. *Journal of Management Information Systems, 18*, 59–86.

Isaksen, S. G., & Parnes, S. J. (1985). Curriculum planning for creative thinking and problem solving. *The Journal of Creative Behavior, 19*, 1–29.

Koestler, A. (1964). *The act of creation*. New York: Dell.

Lackman, R., Lackman, J. L., & Butterfield, E. C. (1979). *Cognitive psychology and information processing: An introduction*. Hillsdale, NJ: Lawrence Erlbaum Associates.

Lamm, H., & Trommsdorff, G. (1973). Group versus individual performance on tasks requiring ideation proficiency (brainstorming): A review. *European Journal of Social Psychology, 3*, 361–388.

Martindale, C. (1995). Creativity and connectionism. In S. M. Smith, T. B. Ward, & R. A. Finke (Eds.), *The creative cognition approach* (pp. 249–268). Cambridge, MA: MIT Press.

Mednick, S. A. (1962). The associative basis of the creative process. *Psychological Review, 69*, 220–232.

Miller, G. A. (1956). The magical number seven, plus or minus two: Some limits on our capacity for processing information. *Psychological Review, 63*, 81–97.

Minsky, M. (1975). A framework for representing knowledge. In P. H. Winston (Ed.), *The psychology of computer vision* (pp. 211–277). New York: McGraw-Hill.

Mobley, M. I., Doares, L. M., & Mumford, M. D. (1992). Process analytic models of creative capacities: Evidence for the combination and reorganization process. *Creativity Research Journal, 5*, 125–155.

Nagasundaram, M., & Dennis, A. R. (1993). When a group is not a group: The cognitive foundation of group idea generation. *Small Group Research, 24*, 463–489.

Neisser, U. (1966). *Cognitive psychology*. New York: Appleton-Century-Crofts.

Nijstad, B. A., Stroebe, W., & Lodewijkx, H. F. M. (2002). Cognitive stimulation and interference in groups: Exposure effect in an idea generation task. *Journal of Experimental Social Psychology, 38*, 535–544.

Nunamaker, J. F., Jr., Dennis, A. R., Valacich, J. S., & Vogel, D. R. (1991). Information technology for negotiating groups: Generating options for mutual gain. *Management Science, 37*, 1325–1345.

Osborn, A. F. (1957). *Applied imagination: Principles and procedures of creative thinking* (2nd ed.). New York: Scribner.

Parnes, S. J., & Meadow, A. (1959). Effects of "brainstorming" instructions on creative problem solving by trained and untrained subjects. *The Journal of Educational Psychology, 50*, 171–176.

Paulus, P. B. (2000). Groups, teams, and creativity: The creative potential of idea-generating groups. *Applied Psychology: An International Review, 49*, 237–262.

Rhodes, M. (1961). An analysis of creativity. *Phi Delta Kappan, 42*, 305–310.

Rickards, T. (1974). *Problem-solving through creative analysis*. New York: Wiley.

Rickards, T. (1988). *Creativity at work*. Borkfield, VT: Gower.

Rossman, J. (1931). *The psychology of the inventor: A study of the patentee*. Washington, DC: Inventors Publishing.

Rothenberg, A. (1986). Artistic creation as stimulated by superimposed versus combined-composite visual images. *Journal of Personality and Social Psychology, 50*, 370–381.

Santanen, E. L., Briggs, R. O., & de Vreede, G.-J. (2002). Toward an understanding of creative solution generation. In J. F. Nunamaker, Jr., & R. H. Sprague, Jr. (Eds.), *Proceedings of the 35th Hawaii International Conference on Systems Sciences* (pp. 221–230). Los Alamitos, CA: IEEE Computer Society Press.

Simon, H. (1960). *The new science of management*. New York: Harper & Row.

Taylor, D. W., Berry, P. C., & Block, C. H. (1958). Does group participation when using brainstorming facilitate or inhibit creative thinking? *Administrative Science Quarterly, 3*, 23–47.

Van Gundy, A. B. (1987). *Creative problem solving: A guide for trainers and management*. New York: Quorum.

Van Gundy, A. B. (1988). *Techniques of structured problem solving* (2nd ed.). New York: Van Nostrand Reinhold.

Woodman, R. W., Sawyer, J. E., & Griffin, R. W. (1993). Toward a theory of organizational creativity. *Academy of Management Review, 18*, 293–321.

Chapter 3

Structuring Creativity: Creative Templates in Negotiation

Jacob Goldenberg
Dina Nir
Eyal Maoz
Hebrew University of Jerusalem

Creativity, in the negotiation context, is considered a key ingredient in the creation of value and in transforming *fixed pie* or even deadlocked situations into integrative, win–win agreements (Fisher, Ury, & Patton, 1991; Pruitt & Carnevale, 1993; Thompson, 2001). Furthermore, creatively constructed, integrative solutions are known to yield higher joint benefits than distributive agreements because they are able to reconcile the parties' needs and interests (Pruitt, 1983a). However, discovering and tapping into the creative potential in any negotiation is a challenge that is easily advocated, but in most organizations hard to implement.

One promising approach to this problem may be found in recent developments in the creativity literature, demonstrating that creative and insightful problem solving can be achieved through systematic inventive thinking (Goldenberg & Mazursky, 2002; Goldenberg, Mazursky, & Solomon, 1999a; Maimon & Horowitz, 1999). The main thesis advanced in this stream of research is that certain structures in creative ideation and problem-solving processes are identifiable, objectively verifiable, and can be studied, generalized, and implemented across various managerial areas. These structures, termed *creativity templates,* can serve as facilitative tools in channeling the ideation process, thereby enabling the negotiator to be more productive and focused in generating creative options and proposals.

The template approach to creativity and problem solving has, so far, been successfully applied in new product development processes (Goldenberg, Mazursky, & Solomon, 1999b), technological innovations (Goldenberg, Mazursky, & Solomon, 1999c), and advertising (Goldenberg, Mazursky, & Solomon, 1999d). The current research is an attempt to bring this innovative technique into the negotiation arena.

ORGANIZATIONS, NEGOTIATIONS, AND CREATIVITY

The rapidly changing and dynamic nature of today's business world, and the growing interdependence of people within and between organizations, implies that negotiating is a fundamental part of everyday business life and a core managerial and leadership activity. In essence, negotiations occur whenever interdependent parties make mutual decisions regarding the allocation of scarce resources (Bazerman, Mannix, & Thompson, 1988). This means that people in the workplace are continuously negotiating to accomplish their goals, whether they are trying to reach a deadline, build team consensus, or market a product.

Negotiating successfully, however, requires the parties to discover integrative solutions that reconcile divergent interests and provide high joint benefit (Pruitt, 1981). This in return strengthens the long-term relationship between the negotiating parties and promotes future cooperation and organizational effectiveness (Pruitt & Carnevale, 1982). The emphasis on reaching integrative solutions, as opposed to reaching distributive outcomes or compromises (i.e., splitting the difference), has brought to the forefront the importance of introducing creativity to negotiation (Fisher, Ury, & Patton, 1991; Pruitt, 1983a, 1983b). Managers who are able to be creative in the process of a negotiation are more likely to reach successful solutions to conflicts, and are better positioned to maximize potential opportunities and achieve personal and organizational objectives.

Considerable research has been conducted to help improve our understanding of the antecedents, conditions, and processes that lead to effective negotiations. However, perhaps less emphasis has been placed on the creative aspect of the negotiation process. Although there is wide agreement concerning the importance of creativity, discovering and tapping into the creative potential in most negotiations remains a challenge that is hard to implement. In practice, negotiators commonly fail to reach creative solutions and win–win agreements, and they tend to settle for ineffective compromises instead (Bazerman & Neale, 1983). As a result, opportunities and resources are left on the table, rather than being used to promote interests and achieve goals. These sometimes ineffective results can be explained by negotiators' tendency to entirely overlook the potential for creative and integrative solutions. Often negotiators assume that the parties' interests are either incompatible or even opposed, when in fact these interests may be similar on many issues (Thompson & Hastie, 1990a, 1990b). It seems negotiators tend to approach negotiations with a fixed pie perception, thinking that the negotiation is a zero-sum game or a win–lose enterprise. This competitive way of thinking tends to inhibit the creative problem-solving processes necessary for the development of integrative solutions (Bazerman, Magliozzi, & Neale, 1985; Thompson & Hastie, 1990b). Consequently, instead of creatively capitalizing on compatible interests and reaching win–win agreements, these commonly held assumptions often lead negotiators to a lose–lose effect (Thompson & Herbec, 1996). Interestingly, some research shows that even negotiators, who are genuinely interested in building a long-term relationship with the other party, have a hard time being creative and often fail to reach integrative agreements (Fry, Firestone, & Williams, 1983; Kurtzberg & Medvec, 1999; Thompson & DeHarpport, 1998). Further, even if negotiators do succeed in improving their efficiency and move toward an improved joint outcome, more often than not they fail to reach optimality and rarely achieve a Pareto optimal solution (Bazerman, 1998; Hyder, Prietula, & Weingart, 2000; Neale & Northcraft, 1986; Pruitt, 1981; Raiffa, 1982).

Over the years, many strategies have been proposed to help negotiators overcome ineffective tendencies and perceptions and to promote creative problem-solving processes. These strategies are aimed at improving negotiators' ability to generate creative options, expand the pie, and reach integrative agreements. In essence, the prevalent strategies emphasize the importance of creating a wide base of information, expanding the issue space, focusing on the differences between the parties (and capitalizing on them), and then creating trade-offs for mutual gain. In the following section, we introduce a new approach to bringing creativity to the negotiation table—the Creative Negotiation Templates (CNT) approach.

CREATIVE NEGOTIATION TEMPLATES (CNT)

Creativity templates can trace their roots to research conducted during the 1940s by Altschuller (1985, 1986), who postulated that repeated patterns or formulas underlie successful ideas. After analyzing and mapping over 200,000 patents and technological innovations, Altschuller succeeded in identifying a number of consistently emerging patterns of innovations. The basic contention was that if these regularities can be identified, they can be used as tools to project new creative product ideas for the future. This framework has since been successfully applied to technological innovations (Maimon & Horowitz, 1999), new product ideation (Goldenberg, Mazursky, & Solomon, 1999b), and advertising (Goldenberg, Mazursky, & Solomon, 1999d), and it has demonstrated that creative and insightful problem solving can be achieved through systematic inventive thinking (Goldenberg

& Mazursky, 2002; Goldenberg, Mazursky, & Solomon, 1999a, 1999c). Further, applying the idea of templates is consistent with the *Restricted Scope* principle to ideation. According to this principle, channeling thinking along predefined inventive routes is more efficient than many other alternatives, such as divergent thinking or unbounded scope (Finke, Ward, & Smith, 1992).

In this chapter, we propose that such inventive routes (templates) also exist in negotiation, and they can be effectively utilized by negotiators seeking new creative solutions. As in the original domains of discovery (new products), the approach is founded on identifying the patterns that underlie recognized creative outcomes—this time in negotiation. Therefore, we started with a detailed mapping of past examples of well-known creative and successful solutions to negotiations. The mapping procedure allowed us to identify, understand, and characterize four main underlying patterns and to produce a systematic way of looking for these types of outcomes in future organizational situations. These four CNTs discovered in the negotiation arena are termed *attribute dependency, multiplication, replacement,* and *displacement.* A prescribed procedure accompanies each of these templates and allows the negotiator to manage the ideation process and produce creative results effectively (Nir, Goldenberg, & Maoz, 2003). It is important to note that using creative templates is not intended to replace other methods and processes for increasing the levels of creativity in a negotiation (e.g., mood; Carnevale & Isen, 1986). Rather, it is our contention that using templates can increase the chances for successful outcomes even when such strategies are employed. Further, because a template is, in essence, a recipe for managing the generation of effective creative ideas, it goes beyond approaches such as ThinkLets (Briggs, Vreede, & Nunamaker, 2003; Hender et al., 2002; Sosik, Avolio, & Kahai, 1997), which suggest that such recipes might be useful, but do not direct negotiators as to "how" specifically to go about the process.

In the next section, we introduce each unique template from three different angles. First, we briefly describe the basic idea behind the template. Then we illustrate how the template exists in the field of new product development—the original field of discovery. Finally, we systematically walk through an example from the negotiation literature to demonstrate the existence of the template in negotiation and to show how this particular template can be implemented.

THE ATTRIBUTE DEPENDENCY TEMPLATE

The basic principle behind attribute dependency involves finding seemingly independent attributes and discovering new, potentially productive dependencies between them. This approach is consistent with earlier work done by

Mednick (1962), who defined the creative process as the forming of associative elements into new combinations. Koestler (1964) viewed creativity in much the same manner and explained the creative process as the *bisociation* of two conceptual matrixes that are not normally associated. Indeed even Albert Einstein elaborated on using combinatory play as a creative, productive process (Ghiselin, 1952). Although both Mednick and Koestler emphasized the importance of these creative cognitive processes, they did not fully explain how these processes actually work or how one may promote their reoccurrence. In this section, we propose the attribute dependency procedure as one possible avenue for reaching these desired results.

Having first been developed in the new product arena, an example of attribute dependency from that field might help clarify the procedure and its characteristics. Consider the problem of dripping wax from a candle. Can attribute dependency help us fix this problematic characteristic and create a clean version of the candle? We can start by listing as many of the attributes of the traditional candle as possible (length, radius, melting temperature, color, etc.), noting that most are unrelated (i.e., same color throughout the length of the candle, same melting temperature throughout its radius). We now, systematically, examine possible dependencies among these attributes. Once we reach the dependency between the radius and the melting point, we can proclaim, "Eureka!" Producing a candle with a lower melting point in its center and a higher melting point in its outer parameter creates the nondrip candle we sought (see Fig. 3.1). By causing a U-shaped dimple in the top surface, we are able to prevent the melted wax from dripping.

This innovative and obviously beneficial structure of a candle can be graphically described as a new dependency between two variables that were previously independent (i.e., the melting point and the candle radius; see Fig. 3.2a). Note that this process was not necessarily specifically focused on solving the candle-dripping problem. Indeed many other new candle products can also emerge from using the attribute dependency template (e.g., a candle with different color wax along its length), and so the nondrip prod-

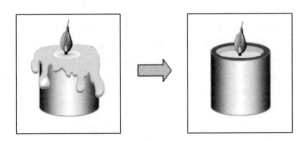

FIG. 3.1. Melting candle example.

uct is just one obviously successful outcome of the many creative options that may be produced through this approach. Creating such a dependency between two previously unrelated attributes is a regularly recurring pattern in successful and innovative new products, and it has been empirically observed across a wide range of product categories (Goldenberg, Mazursky, & Solomon, 1999b).

Attribute Dependency in Negotiation

The attribute dependency template can be used to generate many creative solutions for negotiators. To illustrate the underlying template in the context of negotiation, consider the following example concerning the Mayor of Pageville and Townsend Oil (Fisher, Uri, & Patton, 1991). The Mayor of Pageville intends to raise tax rates on local businesses. The mayor is also interested in encouraging industrial expansion to provide new jobs and strengthen the city's economy. Under this new policy, Townsend Oil, a local refinery, will experience a tax increase from $1 million to $2 million a year. Townsend Oil is presently considering a major refurbishment and expansion of the plant and has been encouraging a plastic plant they work with to relocate nearby and so lower their costs. With the threat of increased taxation, both initiatives may be halted. A creative solution was reached when the mayor agreed to implement a tax holiday of 7 years for new industries and a reduction in tax for existing industries that choose to expand. Thus, the town will be encouraging Townsend Oil to expand its plant and introduce more industries to the area while meeting its true objectives.

This example illustrates an attribute dependency outcome—because a relationship was created between two previously unrelated variables (see Fig. 3.2b for graphic representation of this example). Before the new dependency, the tax level was related only to standard economical criteria, and not to type of company (new vs. existing or expanding vs. nonexpanding). Graphically, this nonrelationship is represented by a straight line in the two-attribute space. The new dependency creates a link between these variables—tax level and type of company—and is described as a step function in Fig. 3.2b.

In addition to the solution reached by both parties in this example, using the attribute dependency template can offer a wide range of creative and potentially beneficial options that could reconcile the interests of both city and industry. Consider, for example, creating a new dependency between the level of tax and the number of local workers Townsend would employ (the more they employ, the lower the level of taxes). Another option could be creating a new dependency between the timing of the expansion and the number of years they receive a tax reduction (the quicker they start expanding, the longer their tax reduction period will be).

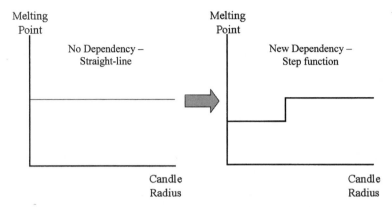

FIG. 3.2a. Attribute dependency in the candle example.

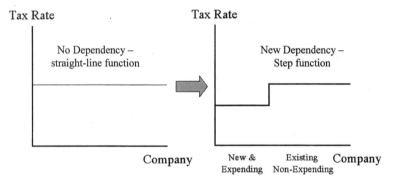

FIG. 3.2b. Attribute dependency in the Pageville and Townsend case.

To develop trade-off offers through the attribute dependency template, a negotiator should start by assembling a list of as many relevant variables that exist within the negotiation context (internal variables) and its immediate surroundings (external variables). The main distinction between internal and external variables is that internal variables are under the direct control of at least one of the parties in the negotiation, whereas external variables are not controlled by either party, yet are part of the immediate environment (see Table 3.1 for a list of these variables in the case of Townsend Oil and the City of Pageville).

After defining the variable space, an initial, internal forecasting matrix may be constructed to start managing the ideation process. The internal forecasting matrix has all the internal variables (of both parties) in both the rows and the columns (see partial matrix in Table 3.2) and contains *all* the possible trade-offs the parties can reach without including variables that are not under their control. We now turn our attention to the numerous inter-

TABLE 3.1
Partial List of Internal and External Variables
in the Pageville and Townsend Oil Case

Internal Variables Under the Control of Townsend	Internal Variables Under the Control of Pageville	External Variables in the Immediate Environment
Plant size	City tax rate	Time
Number of employees	Tax payment terms	City tax rates in neighboring towns
Community projects	Service levels	State of the economy
Political contributions	Investment in infrastructure	State and federal tax levels
Investment in growth	Community activities	Existing versus new companies
. . .	. . .	. . .

TABLE 3.2
A Partial Matrix of the Townsend Oil Case

	A Plant Size	B Investment in Growth	C ...	D City Tax Rate	E Tax Payment Terms	F ...
1 Plant size	X	X	X	X	X	X
2 Investment in growth	1	X	X	X	X	X
3 ...	0	0	X	X	X	X
4 City tax rate	0	0	0	X	X	X
5 Tax payment terms	0	0	0	1	X	X
6 ...	0	0	0	0	0	X

actions inherent in the matrix. First, interactions between the same variables are marked with an X, as are the redundant cells on the top right of the matrix. When an existing dependency between two variables is identified in the matrix, the relevant cell is marked with a "1." For example, in Table 3.2, if different tax rates result in different payment schedules, then a dependency already exists between the two variables, and so Cell D5 must be marked as "1." Similarly, the number "1" in Cell A2 denotes an existing dependency between plant size and the required investment. When a dependency is not identified, the relevant cell is marked with a "0." For example, there is no dependency between the tax rate and the plant size of a company, and therefore Cell A4 is marked "0."

After all the cells in the matrix are filled, the matrix becomes a tool for systematically scanning all null cells for potential integrative trade-offs.

Each zero-mode cell is an opportunity to define a new dependency. All we need to do is preliminarily examine whether the situation is able to sustain the added dependency and then identify the benefits of the new idea in terms of a trade-off offer. What would the advantages be for the parties implementing this offer? Would this option satisfy their interests? Here each party draws on their different capabilities, resources, attitudes, and preferences, and examines whether the specific trade-off on hand would effectively satisfy their own interests. For example, let us examine Cell B4. We can create a dependency between investment in growth and tax rates. That is, companies committed to substantial growth would pay a lower tax rate than other companies. The benefits of this offer to both parties are easy to see. Cell A5 suggests a dependency between plant size and payment terms, thus different sized companies can pay on different schedules (or get different cash incentives). Obviously, every dependency identified in this manner means changing the number in the matrix from "0" to a "1."

After examining the possible dependencies inherent in the internal forecasting matrix, it is time to move into the third dimension. This is done by crossing the internal matrix with the external variables. Thus, every identified dependency (cell with a "1") in the initial matrix can also be dependent on an external variable. For example, the dependency suggested earlier between growing companies and tax rates is problematic in one regard: Is a current investment in growth worth a lifetime tax reduction? Obviously, this offer would benefit if we add time into the equation (e.g., provide a tax break for 7 years only). Additional two-dimensional trade-offs, this time between internal and external variables, may be introduced as well. For example, creating a dependency between tax rate and new versus existing companies would encourage Townsend's customers to relocate to the area and, at the same time, increase employment and create future income for the city.

As we have illustrated in this case, when using the attribute dependency template, our aim is to read the information already embedded in the negotiation context and its immediate environment, and seek new and insightful ways to combine this information. Therefore, we propose that using this structured technique is bound to result in the creation of numerous, innovative, and effective trade-off options.

THE MULTIPLICATION TEMPLATE

The multiplication template involves multiplying a component once or more to create different subfunctions that contribute synergistically to the accomplishment of the main desired function. The additional component does not carry the same exact function as its parent. Rather, with a modification in its parameters, it carries a different function to obtain a synergetic or additive effect. A classic example is the double-bladed razor. The first blade's function was to shave the hair off the face. Simply adding an extra blade to provide another shaving surface is not very useful. However, adding an extra blade at a slight angle that shaves, but also raises whiskers so that the other blade can cut them cleanly, has tremendous value to shavers (see Fig. 3.3a for graphic representation of this example).

Multiplication in Negotiation

The example we have chosen to depict the multiplication template is that of management's attempt to introduce a new salary scheme in an insurance agency (Lewicki, Saunders, & Minton, 1999). An independent insurance agent in a small town discussed the difficulty of moving some of the agency staff from a straight salary compensation system to a base salary and performance pay beyond that, with no limits to the amount they could make. The agent was surprised to discover a lot of resistance among the sales representatives. The representatives were afraid of losing the guaranteed base pay, without knowing how much money they would really make under the new system. The problem was that the representatives did not trust the system and did not trust in their ability to earn the performance-based income. The problem was solved when the agency agreed to maintain the old system, but also keep a new set of records, as if they were already on the new system. During this time, the staff could see actual results and compare the two systems (see Fig. 3.3b for graphic representation of this example).

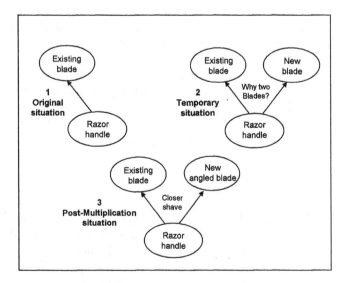

FIG. 3.3a.   Multiplication template in the razor example.

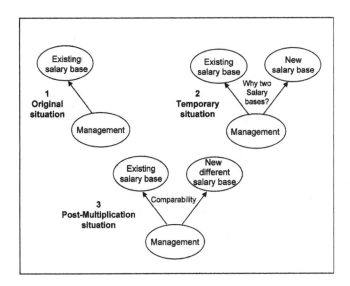

FIG. 3.3b.   Multiplication template in the salary base example.

This example illustrates a creative multiplication that enabled the insurance company to prove their system is advantageous to their employees before actually transferring to the new system. Obviously, the salary system was the component that was multiplied. However, it was multiplied with a modification, and so created two parallel salary systems that could be compared. Consider the benefits of using multiplication even further and multiplying the salary system more than once. This would create a comparison across multiple salary schemes, and so allow the insurance company (and salespersons) to discover the optimal scheme.

THE REPLACEMENT TEMPLATE

The replacement template is based on removing an intrinsic element in the negotiation and replacing it with another element that fulfills the same function. The replacement element is a resource or component that exists in the immediate environment of the negotiated context. Basically, we look for a component of the negotiation that is used to achieve some goal of one or more of the parties. The first step toward implementing the template is to eliminate a valuable component from the situation while retaining the component's function. This operation creates a temporarily inconsistent structure, which is then remedied by finding another way to fulfill the same goal—using other components that exist in the negotiated space.

For an example from the new product design field, consider a manufacturer of children's products applying this template. The manufacturer could visualize a kitchen high chair and remove an essential internal component (e.g., the chair legs). Removal of the legs from the chair (while maintaining their function) would leave the chair floating in the air at a desired height. This seemingly inconsistent thought construct serves to complete the replacement template. The aim at the second stage would be to replace the chair legs with an existing external component that would keep the seat at the proper height constantly. One creative option would be to attach the chair to a table; consequently, the table replaces the missing component (the legs) and a new product emerges—a lightweight, easy-to-carry, baby's high chair that can fit any table (for graphic representation of this example, see Fig. 3.4a). Another benefit of this product is that, no matter what the height of the table may be, the baby seat is always positioned at the appropriate convenient height in relation to the table.

Replacement in Negotiations

Resource shortage is a constant issue of conflict in most organizations. Consider, for example, a case where two departments in a large consulting firm are fighting over an adjacent room that had recently become vacant (The Space Wars Case; Nir et al., 2003). The room was originally designated by management to be evenly distributed between the two departments. Although the Information Technology Department had long been depending on this area for a much needed conference room, the Accounting De-

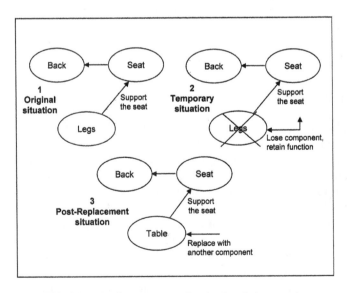

FIG. 3.4a.   Replacement template in the chair example.

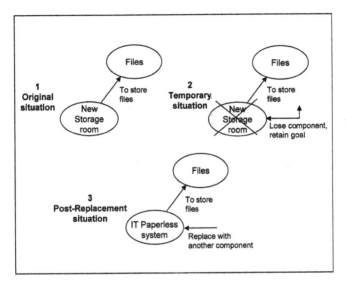

FIG. 3.4b.   Replacement template in the Space Wars case.

partment was desperate to get its hands on the same space to alleviate its problem of overflowing archives. Dividing the room between the two departments could not solve either party's needs because the space was not big enough to maintain both functions at the same time. The solution in this case was for the Information Technology Department to design and help implement a new paperless storage system for the Accounting Department's overall needs, and in return the Accounting Department would relinquish its hold on the new room. Thus, the Information Technology Department obtained the entire room and transformed it into the meeting room they needed all along, and the Accounting Department would gain an efficient, long-term solution for its overflowing archives. Further benefits were created because the Accounting Department was able to increase its available space even further by transferring most of its existing files to the paperless system. Moreover, both parties agreed that the Accounting Department could use the meeting room for its own needs whenever it was free.

In this case, beginning the replacement template process would involve the removal of an intrinsic component from the configuration, which would be the Accounting Department's intended new archive room. However, this leaves the department with all the overflowing cabinet files in the air because the need for extra storage still exists. Then the missing component is replaced by another component existing in the immediate (yet not obvious) environment—the Information Technology's ability to construct a paperless filing system (see Fig. 3.4b). In hindsight, this solution obviously works well for all concerned, but often these creative options elude negotiating parties centered on dividing the pie rather than on its possible expansion.

THE DISPLACEMENT TEMPLATE

The displacement template states that a component may be eliminated from the configuration of a system along with its functions, and thus a new solution is created. As in the case of the replacement template, here too an essential internal component (element) is removed from the configuration. However, in contrast to the replacement template, its associated function (goal) is removed as well.

In the example of the chair we presented earlier, the legs were removed from the configuration of the chair while retaining their function (which is to support the seat at a certain height). In the displacement template, however, the function of the missing component is excluded as well. The chair does not hang in mid-air as it did in the replacement template, but rather the chair seat is now at ground level (the legs and their function are gone). But what benefits can emerge from a legless chair? Actually, this configuration of a legless chair is widely used for sitting on the sand at the beach, where it solves the problem of legs digging into the sand and causing regular chairs to be unstable and uncomfortable to sit on (see Fig. 3.5a). Such a chair has an additional advantage: It is easy to carry.

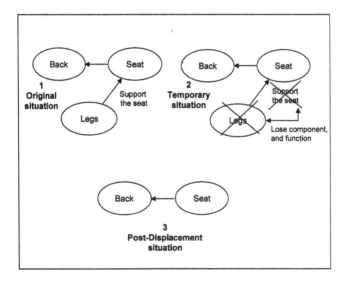

FIG. 3.5a.   Displacement template in the chair example.

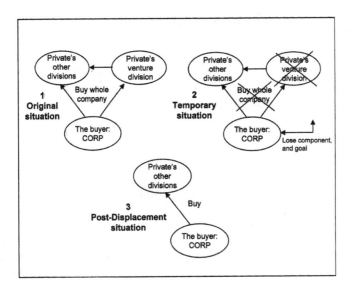

FIG. 3.5b.   Displacement template in the Corp and Private case.

Displacement in Negotiation

Consider, for example, the following negotiation between two companies (Bazerman & Neale, 1992): A large corporation (Corp) wanted to make a friendly acquisition of one of its suppliers, a privately held company (Private). Corp offered $14 million for Private, but Private insisted on $16 million. Neither side found a $15 million price tag acceptable. The two parties had different views about a new high-tech entrepreneurial division (Venture) of Private. Corp considered Venture to be worth only $1 million (of the $14 million they offered), whereas Private truly believed in the viability of the new products under development and had valued this division at $6 million. An agreement was reached where Corp agreed to acquire Private for $12 million ($2 million less than they offered, while losing only a $1 million asset from their perspective), but the owners of Private would retain control of the entrepreneurial division (Venture). From Private's perspective, this agreement would be better than the $16 million it had demanded because it received $12 million and it still owned Venture, which it valued at $6 million. Therefore, its total value stands at $18 million. The agreement reached in this example depicts the thought process of the displacement template while successfully expanding the pie for both parties. As described earlier, a displacement would occur due to the elimination of a significant component along with its functions from the configuration of a system (see Fig. 3.5b). Indeed, in this case, the entrepreneurial division (Venture) was eliminated from the deal, and so the companies were able to reach an agreement with higher utility for both sides compared with a compromise on price. The added value was reached due to the different views regarding the worth of the entrepreneurial division, but it was the removal of the division that enabled these benefits to be seized. In the next section, we present the results of a study aimed at exploring and verifying the prevalence of these templates in the negotiation context.

MAPPING STUDY

Altschuller (1985, 1986) employed a mapping of patents and technological inventions to formulate patterns of inventions. A similar mapping technique was later used to identify templates in the engineering, new product development, and advertising fields (Goldenberg, Mazursky, & Solomon, 1999b; Maimon & Horowitz, 1999). Thus, it seems only logical to use the same procedure to ascertain whether, as we posit, certain templates underlie negotiated outcomes. Further, the study was also designed to test the hypothesis that agreements displaying a template would, on average, be judged more creative than nontemplate-based agreements. The basic approach to this study was one similar to that used in the marketing area for mapping new products and advertising campaigns—that is, using judges to pigeonhole a wide variety of negotiated agreements into templates bins (including a no-template bin) and then using different judges for the creativity evaluations.

Procedure

A set of 40 examples of negotiations and their corresponding negotiated (or proposed) agreements were collected from the negotiation literature. The negotiated situations ranged from personal home situations to negotiations among organizations, businesses, and countries. Each sample case was rewritten, for the purpose of the current study, in a fixed two-part format, keeping the text as close as possible to the original narrative. The first of the two parts explained the negotiated situation and included background information, whereas the second part presented the agreement actually reached or the one proposed by the original authors.

Each of the 40 cases was presented to judges on a separate page to be classified according to the underlying template identified in the agreement—if such a template were recognized. Three judges who were chosen due to their ample experience in the creativity templates approach to new product development and ideation took part in this part of the study. Training the judges in identifying templates in the negotiation context involved a 15-minute session in which examples of templates in this milieu were demonstrated.

The categories used for template classification included four different templates: attribute dependency, multiplication, replacement, and displacement. Obviously, a no-template option was given as well. During the classification task, there was no interaction among the different judges. After the results were returned and analyzed, the judges were presented with the cases on which they disagreed and, through rigorous debates, tried to reach an agreement on the outstanding cases.

Classification Results

The three judges reached unanimous agreement on 32 of the cases. After discussing disagreements, consensus was reached on all but one case (where majority opinion was used). Furthermore, the judges also agreed on there being 2 cases (out of 40) that could be classified by two different templates (attribute dependency and replacement). Thus, 25 out of the 40 cases were classified as having templates, and 15 cases were classified as having no templates. The results of the classifications are summarized in Fig. 3.6.

The mapping shows that templates do indeed underlie many negotiated agreements, and thus can be beneficial for creating such agreements in many future cases. The question still remains regarding whether agreements with underlying templates are more creative and effective than agreements without templates. This question was also addressed in this study and is reported next.

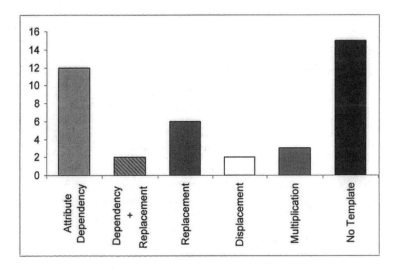

FIG. 3.6.   Results of template classification of cases by judges ($N = 40$).

Judgments of Creativity and Effectiveness

Two judges were presented with the same 40 cases described earlier. The same two-part format of background information and negotiated agreement was maintained. Both judges were experts in negotiation and had at least 10 years experience in teaching negotiation courses to Israeli MBA students. To prevent bias, judges were not exposed to the notion of templates, nor were they aware of the theory of creativity templates in marketing. Following each case, the judges answered a questionnaire containing 10 questions on a scale of 1 to 7. These items were designed to measure three unique constructs regarding the agreement reached in each case: creativity, integrative value, and effectiveness. However, the results of a factor analysis reveal the existence of only two factors with a total communality of 82.7% (the initial principal component factor analysis did not yield a simple structure, and so an oblique rotation was used). Although one of the factors was indeed the creativity construct hypothesized, the other included all of the integrative value and effectiveness items combined. It seems that integrative agreements were deemed as effective by the judges. The list of items loading on each construct is presented in Table 3.3, along with their corresponding intraclass correlation coefficient ($ICC_{(2)}$). As can be seen, interjudge reliability was high ($ICC_{(2)}$ ranging from .69–.84).

Creativity and Effectiveness Results

Next, t tests were run on both constructs to determine whether agreements that have underlying templates were deemed more creative and/or effective by the judges. The results show that cases displaying templates had a

TABLE 3.3
Items Used to Measure Creative and Effective Agreements

Construct	Items	$ICC_{(2)}$
Creativity	1. How innovative is this agreement?	.71
	2. How creative is this agreement?	.81
	3. How original is this agreement?	.74
Effectiveness	4. To what extent have the two parties reached an integrative agreement?	.72
	5. Does this agreement address the issues that are important to both parties?	.84
	6. Would this agreement promote trust between the parties?	.77
	7. Is this a fair agreement?	.69
	8. To what extent does this agreement create value in the negotiation?	.76
	9. How effective is this agreement?	.81
	10. How close is this agreement to a win–win agreement?	.82

mean creativity score of 5.25 (SD = .99), compared with 2.26 (.98) for cases without such structure (t_{38} = 9.32, p < .000, d = 3.03). Further, the results were similar for effectiveness with cases displaying templates having a mean effectiveness score of 5.51 (SD = .89), compared with 3.28 (.91) for cases without such structure (t_{38} = 7.60, p < .000, d = 2.48). Although the sample size is relatively small, the results show a strong effect size for both creativity and effectiveness.

After demonstrating the prevalence of the template structures in the negotiation context, we then turned our attention to the question of whether using templates will indeed facilitate an actual negotiated situation within or between organizations. This course of study (Nir, Goldenberg, & Maoz, 2003) is briefly reported next.

APPLYING CREATIVE TEMPLATES IN NEGOTIATION

The aim of this study was to examine whether negotiators trained in using one creative template—namely, attribute dependency—will generate more creative and effective proposals than negotiators using other creative techniques. Groups of MBA students enrolled in a negotiation class were randomly assigned, by section, to experimental and control groups. The experimental group received a 30-minute lecture on using the attribute dependency template, and the control group received a lecture on using other prevailing creative techniques. Then subjects in both groups were divided into dyads and engaged in a simulated negotiation. The subjects recorded all proposals raised in the course of the negotiation, and at the end of the simulation they rated their experience on multiple semantic differential scales.

First, we compared the total number of proposals raised in the negotiation between the two groups and found that the group using the attribute dependency template created significantly more proposals than the control group. Next, the proposal content was evaluated and classified (by independent judges) as either a trade-off or a single-issue proposal (concession or one-sided demands), and once again a significant difference—in favor of the template manipulation—was found between the two groups. This was mirrored by self-evaluations of the research participants, who also rated the process they went through and the results they reached as being more creative and effective. To determine whether indeed the proposals generated by the experimental group were more creative and effective, external judges analyzed all the proposals obtained from both groups. The results show that the external evaluation reached similar results to the ones obtained internally from the subject. That is, those using the attribute dependency template created proposals that were more creative and effective than the proposals generated by the control group.

DISCUSSION

Past research has demonstrated that negotiators commonly fail to reach creative solutions and integrative agreements. In most cases, negotiators tend to perceive the negotiation as a zero-sum game or a win–lose enterprise. This competitive way of thinking hinders the creative problem-solving process that is necessary to create integrative solutions, and it leads parties to a lose–lose effect. Indeed even when parties are interested in a long-term relationship and are concerned about the other party's needs, they often fail to reach integrative agreements, and at best they tend to settle for compromises instead. Increasing negotiators' ability to be creative is often proposed as the solution to this problem. However, the road to creativity is not always clear to the parties involved.

In this chapter, we propose the application of the creativity templates approach, first put forth in the realm of new product development, to the negotiation arena. We identified and described four creativity templates known in the new product development field as *attribute dependency, multiplication, replacement,* and *displacement,* and we set forth to demonstrate their pervasiveness in the negotiation context. A mapping study indeed verified that creativity templates underlie creative agreements. Furthermore, we found that negotiated agreements that were classified as pertaining to one of these templates were also evaluated as more creative and effective by independent judges. Interestingly, similarly to findings in both the new product and advertising fields, the most pervasive template identified in the mapping study was attribute dependency. This particular template provides a structured approach to creating multiple creative and effective trade-off offers that are considered essential in the formation of creative, win–win agreements. Another recent exploration of the template approach to negotiation set out to examine the actual use of creative negotiation templates (CNT) in a negotiated interorganizational situation. The results demonstrate that dyads using the CNT approach produced significantly more creative offers and more effective trade-offs than those generated by dyads using other prevailing creative strategies.

The CNT approach can be viewed as mapping onto several well-established creativity strategies in negotiation. Specifically, because the procedures pertaining to all four of the templates suggest viewing the negotiation space either in terms of attributes or components, negotiators are encouraged to seek more information within the context of the negotiation, and to assemble and define the issues at hand. As a mechanism for initiating and managing the exchange of information and the expansion of the issues to be traded on, templates can therefore be viewed as mapping onto creativity strategies such as Asking Many Questions, Adding and Creating New Issues, and Unbundling or Unlinking Issues (Lax & Sebenius, 1986; Pruitt,

1981). In general, the CNT approach may enhance strategies pertaining to Building Trust and Sharing Information between the negotiating parties (Bazerman & Neale, 1992; Kemp & Smith, 1994; Thompson, 1991). This may be possible because parties using CNT engage in an agreed-on and prescribed process, and thus are more likely to build trust along the way and share information more readily.

More specifically, working with the attribute dependency template helps generate multiple creative trade-off offers, and therefore facilitates the implementation of strategies such as Building Trade-Off offers for mutual gain and Making Multiple Offers Simultaneously (Bazerman & Neale, 1992; Froman & Cohen, 1970; Pruitt, 1983a). Other creative negotiation strategies, such as Capitalizing on Differences (Lax & Sebenius, 1986), Cost Cutting, and Non-Specific Compensation (Pruitt, 1983a), suggest focusing on specific issues that, in many cases, offer higher potential and, in essence, may hold the key to creating mutual gain. Similarly, the CNT approach provides a mechanism to achieve this goal by focusing the parties on the more potentially profitable areas of the forecasting matrix.

Boden (1991), on reviewing Koestler's bisociative creative thought processes, commented that what is missing from the mix is the *how* component, and that not understanding how these outcomes are arrived at does not allow for complete understanding of their creative potential. Boden asked a simple, yet profound, question regarding how creative ideas are discovered: "How is it that people can notice things they were not even looking for?" (p. 25). What the template approach tries to do is provide negotiators with a solution to this question—a systematic procedure by which to look for these creative and insightful outcomes. Thus, by providing highly formulated directions, the template approach can show negotiators how to manage the construction of creative proposals and mutually beneficial agreements. The template approach offers negotiators a method by which to identify the issues, attributes, components, and goals of the negotiated situation, thus keeping the parties well focused on the task at hand and, through reformulating the relationships between these elements, helping the parties arrive at new, creative solutions they might not have seen before. Furthermore, because each one of the four templates discussed accomplishes this task in a different way, different types of solutions can be derived from applying them individually.

Future research is needed to further evaluate the effectiveness and efficiency of the various creative negotiation templates and to ascertain whether templates unique to the negotiation field can be identified. Other interesting issues to be explored in the near future are the potential benefits of the CNT approach in facilitating mediation processes and the effect of using templates on trust and cooperation between parties engaged in a negotiation. The results to date demonstrate the potential inherent in the creative negotiation templates. These templates bring structure to creativity by providing negotiators with prescribed methodologies and proved paths to follow on the long, and sometimes bumpy, road to a mutually successful outcome.

REFERENCES

Altschuller, G. S. (1985). *Creativity as an exact science.* New York: Gordon & Breach.
Altschuller, G. S. (1986). *To find an idea: Introduction to the theory of solving problems of inventions.* Novosibirsk, USSR: Nauka.
Bazerman, M. H. (1998). *Judgment in managerial decision making* (4th ed.). New York: Wiley.
Bazerman, M. H., Magliozzi, T., & Neale, M. A. (1985). Integrative bargaining in a competitive market. *Organizational Behavior and Human Decision Processes, 35,* 294–313.
Bazerman, M. H., Mannix, E., & Thompson, L. (1988). Groups as mixed-motive negotiations. In E. J. Lawler & B. Markovsky (Eds.), *Advances in group processes: Theory and research* (Vol. 5). Greenwich, CT: JAI.
Bazerman, M. H., & Neale, M. A. (1983). Heuristics in negotiation: Limitations to effective dispute resolution. In M. H. Bazerman & R. J. Lewicki (Eds.), *Negotiation in organizations.* Beverly Hills, CA: Sage.
Bazerman, M. H., & Neale, M. A. (1992). *Negotiating rationally.* New York: The Free Press.
Boden, M. (1991). *The creative mind: Myths and mechanisms.* New York: Basic Books.
Briggs, R. O., Vreede, G., & Nunamaker, J. (2003). Collaboration engineering with ThinkLets to pursue sustained success with group support systems. *Journal of Management Information Systems, 19*(4), 31–64.
Carnevale, P. J., & Isen, A. (1986). The influence of positive affect and visual access on the discovery of integrative solutions in bilateral negotiations. *Organizational Behavior and Human Decision Processes, 37,* 1–13.
Finke, R. A., Ward, T. B., & Smith, S. M. (1992). *Creative cognition.* Cambridge, MA: MIT Press.
Fisher, R. E., Ury, W., & Patton, B. (1991). *Getting to yes: Negotiating an agreement without giving in* (2nd ed.). New York: Penguin.
Froman, L. A., & Cohen, M. D. (1970). Compromise and logroll: Comparing the efficiency of two bargaining processes. *Behavioral Science, 30,* 180–183.
Fry, W. R., Firestone, I. J., & Williams, D. L. (1983). Negotiation process and outcome of stranger dyads and dating couples: Do lovers lose? *Basic and Applied Social Psychology, 4,* 1–16.
Ghiselin, B. (1952). *The creative process.* Berkeley, CA: University of California Press.
Goldenberg, J., & Mazursky, D. (2002). *Creativity in product innovation.* Cambridge, UK: Cambridge University Press.
Goldenberg, J., Mazursky, D., & Solomon, S. (1999a). Creative sparks. *Science, 285*(5433), 1495–1496.
Goldenberg, J., Mazursky, D., & Solomon, S. (1999b, May). Toward identifying the inventive templates of new products: A channeled ideation approach. *Journal of Marketing Research, 36,* 200–210.
Goldenberg, J., Mazursky, D., & Solomon, S. (1999c, May). Templates of original innovation: Protecting original incremental innovations from intrinsic information. *Technology, Forecasting and Social Change, 36,* 200–210.
Goldenberg, J., Mazursky, D., & Solomon, S. (1999d). Creativity templates: Towards identifying the fundamental schemes of quality advertising. *Marketing Science, 18,* 333–351.

Hender, J. M., Dean, D. L., Rogers, T. L., & Nunamaker, J. (2002). An examination of the impact of stimuli type and GSS structure on creativity: Brainstorming versus non-brainstorming techniques in a GSS environment. *Journal of Management Information Systems, 18*(4), 59–86.

Hyder, E. B., Prietula, M. J., & Weingart, L. R. (2000). Getting to best: Efficiency versus optimality in negotiation. *Cognitive Science, 24*, 169–204.

Kemp, K. E., & Smith, W. P. (1994). Information exchange, toughness, and integrative bargaining: The role of explicit clues and perspective-taking. *International Journal of Conflict Management, 5*, 5–21.

Koestler, A. (1964). *The act of creation.* Arkana, England: Penguin.

Kurtzberg, T., & Medvec, V. H. (1999). Can we negotiate and still be friends? *Negotiation Journal, 15*(4), 355–362.

Lax, D. A., & Sebenius, J. K. (1986). *The manager as negotiator.* New York: The Free Press.

Lewicki, R. J., Saunders, D. M., & Minton, J. W. (1999). *Negotiation* (3rd ed.). Singapore: McGraw-Hill.

Maimon, O., & Horowitz, R. (1999). Sufficient condition for inventive ideas in engineering. *IEEE Transactions, Man and Cybernetics, 29*(3), 349–361.

Mednick, S. A. (1962). The associative basis of the creative process. *Psychological Review, 69*(3), 220–232.

Neale, M. A., & Bazerman, M. H. (1991). *Negotiator cognition and rationality.* New York: The Free Press.

Neale, M. A., & Northcraft, G. (1986). Experts, amateurs, and refrigerators: Comparing expert and amateur negotiators in a novel task. *Organizational Behavior and Human Decision Processes, 38*, 305–317.

Nir, D., Goldenberg, J., & Maoz, E. (2003). *Creativity in negotiation through the prism of creative negotiation templates.* Working Paper.

Pruitt, D. G. (1981). *Negotiation behavior.* New York: Academic Press.

Pruitt, D. G. (1983a). Strategic choice in negotiation. *American Behavioral Scientist, 27*, 167–194.

Pruitt, D. G. (1983b). Achieving integrative agreements. In M. Bazerman & R. Lewicki (Eds.), *Negotiating in organizations.* Beverly Hills, CA: Sage.

Pruitt, D. G., & Carnevale, P. J. D. (1982). The development of integrative agreements. In V. Derlega & J. Grzelak (Eds.), *Cooperation and helping behavior: Theories and research.* New York: Academic Press.

Pruitt, D. G., & Carnevale, P. J. D. (1993). *Negotiation in social conflict.* Pacific Grove, CA: Brooks-Cole.

Raiffa, H. (1982). *The art and science of negotiation.* Cambridge, MA: Belknap.

Sosik, J. J., Avolio, B. J., & Kahai, S. S. (1997). Effects of leadership style and anonymity on group potency and effectiveness in a group decision support system environment. *Journal of Applied Psychology, 82*(1), 89–103.

Thompson, L. L. (1991). Information exchange in negotiation. *Journal of Experimental Social Psychology, 27*, 161–179.

Thompson, L. L. (2001). *The mind and heart of the negotiator.* Upper Saddle River, NJ: Prentice-Hall.

Thompson, L. L., & DeHarpport, T. (1998). Relationships, good incompatibility, and communal orientation in negotiations. *Basic and Applied Social Psychology, 20*(1), 33–44.

Thompson, L. L., & Hastie, R. (1990a). Social perception in negotiation. *Organizational Behavior and Human Decision Processes, 47*, 98–123.

Thompson, L. L., & Hastie, R. (1990b). Judgment tasks and biases in negotiation. In B. H. Sheppard, M. H. Bazerman, & R. J. Lewicki (Eds.), *Research on negotiation in organizations.* Greenwich, CT: JAI.

Thompson, L. L., & Herbec, D. (1996). Lose–lose agreements in interdependent decision making. *Psychological Bulletin, 120*, 396–409.

Part II

TEAM AND GROUP DYNAMICS
OF BRAINSTORMING

Chapter 4

Group Brainstorming and Teamwork: Some Rules for the Road to Innovation

Paul B. Paulus
Toshihiko Nakui
Vicky L. Putman
University of Texas at Arlington

A comparison between the groups literature and the individual creativity literature in the early 1990s revealed that they were quite consistent. The individual creativity literature emphasized personal characteristics and experiences related to creativity. There was much evidence that eminence and creativity often involve much solitary persistence. Eminently creative individuals were also renowned for their high level of motivation. They appeared to have a divergent thinking style and generated a high quantity of products (e.g., Simonton, 1988). Studies of groups generally found little basis for creative potential in groups (see Paulus, Brown, & Ortega, 1999, for a review). The most salient literature was that on brainstorming. The consistent finding in that literature was that groups tended to generate fewer ideas and fewer high-quality ideas compared with individual ideation conditions (Mullen, Johnson, & Salas, 1991). Amabile (1983) published her influential book on social context factors in creativity and emphasized that certain controlling factors such as evaluation and the use of reward inhibit intrinsic motivation (and thus creativity). However, she also emphasized how modeling and factors that enhanced intrinsic motivation could enhance creativity. Other scholars also highlighted the positive potential for social and group factors in creativity (Nystrom, 1979; Stein, 1982; West, 1990), and there was in general an increased interest in teamwork and its potential for enhancing productivity and innovation (see Paulus, 2000; West, 2003, for reviews). However, literature surveys yielded few references to group and team creativity or innovation (cf. Paulus et al., 1999). Recently

69

there has been a significant increase in activity in those areas, leading to a volume summarizing research on group creativity (Paulus & Nijstad, 2003). We review the diverse perspectives on group creativity that have evolved over that time in the research on groups and teams. First, we compare the contrasting perspectives on group creativity suggested by the research traditions on groups and teams. Then we examine the factors that influence our perceptions of groups and teams as productive or creative and note that such perceptions may often be incorrect. We evaluate the relative utility of the group and team paradigms for an examination of the creative potential of groups. Then we summarize the findings of laboratory research on group creativity and the related implications for enhancing group creativity. Finally, we evaluate the applicability of the literature on group creativity to organizations. There has been much discussion of the differences between teams and groups. For our purposes, groups consist of three or more individuals focused on some common activity. Teams are generally longer term groups that have interrelated roles and are part of a larger organization. Groups research has typically focused on short-term tasks, whereas team research has typically examined groups engaged in activities that are extended over time.

WHY ARE GROUPS BAD FOR CREATIVITY?

The overwhelming thrust of the literature on groups is that groups are bad for creativity. Groups appear to reduce the motivation to share divergent ideas. The classic research on groupthink has shown that groups may inhibit the sharing of perspectives that go against the dominant group view (Janis, 1982). Moreover, there is a general tendency of groups to exchange information or ideas that they have in common rather than unique information (Stasser & Birchmeier, 2003). Group members may also be concerned about the evaluation of their ideas by other group members. This may be particularly true of group members who tend to be uncomfortable or anxious in groups (Camacho & Paulus, 1995). Another factor that contributes to the low creativity in groups is social interference or production blocking (Nijstad, Diehl, & Stroebe, 2003). When group members share ideas in groups, they can do so effectively only one at a time. Much time in groups is spent waiting one's turn or listening to ideas presented by others. During this process, one may be distracted from a potentially fruitful line of thought or may forget what one was planning to share. One may simply become frustrated by the difficulty of sharing one's ideas and become less motivated to share creative ideas. Finally, the performance of individual group members is likely to be influenced by the performance of others in the group. Because the various procedural limitations of the group sharing process lead to a generally low level of performance, there may be a general tendency for group members to move in the direction of a low group performance norm (Paulus & Dzindolet, 1993). Thus, there is much evidence that group interaction can inhibit the generation of creative ideas in groups.

TEAMS ARE GOOD FOR CREATIVITY

Work teams are prevalent in organizations in large part because of presumptions about their positive impact on productivity and innovation (Devine, Clayton, Philips, Dunford, & Melner, 1999). Teams may be a source of motivation, especially when they have a lot of autonomy (Cohen & Bailey, 1997). They may also be sources of innovation because they can take advantage of the diverse skills and information in developing new ideas or initiatives (Drach-Zahavy & Somech, 2001). Much of the research on teamwork has focused on the team characteristics and contextual factors that influence team effectiveness. Although the research on team productivity is mixed (Naquin & Tynan, 2003; Paulus, 2000), much research has focused on factors that enhance team innovation, such as organizational support, autonomy, and interteam communication (Amabile, Conti, Coon, Lazenby, & Herron, 1996; Ancona & Caldwell, 1992; West, 2003). A critical aspect of innovative teamwork is the team meeting. At this time, much of the information exchange, social influence, conflict, and negotiation take place. These processes can be critical for team innovation (Drach-Zahavy & Somech, 2001).

We briefly highlight a few examples of this type of research. West's (2003) research has focused on teams that are tasked with developing innovations for hospitals and manufacturers. He has found that teams that have challenging tasks, appropriate leadership, innovative members, diverse membership, a supportive organizational culture, and external demands are most likely to be innovative. He has championed the role of reflexivity—a measure of reflectiveness and adaptability in the ability of teams to develop innovative ideas.

Dunbar (1995, 1997) focused on scientific teams. He studied more than 11 of these around the world and found that a variety of group and analytic factors influence the extent to which these teams come up with major discoveries. A major determinant of these teams' effectiveness was the group process during the team meetings. Successful teams were those that dealt effectively with contradictory results, had some diversity in their makeup, and engaged in effective collaborative reasoning.

Drach-Zahavy and Somech (2001) examined elementary school staff teams for factors related to their innovation. Team innovation was based on ratings by team members and school principals, and measures of team processes were also based on self-report measures. They found that frequency of team meetings, diversity of organizational roles represented by team members, and team processes such as exchanging information, learning, motivating, and negotiating were related to measures of team innovation. Many studies of teams have examined ad hoc groups in short-term problem-solving or task performance settings (Ellis et al., 2003; LePine, 2003; Swezey & Salas, 1992). These studies are able to obtain objective measures of performance on the team tasks. The focus of these studies has been the role of team member characteristics. It appears that high levels of cognitive ability, openness to experience, and a clearly structured team interaction process (e.g., interaction among pairs of team members) are related to enhanced team performance.

ILLUSION AND REALITY

Our review thus far indicates that groups can be bad for creativity, but that teams may be innovative under certain conditions. How can these two perspectives be reconciled? We examine this issue in some detail, but first we address some of the factors that contribute to the perception of creativity or productivity in groups. These perceptions may in part be responsible for the apparent discrepancy. Thus, the popularity of teamwork in organizations may largely be based on mythical beliefs about its efficacy (Hackman, 1998; Thompson, 2004). We briefly examine those factors that influence perception of group effectiveness. In the rest of the chapter, we try to come to an objective perspective about the reality of group creativity and team innovation.

People seem to have a positive bias about the performance of groups and teams (Naquin & Tynan, 2003; Paulus, Larey, & Ortega, 1995), and there are many books and articles that promote the use of collaborative groups or teams in organizations (cf. Paulus, 2000; West, 2003). The ability to work in teams is one of the more important characteristics that corporations look for in their employees (Bradley, White, & Mennecke, 2003). Participants in teams also appear to have positive feelings about the effectiveness of teams (Cotton, 1993). For example, Sutton and Hargadon (1996) reported that both participants and observers of the brainstorming process in the IDEO Corporation had positive feelings about the efficacy of the process. These positive feelings might be justified, but could also reflect biased perceptions based on exposure to proteam propaganda or social influence processes.

One of the problems in evaluating the illusion issue is the criteria respondents are using and which criteria we should use to evaluate the adequacy of team or group work. As pointed out by other scholars (e.g., Furnham, 2000), productivity is only one criterion for evaluating the usefulness of different forms of group work. Enhanced group morale and motivation, opportunities to develop social and intellectual skills, commitment to decisions that come out of group processes, and opportunities to learn to work with diverse group members are just a few of these. In this chapter, we focus on performance and the perception of performance because the most extensive literature exists on this topic. Participants in face-to-face idea-generation groups appear to rate their performance more favorably than those who perform in isolation even though their performance is inferior. Participants in electronic brainstorming groups tend to rate their performance more favorably than those in face-to-face situations, but this may in part be related to the novelty of working on computers (Pinsonneault, Barki, Gallupe, & Hoppen, 1999). Often participants are not able to accurately judge the extent to which their performance is at a high level (Connolly, Jessup, & Valacich, 1990).

Research suggests that perception of performance is based on a number of social and task characteristics. Part of the task judgment in groups seems to be related to the social context. Individuals in groups can use other group members as a reference point for assessing their own performance. Individuals tend to compare to similar others (Festinger, 1954; Goethals & Darley, 1987), so coworkers are a natural basis for comparison. Comparisons may influence both perceptions and motivation. If someone discovers their performance level is below that of coworkers, this person should negatively evaluate their performance and be motivated to increase their level of effort. Conversely, if they are doing better than coworkers, they should evaluate their performance favorably and have a reduced motivation for performance. This perspective suggests a tendency for performance of individual group members to flow toward a group norm (the average of the group members' performance). Group members should then evaluate their performance as generally adequate because it is typically close to the group norm. In contrast, individuals performing alone have no such reference point for their performance or judgment, and they may feel some uncertainty about the adequacy of their performance.

The performance evaluation process is affected by the personal motivations of the individuals and the social context. If individuals are achievement-oriented, they should be particularly interested in social comparison with other group members and be motivated to exceed the group norm. Others may be more concerned with just getting by (satisficers; Schwartz et al., 2002) and may be happy as long as their performance is in the general range of the group norm. This individual tendency is likely to be influenced by cultural mores, as exemplified by cultural differences in social loafing (Karau & Williams, 1993). However, such external influences may also occur in organizational or laboratory contexts in which the motivational structure is varied. An emphasis on competition and individual achievement should lead to a tendency toward upward comparison in which individuals are more concerned with showing off their abilities than in matching the group norm (Paulus, Dugosh, Dzindolet, Coskun, & Putman, 2002; Sutton & Hargadon, 1996). In contrast, in an environment that focuses on the group or team performance, there may actually be a downward comparison tendency in which the low performers in the group set the standard. Although performance of those who compare downward should be inferior to those of upward comparers, they should feel more positive about their performance because they have a low comparison standard.

Beliefs about group efficacy can also be affected by prescriptive ideals in the organizational or broader culture. As mentioned, there is much emphasis on the importance and effectiveness of teamwork in the popular literature. When team members or outside evaluators are asked to evaluate the effectiveness of a particular team, one would expect an evaluation in the direction of the organizational bias. Moreover, one would expect that factors such as degree of organizational support, psychological safety, and external demands would have a positive influence on evaluations of team performance (West, 2003).

COMPARISON OF THE GROUP
AND TEAM PARADIGMS

The research on group creativity and team innovation discussed thus far has presented rather divergent perspectives on the potential for group/team-based creativity. The research on face-to-face interactive groups has highlighted the many ways group interaction limits the creative potential of group members. The team innovation literature has focused on contextual, personal, and process factors related to enhanced performance and innovation. The divergent perspectives provided by these two traditions can be seen as (a) representing an empirical or theoretical conflict as to the nature of the group creative process, (b) unrelated sets of findings from two different research traditions, or (c) evidence for the illusion of teamwork effectiveness. Alternatively, it may be possible to integrate these findings into a broader perspective of team innovation and creativity. Recent studies of brainstorming have provided some evidence for synergistic effects in interactive groups (Dugosh, Paulus, Roland, & Yang, 2000; Paulus & Yang, 2000) and support such an optimistic conclusion.

We first examine important differences between the paradigms. Then we examine recent findings on group creativity that suggest a more positive perspective. Next we summarize factors that are important for enhancing group creativity and compare the current status of research on group creativity with that on team innovation. Then we relate our findings to practice in organizations.

The typical features of laboratory research on group creativity have included the following: experimental, random assignment, use of noninteractive control groups, short sessions, use of student participants, primarily a focus on ideation, assigned problems, broad domain problems, no self-selection, no facilitators, and objective outcomes. Studies of team innovation tend to have the following characteristics: longer term groups, nonexperimental or quasiexperimental, lack of nonteam control groups, self-selection or selection based on task, relevant problems, limited domain problems, multiple phases, facilitators, self-managing, and self-report measures of performance.

The focus of group creativity research has been on comparing the group ideation process with individual ideation. The focus of team research has been in the innovation process rather than the ideation process. The innovation process is concerned with implementation of ideas. This involves generation of ideas and subsequent selection of ideas for implementation. The team research has not assessed whether teams are creative relative to nonteamwork approaches. Team innovation is assumed to occur, and the interest is in those factors that influence the extent of innovation.

Participants in these two camps obviously have somewhat different perspectives about the relative value of these approaches. Team innovation researchers tend to point to the limitations of the experimental approach (Ford, 1999). Because this research has been done primarily with college students exchanging ideas on topics of questionable import in brief sessions in groups of strangers, it may not be a good approximation of the types of groups and group processes involved in creative processes in longer term groups working on meaningful tasks (e.g., work or scientific tasks; Dunbar, 1997; West, 2003). West claimed that it is easy to come up with ideas, but much harder to innovate or implement those ideas (West, 2003). Sutton and Hargadon (1996) suggested the experimental work is misguided in its focus on performance. They noted that a broader range of outcomes should be considered in evaluating the benefits of brainstorming. For example, they noted that a successful product development company found brainstorming useful for the development of innovative products, but also for such outcomes as enhancing organizational memory, the experience of skill variety, status competition, "showing off" to clients, and earned income for these activities. They emphasized the importance of the role of organizational context and the need to assess a broad range of consequences of social interventions. They also questioned whether brainstorming is really as prevalent in organizations as often claimed.

The groups researchers have noted that it is difficult to make causal statements from many of the team studies that are of a correlational nature (Paulus, 2000). Organizations with self-managed teams may be different in many ways from those that use different forms of work organization (e.g., leadership style, compensation practices, use of team facilitators). Moreover, there have been no studies as far as we know that have examined the effects of self-managed teamwork without the confounding effects of other organizational differences or possible contributions of self-fulfilling prophecies (expectation effects).

Team studies that are not done in controlled laboratory conditions typically rely on subjective measures of both processes and outcomes (e.g., Caldwell & O'Reilley, 2003; Drach-Zahavy & Somech, 2001). Thus, there is often a problem of shared method variance. In addition, such measures could be subject to a variety of biases that are favorable toward groups or teams (Naquin & Tynan, 2003; Paulus, Dzindolet, Poletes, & Camacho, 1993). Moreover, some studies of scientific teams have reported only observational data (Dunbar, 1995, 1997).

The presumption of this chapter is that laboratory research on group creativity is indeed quite relevant to an understanding of functioning of groups and teams in more realistic settings. The group research provides information about the potential effectiveness of meetings in which ideas are being exchanged. This is an important part of the team innovative process (Dunbar, 1997). Better understanding of the group ideation process and how to enhance it should provide useful information to those concerned with managing team innovation. Although it is often argued that research in realistic settings is more generalizable than experimental lab research, some reviews have indicated that findings from experimental research in social psychology are often quite consistent with those from field research (Anderson, Lindsay, & Bushman, 1999).

Some have emphasized that innovation is more critical than creativity in organizations (e.g., West, 2003), but it should be noted that the gap between ideation and implementation varies depending on the constraints of the problem and organizational context. Some problems have many options and alternatives, and therefore should be more amenable to brainstorming than those that have only limited options. The connection between ideas generated and their implementation also depends on the number of organizational layers between the idea people and the implementation people and the various financial and political constraints. Brainstorming should be more beneficial in environments in which there are few constraints on implementation of good ideas.

LABORATORY RESEARCH ON GROUP CREATIVITY

Research on laboratory groups has allowed us to gain considerable knowledge about the information exchange process in various modalities. We summarize some of this research and highlight procedures that can enhance the group ideation process.

Most brainstorming research suggests that it is best to do it alone or at the most in pairs (Mullen et al., 1991). This presumes that groups are a source of various factors that inhibit productivity, such as production blocking, social loafing, and evaluation apprehension (Diehl & Stroebe, 1987). Generation of ideas is also influenced by a variety of other social factors. Providing groups or individuals with challenging goals or high norms increases idea generation (Larey & Paulus, 1995; Paulus & Dzindolet, 1993). Simply having the opportunity to compare one's performance with other group members enhances the number of ideas generated (Paulus, Larey, Putman, Leggett, & Roland, 1996; Roy, Guavin, & Limayem, 1996).

Intergroup comparisons appear to have similar positive benefits, particularly when a group is given feedback that it performed more poorly than other groups (Coskun, 2000). Group composition is also important. There is some evidence that some degree of ethnic diversity seems to enhance performance in brainstorming groups (McCleod, Lobel, & Cox, 1996), but the effect of diversity is complicated by negative social or affective reactions to a number of dimensions of diversity (Milliken, Bartel, & Kurtzberg, 2003). Although it would seem obvious that diversity or complementarity of knowledge or expertise in a group will enhance its creativity, thus far the evidence for this is not very convincing (Brown & Paulus, 2002; Cady & Valentine, 1999). It is of course possible that biases toward common rather than unique information in groups (Stasser & Birchmeier, 2003) will limit the beneficial effects of knowledge diversity in groups. Group composition based on differences in personality or attitudes can also affect the performance of groups, particularly if these traits have some relevance for the various social and cognitive processes that influence idea generation. Groups composed of members who are high in social anxiety tend to perform poorly in comparison with groups composed of members low in social anxiety (Camacho & Paulus, 1995). This is consistent with the idea that evaluation apprehension inhibits brainstorming. Groups composed of individuals who have a preference for working in groups tend to perform better (Larey & Paulus, 1999). Of the Big Five personality traits, we have found that *extraversion* and *intellect/imagination* are related to higher levels of idea generation (Putman & Paulus, 2002).

Although social factors and group member characteristics tend to influence group creativity, features of the task appear to be even more important. Allowing group members to exchange ideas by means of writing or computers avoids production blocking and allows groups to demonstrate enhanced performance in comparison with nominal groups (the highly sought evidence of group synergy; Dennis & Williams, 2003; Paulus et al., 2002). These benefits of group interaction are evident both during group brainstorming and in solitary ideation sessions after group brainstorming (Dugosh et al., 2000; Paulus & Yang, 2000). Some type of task decomposition seems to be beneficial as well. Presenting the problem one component at a time (Coskun, Paulus, Brown, & Sherwood, 2000; Dennis, Valacich, Connolly, & Wynne, 1996), rather than all at once, seems to enhance the number of ideas generated. Priming individuals with ideas during the idea-generation process appears to increase the overall number of ideas generated. Contrary to what one might expect, common ideas tend to have more stimulation value than unique ones, but presenting unique categories is more stimulating than presenting more common categories (Dugosh & Paulus, 2005).

Performance in brainstorming declines over short periods of time, and shifting from one mode of brainstorming to another may help maintain task motivation as well as provide cognitive benefits. We have found that brief breaks within brainstorming sessions can enhance brainstorming (Paulus & Brown, 2003). Shifting from one type of brainstorming to another would inevitably be accompanied by brief breaks in the task process. So shifting brainstorming modality (to alone or group or even from oral to written or computer) at a point when the brainstormers appear to be slowing down in the generation process may be quite helpful. However, too many breaks or premature breaks may be more disruptive than helpful.

GROUP AND INDIVIDUAL BRAINSTORMING

One of the frequent comments about group brainstorming is that, although group brainstorming may not be more effective than individual brainstorming, groups may be motivating, and ideas that come from group interaction may have more support than those that come from individuals (Furnham, 2000; R. I. Sutton, personal communication, October 2002). Yet the reality of work life is that people go back and forth from individual to group activities. When people come together to discuss ideas, they typically have thought about the issue prior to the meeting. At the meeting, knowledge and ideas are exchanged and probably evaluated. Afterward individuals may reflect on the exchanged information and related evaluations. In a subsequent group meeting, there may be a reassessment of the issue in which such second thoughts can be shared and a final decision made (Janis & Mann, 1977). Similarly, Osborn (1957, 1963) proposed that some alternation between group and individual brainstorming might be optimal. Thus, a critical issue for group ideation and innovation is as follows: How should the time for dealing with an issue be allocated to individual or group efforts? That is, what is the optimum sequence of individual to group consideration of the issues?

Some research suggests that the benefits of group idea exchange may be most evident after a subsequent period of individual incubation or reflection (Dugosh et al., 2000; Paulus & Yang, 2000). Therefore, the best sequence may be one in which group brainstorming is followed by individual brainstorming (Brown & Paulus, 2002). However, there may also be benefits from generating ideas privately before group brainstorming (Paulus et al., 1995). This allows one to more easily access a large number of ideas during the subsequent group sharing session, and this could help minimize the impact of negative factors in group brainstorming. It also makes it more likely that group members will respond positively to ideas that they did not think of in the prior session (i.e., there is more recognition of uniqueness; Putman & Paulus, 2002). So we would predict that some type of alone/group alternation process would increase the overall productivity of a brainstorming session. Unfortunately, data on the effects of individual and group brainstorming sequence are rather mixed (Paulus et al., 1995). There are no empirical data on exactly how much time should be allocated to each of these phases.

BRAINSTORMING RULES

Another critical issue for creativity ideas is the use of rules. Brainstorming research indicates that it is important to use brainstorming rules in meetings if one wants to optimize the number of ideas generated. This involves separating presentation of ideas and their evaluation and focusing on generating as many ideas as possible without concern for quality (Osborn, 1957). The purpose is to stimulate the exchange of as many ideas as possible before evaluating their efficacy. Even bad ideas may stimulate others to come up with new insights. Studies have found that quantity and quality of ideas are in fact strongly correlated (Dennis et al., 1996; Mullen et al., 1991). Studies have also shown that groups which use brainstorming rules generate more ideas than those who do not (Parnes & Meadow, 1959).

We do not know of any study that has examined the impact of the four different rules. Each has a somewhat unique focus. The "don't criticize" rule should reduce evaluation apprehension. The "focus on quantity" rule should motivate participants to generate a large number of ideas, rather than worrying about impressing others with the quality of one's ideas. The "say everything you think of" rule also serves the quantity aim and encourages individuals not to self-censor. The "build on others' ideas" rule should encourage participants to attend to others' ideas and relate them to their own store of knowledge and ideas. We have found careful attention to the ideas of others is important for deriving benefits of idea sharing (Dugosh et al., 2000).

Although these rules facilitate group brainstorming, brainstorming groups still perform rather poorly compared with individual brainstorming comparisons. One major factor in this poor performance appears to be production blocking—the fact that when one group member shares ideas, others are not able to do so. Contributing to the impact of production blocking is the fact that group participants often tend to elaborate their ideas or tell stories in communicating their ideas to others. Other group members may chime in with similar stories, and much of the idea-generation session may be taken up by filler rather than pure ideas. This increases the cognitive load of individuals in groups as they attempt to process the shared ideas in addition to generating their own ideas. In one study, we found that exposing individuals to pure ideas led to stimulation of more ideas than exposing them to a similar number of ideas with the typical filler material (Dugosh et al., 2000). One way to enhance group brainstorming might be to add some rules emphasizing that group members should be efficient in the sharing of their ideas. We have done this in several studies (Paulus et al., 2002). In one study, we compared interactive and nominal groups who were either given Osborn's four rules or were given four additional rules. The additional rules were derived from a survey of facilitator practice and used in a facilitator study by Oxley, Dzindolet, and Paulus (1996). Two of the rules emphasized staying focused on the task. Participants were instructed not to tell stories or explain their ideas. A third rule instructed them to keep brainstorming going during lulls in the conversation by restating the problem and trying to think of additional ideas. This rule was designed to encourage participants to persist through gaps in the idea-generation process, rather than using these as cues to stop the session. The fourth rule suggested that when they could not think of additional ideas, they should consider going back to previous categories of ideas. It was felt that this process might help prime additional ideas in this as well as other categories (Coskun et al., 2000). We have found that the use of additional rules enhances the number of ideas generated for both interactive and nominal groups. Moreover, this benefit transfers over sessions as groups/ individuals brainstorm on different problems. The benefit was quite strong, with a 79% increase for the group brainstorming condition. The presence of an experimenter or a facilitator who enforces the rules has little additional benefit. The use of additional rules also enhances idea generation in electronic brainstorming (Paulus et al., 2002).

What is the basis for this enhanced performance with additional rules? One factor appears to be that participants are in fact more efficient in sharing their ideas with additional rules. With both oral and electronic brainstorming, group and nominal participants use considerably fewer words in expressing their ideas. In one preliminary study, in which we examined the impact of the individual rules, we found that the focus rules had the most impact. It is possible, however, that all of the four additional rules have some impact in motivating participants to work harder and more effectively on the brainstorming task. A clear conclusion one can draw from this study is that brainstorming instructions are an important feature of the effectiveness of the brainstorming session. It would be worthwhile to discover the essential rules that are critical to effective brainstorming.

THEORETICAL INTEGRATION

What does all this mean theoretically? Not all of the findings cited fit neatly into a consistent theoretical model, but we have generally explained the brainstorming findings from a social influence/information-processing perspective (Brown & Paulus, 2002; Paulus et al., 2002). Effective idea generation in groups requires a clear task focus, motivation to perform at a high level, and the ability to process others' ideas. Task focus is obtained by setting clear goals, providing clear instructions, subdividing the task, and instructing participants to attend carefully to the shared ideas. Motivation is increased by increasing within-group or between-group competition, setting high goals, encouraging groups to develop high performance norms, or selecting group members who enjoy group interaction or creativity tasks. The ability to process information in a group sharing paradigm is enhanced by allowing the use of writing and computer modalities, providing periodic stimuli to maintain the ideation process, providing opportunities for incubation after group sharing, instructing participants to express their ideas without unnecessary elaboration (reduce cognitive load), and providing brief breaks to allow diffusion of cognitive inhibition processes (Smith, 2003). Although we have never used all or a large subset of these conditions in one study, it would seem likely that high levels of performance could be attained when groups and/or facilitators follow the guidelines implicit in the previously mentioned factors.

GROUP CREATIVITY IN ORGANIZATIONS

Opportunities for group creativity in organizations occur whenever there are meetings or team interactions. What are the implications of the research we have cited for such meetings and teamwork activities? It is presumed that meetings are an important component of most knowledge teams because they are a convenient way to share perspectives and knowledge (Dunbar, 1997). Workers in some companies spend a large amount of time in meetings. For example, in 1 year, Xerox Corporation had about 4,500 meetings a week in their manufacturing section—at a cost of $100 million in wages (Kayser, 1995). The brainstorming literature provides a fertile basis for developing procedures for effective meetings. It is suggested that anything we can do to make meetings more efficient and effective will enhance the development of novel ideas, the selection of good ideas for innovation, and the overall effectiveness of the team and organization (Paulus & Brown, 2003).

A casual review of the teamwork literature also makes it evident that most of the factors that are important in the productivity of brainstorming groups are also influential in determining the productivity of teams. Goal setting, a supportive environment, psychological safety, norms, group member characteristics, diversity, training, and the use of trained facilitators have been related to effective teamwork (cf. Bradley et al., 2003; Hoegl & Parboteeah, 2003; West, 2003). The results for diversity are generally mixed (Cady & Valentine, 1999), as they are in the case of short-term groups. It remains to be seen whether some of the other factors found to be important in brainstorming groups do indeed influence the effectiveness of team meetings and their resultant productivity.

A number of scholars have questioned the relevance of experimental research on brainstorming for organizational practice. Sutton and Hargadon (1996) argued that productivity is only one factor that should be considered in evaluating the utility of brainstorming sessions in organizations. Kramer, Fleming, and Mannis (2001) pointed out that most brainstorming in organization involves facilitators, whereas most brainstorming research does not. Furthermore, brainstorming in organizations typically involves people who are already acquainted, have specific roles, and have diverse knowledge or expertise. Experimental research typically involves strangers who have no specific roles or expertise. There are only a few experimental studies that have been done in organizational settings. One of those studies demonstrated that conventional brainstorming in groups is associated with production losses in groups composed of coworkers who are brainstorming about issues related to their organization (Paulus et al., 1995).

Although there is not much controlled research in organizational settings, a survey of the organizational literature reveals much evidence for the active use of group brainstorming in organizations. A survey of the Business Source Premier database since 1990 yielded about 540 papers dealing with brainstorming. A casual survey of some recent articles by practitioners promoting techniques for effective brainstorming yielded a large number of suggestions for effective brainstorming. Among these were setting goals, group member diversity, facilitators, motivational techniques, directive cuing, task structure (writing, practice), a creative/relaxed context, fun, using multiple senses, and selecting creative people. It is interesting to compare the list of practitioner recommendations with those that can be derived from experimental research. We have reviewed supporting evidence for all of the items on the list except for fun and multisensing. However, it is important to realize that these various procedures seem to facilitate brainstorming in general. We have not found any that give group brainstorming a unique advantage over individual brainstorming except for exchange of ideas by means of writing or computer.

SUMMARY

The main conclusions of our chapter are as follows. Face-to-face meetings for brainstorming or innovation may be much less productive than most people believe. Brainstorming sessions can be greatly enhanced by the judicious use of procedures that eliminate the negative aspects of group interaction and accentuate the positive ones. So there is some basis for optimism about the potential of the group ideation process. Team research has demonstrated that team innovation can be enhanced by a variety of external conditions and for certain group compositions. Group creativity research has demonstrated that group interaction can have synergistic effects on the generation of ideas. We need to discover the best combination of individual- and team-based work for different types of creative tasks. Organizational researchers believe it is important to consider outcomes of teamwork other than performance, such as satisfaction, knowledge sharing, and acceptance of ideas. An integration of the research on group creativity research, research on team innovation, and organizational practice should provide a useful basis for enhancing creativity and innovation in organizations.

REFERENCES

Amabile, T. M. (1983). *The social psychology of creativity*. New York: Springer-Verlag.

Amabile, T. M., Conti, R., Coon, H., Lazenby, J., & Herron, M. (1996). Assessing the work environment for creativity. *Academy of Management Journal, 39*, 1154–1184.

Ancona, D. F., & Caldwell, D. F. (1992). Bridging the boundary: External activity and performance in organizational teams. *Administrative Science Quarterly, 37*, 634–665.

Anderson, C. A., Lindsay, J. J., & Bushman, B. J. (1999). Research in the psychological laboratory: Truth or triviality? *Current Directions in Psychological Science, 8*, 3–9.

Bradley, J., White, B. J., & Mennecke, B. E. (2003). Teams and tasks: A temporal framework for the effects of interpersonal interventions on team performance. *Small Group Research, 34*, 353–387.

Brown, V. R., & Paulus, P. B. (2002). Making group brainstorming more effective: Recommendations from an associative memory perspective. *Current Directions in Psychological Science, 11*, 208–212.

Cady, S. H., & Valentine, J. (1999). Team innovation and perceptions of consideration: What difference does diversity make? *Small Groups, 30*, 730–750.

Caldwell, D. F., & O'Reilly, C. A., III. (2003). The determinants of team-based innovation in organizations: The role of social influence. *Small Group Research, 34*, 497–517.

Camacho, L. M., & Paulus, P. B. (1995). The role of social anxiousness in group brainstorming. *Journal of Personality and Social Psychology, 68*, 1071–1080.

Cohen, S. G., & Bailey, D. E. (1997). What makes teams work: Group effectiveness research from the shop floor to the executive suite. *Journal of Management, 23*, 239–290.

Connolly, T., Jessup, L. M., & Valacich, J. S. (1990). Effects of anonymity and evaluative tone on idea generation in computer-mediated groups. *Management Science, 36*, 689–703.

Coskun, H. (2000). *The effects of outgroup comparison, social context, intrinsic motivation, and collective identity in brainstorming groups.* Unpublished doctoral dissertation, University of Texas at Arlington.

Coskun, H., Paulus, P. B., Brown, V., & Sherwood, J. J. (2000). Cognitive stimulation and problem presentation in idea generation groups. *Group Dynamics: Theory, Research, and Practice, 4*, 307–329.

Cotton, J. L. (1993). *Employee involvement.* Newbury Park, CA: Sage.

Dennis, A. R., Valacich, J. S., Connolly, T., & Wynne, B. E. (1996). Process structuring in electronic brainstorming. *Information Systems Research, 7*, 268–277.

Dennis, A. R., & Williams, M. L. (2003). Electronic brainstorming: Theory, research, and future directions. In P. B. Paulus & B. A. Nijstad (Eds.), *Group creativity: Innovation through collaboration* (pp. 32–62). New York: Oxford University Press.

Devine, D. J., Clayton, L. D., Philips, J. L., Dunford, B. B., & Melner, S. B. (1999). Teams in organizations: Prevalence, characteristics, and effectiveness. *Small Group Research, 30*, 678–711.

Diehl, M., & Stroebe, W. (1987). Productivity loss in brainstorming groups: Toward the solution of a riddle. *Journal of Personality and Social Psychology, 53*, 497–509.

Drach-Zahavy, A., & Somech, A. (2001). Understanding team innovation: The role of team processes and structures. *Group Dynamics: Theory, Research, and Practice, 5*, 111–123.

Dugosh, K. L., & Paulus, P. B. (2005). Cognitive and social comparison processes in brainstorming. *Journal of Experimental Social Psychology, 41*, 313–320.

Dugosh, K. L., Paulus, P. B., Roland, E. J., & Yang, H.-C. (2000). Cognitive stimulation in brainstorming. *Journal of Personality and Social Psychology, 79*, 722–735.

Dunbar, K. (1995). How scientists really reason: Scientific reasoning in real-world laboratories. In R. J. Sternberg & J. E. Davidson (Eds.), *The nature of insight* (pp. 365–395). Cambridge, MA: MIT Press.

Dunbar, K. (1997). How scientists think: On-line creativity and conceptual change in science. In T. B. Ward, S. M. Smith, & J. Vaid (Eds.), *Creative thought: An investigation of conceptual structures and processes* (pp. 461–493). Washington, DC: American Psychological Association.

Ellis, A. P. J., Hollenbeck, J. R., Ilgen, D. R., Porter, C. O. L. H., West, B. J., & Moon, H. (2003). Team learning: Collectively connecting the dots. *Journal of Applied Psychology, 88*, 821–835.

Festinger, L. (1954). A theory of social comparison processes. *Human Relations, 7*, 117–140.

Ford, C. M. (1999). Thinking big about small groups in the real world: Comment on Craig & Kelly (1999). *Group Dynamics: Theory, Research, and Practice, 3*, 257–262.

Furnham, A. (2000). The brainstorming myth. *Business Strategy Review, 11*, 21–28.

Goethals, G. R., & Darley, J. M. (1987). Social comparison theory: Self-evaluation and group life. In B. Mullen & G. R. Goethals (Eds.), *Theories of group behavior* (pp. 22–47). New York: Springer-Verlag.

Hackman, J. R. (1998). Why teams don't work. In R. S. Tindale & L. Heath (Eds.), *Theory and research on small groups* (pp. 245–267). New York: Plenum.

Hoegl, M., & Parboteeah, P. (2003). Goal setting and team performance in innovative projects: On the moderating role of teamwork quality. *Small Group Research, 34*, 3–19.

Janis, I. (1982). *Groupthink* (2nd ed.). Boston: Houghton-Mifflin.

Janis, I., & Mann, L. (1977). *Decision making: A psychological analysis of conflict, choice, and commitment.* New York: The Free Press.

Karau, S. J., & Williams, K. D. (1993). Social loafing: A meta-analytic review and theoretical integration. *Journal of Personality and Social Psychology, 65*, 681–706.

Kayser, T. A. (1995). *Mining group gold: How to cash in on the collaborative brain power of a group.* Chicago: Irwin.

Kramer, T. J., Fleming, G. P., & Mannis, S. M. (2001). Improving face-to-face brainstorming through modeling and facilitation. *Small Group Research, 32,* 533–557.

Larey, T. S., & Paulus, P. B. (1995). Social comparison and goal setting in brainstorming groups. *Journal of Applied Social Psychology, 25,* 1579–1596.

Larey, T. S., & Paulus, P. B. (1999). Group preference and convergent tendencies in small groups: A content analysis of group brainstorming performance. *Creativity Research Journal, 12,* 175–184.

LePine, J. A. (2003). Team adaptation and postchange performance: Effects of team composition in terms of members' cognitive ability and personality. *Journal of Applied Psychology, 88,* 27–39.

McLeod, P. L., Lobel, S. A., & Cox, T. H. (1996). Ethnic diversity and creativity in small groups. *Small Group Research, 27,* 248–264.

Milliken, F. J., Bartel, C. A., & Kurtzberg, T. R. (2003). Diversity and creativity in workgroups: A dynamic perspective on the affective and cognitive processes that link diversity and performance. In P. B. Paulus & B. A. Nijstad (Eds.), *Group creativity: Innovation through collaboration* (pp. 32–62). New York: Oxford University Press.

Mullen, B., Johnson, C., & Salas, E. (1991). Productivity loss in brainstorming groups: A meta-analytic integration. *Basic and Applied Social Psychology, 12,* 3–23.

Naquin, C. E., & Tynan, R. O. (2003). The team halo effect: Why teams are not blamed for their failures. *Journal of Applied Psychology, 88,* 332–340.

Nijstad, B. A., Diehl, M., & Stroebe, W. (2003). Cognitive stimulation and interference in idea-generating groups. In P. B. Paulus & B. A. Nijstad (Eds.), *Group creativity: Innovation through collaboration* (pp. 137–178). New York: Oxford University Press.

Nystrom, H. (1979). *Creativity and innovation.* New York: Wiley.

Osborn, A. F. (1957). *Applied imagination* (1st ed.). New York: Scribner.

Osborn, A. F. (1963). *Applied imagination* (2nd ed.). New York: Scribner.

Oxley, N. L., Dzindolet, M. T., & Paulus, P. B. (1996). The effects of facilitators on the performance of brainstorming groups. *Journal of Social Behavior and Personality, 11,* 633–646.

Parnes, S. J., & Meadow, A. (1959). Effect of "brainstorming" instructions on creative problem-solving by trained and untrained subjects. *Journal of Educational Psychology, 50,* 171–176.

Paulus, P. B. (2000). Groups, teams and creativity: The creative potential of idea generating groups. *Applied Psychology: An International Review, 49,* 237–262.

Paulus, P. B., & Brown, V. (2003). Ideational creativity in groups: Lessons from research on brainstorming. In P. B. Paulus & B. A. Nijstad (Eds.), *Group creativity: Innovation through collaboration* (pp. 110–136). New York: Oxford University Press.

Paulus, P. B., Brown, V., & Ortega, A. H. (1999). Group creativity. In R. E. Purser & A. Montuori (Eds.), *Social creativity* (Vol. 2, pp. 151–176). Cresskill, NJ: Hampton.

Paulus, P. B., Dugosh, K. L., Dzindolet, M. T., Coskun, H., & Putman, V. L. (2002). Social and cognitive influences in group brainstorming. Predicting production gains and losses. *European Review of Social Psychology, 12,* 299–325.

Paulus, P. B., & Dzindolet, M. T. (1993). Social influence processes in group brainstorming. *Journal of Personality and Social Psychology, 64,* 575–586.

Paulus, P. B., Dzindolet, M. T., Poletes, G., & Camacho, L. M. (1993). Perception of performance in group brainstorming: The illusion of group productivity. *Personality and Social Psychology Bulletin, 19,* 78–89.

Paulus, P. B., Larey, T. S., & Ortega, A. H. (1995). Performance and perceptions of brainstormers in an organizational setting. *Basic and Applied Social Psychology, 17,* 249–265.

Paulus, P. B., Larey, T. S., Putman, V. L., Leggett, K. L., & Roland, E. J. (1996). Social influence process in computer brainstorming. *Basic and Applied Social Psychology, 18,* 3–14.

Paulus, P. B., Nakui, T., Putman, V. L., & Brown, V. (2002). *The effects of task instructions and brief breaks on brainstorming.* Unpublished manuscript, University of Texas at Arlington.

Paulus, P. B., & Nijstad, B. (Eds.). (2003). *Group creativity: Innovation through collaboration.* New York: Oxford University Press.

Paulus, P. B., & Yang, H. C. (2000). Idea generation in groups: A basis for creativity in organizations. *Organizational Behavior and Human Decision Processes, 82,* 76–87.

Pinsonneault, A., Barki, H., Gallupe, R. B., & Hoppen, N. (1999). Electronic brainstorming: The illusion of productivity. *Information Systems Research, 10,* 110–133.

Putman, V. L., & Paulus, P. B. (2002). *Brainstorming and decision making.* Unpublished manuscript, University of Texas at Arlington.

Roy, M. C., Gauvin, S., & Limayem, M. (1996). Electronic group brainstorming: The role of feedback on productivity. *Small Group Research, 27,* 215–247.

Schwartz, B., Ward, A., Monterosso, J., Lyumbomirsky, S., White, K., & Lehman, D. R. (2002). Maximizing versus satisficing: Happiness is a matter of choice. *Journal of Personality and Social Psychology, 83,* 1178–1197.

Simonton, D. K. (1988). *Scientific genius. A psychology of science.* New York: Cambridge University Press.

Smith, S. (2003). The constraining effects of initial ideas. In P. B. Paulus & B. A. Nijstad (Eds.), *Group creativity: Innovation through collaboration* (pp. 15–31). New York: Oxford University Press.

Stasser, G., & Birchmeier, Z. (2003). Group creativity and collective choice. In P. B. Paulus & B. A. Nijstad (Eds.), *Group creativity: Innovation through collaboration* (pp. 85–109). New York: Oxford University Press.

Stein, M. I. (1982). Creativity, groups, and management. In R. A. Guzzo (Ed.), *Improving group decision making in organizations* (pp. 127–155). New York: Academic Press.

Sutton, R. I., & Hargadon, A. (1996). Brainstorming groups in context. *Administrative Science Quarterly, 41,* 685–718.

Swezey, R. W., & Salas, E. (Eds.). (1992). *Teams: Their training and performance.* Norwood, NJ: Ablex.

Thompson, L. (2004). *Making the team: A guide for managers* (2nd ed.). Upper Saddle River, NJ: Prentice-Hall.

West, M. A. (1990). The social psychology of innovation in groups. In M. A. West & J. L. Farr (Eds.), *Innovation and creativity at work: Psychological and organizational strategies* (pp. 309–334). London: Wiley.

West, M. A. (2003). Innovation implementation in work teams. In P. B. Paulus & B. A. Nijstad (Eds.), *Group creativity: Innovation through collaboration* (pp. 245–276). New York: Oxford University Press.

Chapter 5

Membership Change in Groups: Implications for Group Creativity

Hoon-Seok Choi
Sungkunkwan University

Leigh L. Thompson
Northwestern University

Creativity is one of the most sought after of team skills and management competencies. A walk through a local bookstore suggests that creativity and innovation are experiencing nothing short of a heyday in the business world. In 2002 alone, over 25 books were launched on creativity and innovation, brandishing titles like *Weird Ideas That Work: 11½ Ideas for Promoting, Managing and Sustaining Motivation* (Sutton, 2002) and *The Do It Yourself Lobotomy: Open Your Mind to Greater Creative Thinking* (Monahan, 2002). In fact, since 1996, over 250 books on creativity and innovation have been released, each with its own take on creativity, ranging from jazz (e.g., *Jamming*; Kao, 1996) to the practices followed by a given company (e.g., *The Art of Innovation*; Kelley, 2001). A recent *BusinessWeek* article touted creativity as the single most important skill for the new business era (July 2002).

The renewed interest in team creativity is likely the result of many factors, including the fact that as markets become more commoditized, the only way to differentiate products is to either develop a new product or leverage the product's unique capabilities, such as service. Moreover, the information age has fueled renewed interest in creativity as new economies are requiring solutions to unprecedented technological challenges and possibilities.

The business community has not been reluctant to attempt to meet the challenge of the new creativity era, as judged by the volume of creativity and innovation seminars and training programs. A key component of many of these programs centers on constructing the proper environment for teams to work (for a review, see Thompson, 2003). Several companies have invested millions of dollars in the creative enterprise. Steelcase, Inc. has designed multimillion dollar "innovation spaces" (Brown, 2002). Procter & Gamble fitted all of its campus buildings in Cincinnati with escalators rather than elevators. IBM, 3M, and Aurora Foods use special electronic whiteboards. Some companies go for the outrageous, such as Southern California's Foote, Cone & Belding advertising agency, which adorned the walls of its boardroom with 156 surfboards, removed all doors from offices, and installed Italian bocce ball courts for creative brainstorming.

In this chapter, we suggest that it behooves managers and their companies to consider group design and, in particular, group composition as key in the creative process (see also Ancona & Bresman, chap. 9, this volume; Nijstad, Rietzschel, & Stroebe, chap. 8, this volume; Paulus, Nakui, & Putman, chap. 4, this volume). This is not to argue that group composition is the only factor that affects group creativity. Rather, we focus on group composition as one of many group-related issues (e.g., member characteristics, group process, and organizational context) that affect the creativity of groups (see Ancona & Bresman, chap. 9; Nijstad et al., chap. 8; Paulus et al., chap. 4; West et al., chap. 7, this volume). We argue that group composition is not synonymous with understanding the creative potential or style of a particular individual. Instead we focus on the group as a dynamic entity. Our arguments are both theoretical as well as practical. Theoretically, we suggest that the composition of the group, which is distinct from the talents of its members, is a key factor in group creativity. On a practical level, group composition represents something that is more efficient to change and under the control of most group leaders (as opposed to multimillion dollar structures).

OVERVIEW

We begin by defining what we mean by *group composition*. In so doing, we discuss a particular group composition issue—membership change. Specifically, we discuss four types of membership change and their effects on group functioning. From this we derive two theoretical views about the consequence of membership change in groups: the disruption perspective and the stimulation perspective. We ultimately argue that membership change stimulates the creative process in groups and enhances group creativity. We then provide a description of our program of research on membership change in groups and its positive impact on creativity.

GROUP COMPOSITION

Group composition refers to the representation and balance of people in a group (cf. Moreland & Levine, 1992). A variety of research exists on group composition (for extensive overviews, see Jackson, May, & Whitney, 1995; Levine & Moreland, 1998; McGrath, 1998; Moreland & Levine, 1992, 2003; Neale, Mannix, & Gruenfeld, 1998). The common approach to group composition involves how the composition on a given attribute affects group performance. These attributes include member ability (e.g., knowledge, skill, task experience), belief system (e.g., value, attitude, culture), member styles (e.g., personality, cognitive and behavioral style), and demographic characteristics (e.g., race, gender, ethnicity). Some of these attributes (e.g., demographic characteristics) are more visible than others (e.g., personality), and, all else being equal, visible attributes have a stronger and more immediate impact on groups than do less visible attributes (Milliken, Bartel, & Kurtzberg, 2003; Moreland & Levine, 1992; Williams & O'Reilly, 1998). Although group composition has typically been treated as a causal factor that influences groups, other analytic frameworks can also be used. For example, group composition can be viewed as a consequence of the operation of other social psychological processes or a context that moderates the relationship between other variables (Moreland & Levine, 1992).

The vast majority of work involving the link between group composition and creativity has dealt with how diversity in member attributes relates to the creativity of groups. Previous work in this research tradition generally supports the notion that diversity is a mixed blessing (Williams & O'Reilly, 1998). Studies of group brainstorming, for example, suggest that diversity in skills and knowledge background can enhance groups' ability to generate creative ideas, but this benefit can be offset by increased difficulty in communication, decreased social interaction between people, and bias in groups to focus more on shared information than unique information (Paulus, Larey, & Dzindolet, 2001). Similarly, studies of diversity in organizational work groups documented that diversity promotes group creativity through a wide range of ideas and perspectives that members bring to the task, but is associated with less desirable outcomes such as low member satisfaction, weak identification with the group, greater emotional conflict, and turnover (Jackson, Brett, Sessa, Cooper, Julin, & Peyronnin, 1991; Levine & Moreland, 1998; Milliken et al., 2003; Williams & O'Reilly, 1998).

Although previous research on diversity offers useful insights into the composition–creativity link in groups, our understanding of the phenomenon is still limited for two major reasons. First, there are limits in terms of the kinds of composition dimensions being studied, with the result that some aspects of group composition (e.g., demographic diversity) received far more attention than others (e.g., diversity in cognitive styles; cf. McGrath, 1998). Second, and more important for the purpose of the present chapter, much of the research investigations involves the impact of diversity (composition) on creativity at a particular point in time, as opposed to taking a developmental perspective. This is particularly problematic because groups are not static entities, but instead undergo changes in their composition in dynamic ways (Arrow & McGrath, 1995; Levine & Choi, 2004; McGrath, 1998; Moreland & Levine, 1982, 1992). Obviously, group composition varies over time as new members join and/or old timers leave the group. Even if there is no change in terms of who makes up the group, several aspects of group composition (e.g., abilities, opinions, job responsibilities) naturally change as a function of time or social influence processes within the group (Moreland & Levine, 1992; Moreland, Levine, & Wingert, 1996). Moreover, the impact of group composition on group functioning can vary as groups pass through a set of developmental stages (cf. Milliken et al., 2003; Watson, Kumar, & Michaelson, 1993). In this chapter, we focus on one of those issues in detail: the impact of membership change on group creativity.

MEMBERSHIP CHANGE

One of the defining characteristics of groups is that they are bounded (Guzzo & Dickson, 1996; Hackman, 1987; Sundstrom, 1999). That is, there is a shared perception of who is a group member. In a similar vein, Campbell's (1958) treatment of "group entitativity" made the point that groups do not have quite the same status as individuals in terms of being indisputable entities, but that, despite their semiephemeral nature, they are indeed entities. Collectively, these treatments of group boundaries suggest that groups have stability in terms of membership. Yet the reality is that groups experience changes in their membership over time and their boundaries are often permeable. In fact many organizations utilize a variety of compositional techniques that involve temporary changes in group membership to better accomplish group goals (Ancona & Caldwell, 1998; Gruenfeld, Martorana, & Fan, 2000).

Simply stated, *membership change* refers to changes in a group's membership structure. There are four key types of membership change in groups: upsizing, downsizing, reorganization (cf. Arrow & McGrath, 1995; Ziller, 1965), and a change in function.[1] *Upsizing* involves entry of newcomers to

---

[1]Most treatments of membership change have focused on the first three types: newcomer entry, member exit, and member replacement. We add the concept of functional change to our treatment.

an existing group, whereas *downsizing* involves exit of a subset of existing members. *Reorganization* involves the departure of a subset of existing members and entry of newcomers. A final type of membership change concerns the case in which the members of the group do not change per se, but there is a change in one (or more) member's status, function, or reporting relationships. As an example, consider a situation in which one member of a previously self-directed team is appointed to be leader of the group. In this sense, the member of the group may in fact undergo a virtual change in terms of the knowledge or processes used in the group. For the purposes of this chapter, we focus on one of the four types of membership change: reorganization. Reorganization often occurs in open groups (Ziller, 1965) whose boundaries are more or less permeable and, in effect, involves the departure of old timers and entry of newcomers.

COMPETING PERSPECTIVES REGARDING THE IMPACT OF MEMBERSHIP CHANGE IN GROUPS

Membership change can have important consequences for group functioning because it alters both the distribution of knowledge within the group and relations among members (Levine, Choi, & Moreland, 2003; Levine & Moreland, 1994; Moreland & Levine, 1982). Thus, it has cognitive as well as socioemotional consequences. The groups literature on balance would seem to favor that membership change would have negative consequences. However, there are some notable exceptions. In the following, we distinguish two broad perspectives concerning how membership change affects group functioning: the disruption perspective and the stimulation perspective.

Disruption Perspective

The disruption perspective focuses on the negative consequences of membership change. One such consequence is lowered group performance due to changing membership. This can happen for several reasons. For example, newcomers often lack task-relevant experience and thus undermine the group's ability to perform its task. Moreover, newcomers often interfere with existing work practices because they require the group to spend a substantial amount of time and effort on socialization. In line with this reasoning, research on turnover in small groups indicates that turnover is harmful for group performance (e.g., Goodman & Leyden, 1991; Mathiyalakan, 2002; Rogers, Ford, & Tassone, 1961; for a review, see Argote & Kane, 2003). Moreover, findings suggest that turnover can be more detrimental to group performance when the quality of replacements is inferior to the people being replaced (Naylor & Briggs, 1965; Trow, 1960), when turnover rates are greater than usual (Trow, 1960), when members work interactively rather than independently (Naylor & Briggs, 1965), when the group has low rather than high structure (Devadas & Argote, 1995), and when the task is simple rather than complex presumably because task knowledge changes more slowly on simple tasks than complex tasks, and thus the departure of existing members is often more costly in the former than in the latter (Argote, Insko, Yovetich, & Romero, 1995). It is worth noting that most of the research investigations on the impact of turnover in groups have focused on group performance in general, as opposed to particular measures of group creativity. Thus, although useful, this line of work does not tell us much about how membership change affects group creativity.

Another line of research involving the negative consequence of membership change centers around the work of transactive memory and shared mental models in teams. The research on transactive memory in groups (Austin, 2003; Liang, Moreland, & Argote, 1995; Moreland, 1999; Moreland, Argote, & Krishnan, 1998) suggests that the stability in group membership allows groups to develop and utilize transactive memory systems that aid in problem solving. Thus, when this process is disrupted through the exit or addition of new members, one would expect that the cognitive integrity of groups may be threatened. Similarly, the research on shared mental models (for reviews, see Salas & Cannon-Bowers, 2001; Thompson & Fine, 1999) suggests that one of the essential features of groups is the development of collective mental models that influence the ways in which members engage in coordinated actions and perform their tasks. Further, shared mental models are built implicitly through repeated interaction among group members (Klimoski & Mohammed, 1994).

Thus far, the research evidence would seem to be nearly uniform in suggesting that membership change can only hurt group effectiveness. We disagree and suggest that when the task at hand primarily requires the kind of coordination that is prescribed by transactive memory or shared mental models, such as in the construction of radios (cf. Moreland et al., 1998), membership change would be disruptive. However, we argue that the memory-type tasks used in investigations of transactive memory as well as construction-tasks are largely convergent tasks requiring coordinated actions to solve a problem that usually has a single solution set. In contrast, we suggest that creative tasks often require divergent thought processes, and it is precisely the lack of shared mental models or scriptlike knowledge system that may facilitate creativity. In the next section, we explore this in detail.

Stimulation Perspective

A quite different perspective is the stimulation perspective. This view states that membership change can have positive consequences. One such consequence of membership change, of course, is simply that newcomers replace ineffective old timers whose presence harmed the group. Below we summarize four distinct lines of research that support the notion that membership change can be beneficial for groups: newcomer innovation, group reflection, group problem solving, and knowledge transfer.

Newcomer Innovation. Membership change can be a stimulating event in a group's life for the facilitative role that newcomers play in producing innovations. Though newcomers are often submissive and susceptible to old timers' influence attempts (Moreland & Levine, 1989; Wanous & Colella, 1989), they are not always passive recipients of influence from a group. Instead, they can play a more active role, introducing innovations in group structure or process that help the group perform its task more effectively (Choi & Levine, 2004; Levine et al., 2003; Levine & Moreland, 1985). The success of newcomers in producing innovations depends on a variety of newcomer characteristics, including motivation to introduce changes into the group, their ability to generate innovative ideas, and their ability to convince old timers to adopt these ideas (see Levine et al., 2003). Newcomers' motivation and ability to produce innovations can depend on several factors. For example, newcomers' motivation to introduce innovation varies positively with their commitment to the group, their belief that they can successfully implement new ideas, and their perception that their innovation efforts will be rewarded by the group. Newcomers' ability to produce innovation can depend on a variety of group characteristics as well. For example, newcomers' innovation attempts would be more successful when groups are understaffed rather than adequately staffed, during earlier rather than later stages of group development, when groups are performing poorly rather than well, when groups are not committed to their current task strategies, and when groups experience high rather than low rates of turnover.

Considering newcomers as innovation agents is also consistent with a large body of literature on minority influence (Moscovici, 1985; Moscovici, Mucchi-Faina, & Maass, 1994). That is, newcomers are often numerical minorities in a group, and therefore innovations produced by newcomers can be viewed as a special kind of minority influence (Choi & Levine, 2004; Gruenfeld & Fan, 1999; Levine et al., 2003; Levine & Moreland, 1985). It is well known that a dissenting minority stimulates a majority to engage in a divergent thinking process, which in turn results in better performance, decision making, and creativity (Nemeth, 1992; Nemeth & Owens, 1996). Insofar as newcomers are motivated and able to introduce changes in the groups they join (cf. Bauer, Morrison, & Callister, 1998; Levine et al., 2003), an exposure to such newcomers (i.e., a minority) can stimulate creative thinking processes on the part of old timers (i.e., a majority) by promoting the consideration of multiple perspectives and deeper analyses of the given problem.

Group Reflection.   Groups do not always engage in reflective processes on their own, although they are critical for group effectiveness (Hackman, 1987; Schippers, Den Hartog, Koopman, & Wienk, 2003; Swift & West, 1998; West, 1996, 2000). Moreover, much of the social interactions in groups is routinized (Gersick & Hackman, 1990; Weiss & Ilgen, 1985), and the patterns of social interactions tend to be resistant to change (Brawley, Carron, & Widmeyer, 1988; Kelly, 1988; McGrath & Kelly, 1986). The lack of reflective activities, coupled with the forces toward routinization, poses problems especially when the group task requires creativity or when the nature of the task changes rapidly. To the extent that membership change necessitates changes in a group's existing work practices (Moreland & Levine, 1982), it can facilitate reflective processes in groups and help groups perform their task more effectively. Along these lines, some evidence suggests that membership change stimulates cognitive reflection by group members. Arrow and McGrath (1993), for example, reported that the quality of group reflection involving the activities that are related to the group's task was higher during weeks in which groups experienced a member replacement than during weeks in which their membership was intact. Similarly, Levine and Choi (2004) discovered that groups which experienced membership change engaged in more cognitive activities involving their task strategy than those which did not experience such change.

Group Problem Solving.   In most of the research on group problem solving, groups do not experience membership change during the course of interaction. In fact membership is typically considered something that must be controlled or held constant (cf. Moreland & Levine, 1992), and researchers do not actively pursue potential impact of changing membership on groups' ability to solve problems. Despite this dominant trend, several exceptions exist. For example, Torrance (1955) examined problem solving in temporary and permanent groups. He found that military air crews in which membership was determined on a temporary basis reached better solutions than did crews composed of permanent members.

A rather unique approach to group problem solving involving membership change can be found in the studies of stepladder groups (Rogelberg, Barnes-Farrell, & Lowe, 1992; Rogelberg & O'Connor, 1998; Rogelberg, O'Connor, & Sederburg, 2002). In the typical paradigm used to study stepladder groups, initially two group members (i.e., the initial core) work together on the problem at hand, and then a third and a fourth member sequentially joins the core group. Thus, stepladder groups are a special case of membership change that involves linear addition of new members to an existing group. Using this procedure, Rogelberg and colleagues demonstrated that, compared with conventional four-person groups, in which all members performed the task from the outset, stepladder groups produced higher quality solutions. Several explanations exist as to why stepladder groups produce quality solutions compared with conventional groups (Rogelberg et al., 1992, 1998). For example, stepladder procedure promotes communication via constant verbalization and reiteration of the ideas due to the requirement that the entering member and the core group explain their solutions. In addition, stepladder groups typically feel less pressure to conform to the group norm due to the changing nature of group membership. This reduced social pressure, in turn, can stimulate critical evaluations of ideas, encourage disagreements, and allow the best member to exert greater influence on the group's final solution.

Knowledge Transfer. One of the most daunting challenges in organizations is to facilitate knowledge transfer among groups. This is particularly so given groups' inability to learn from one another (Argote, 1999; Szulanski, 1996). As an attempt to overcome this hurdle, a variety of compositional techniques have been proposed (see Ancona & Caldwell, 1998; Mohrman, Cohen, & Mohrman, 1995). One such technique involves rotating members who have particular knowledge or task experience. Ancona and Caldwell (1992), for example, found that replacing the leader of a product development team with a member of a manufacturing department not only increased the team's knowledge about the manufacturing, but also created new links to that department. Although the exact nature of the link between member rotation and knowledge transfer in organizations is still debatable (cf. Gruenfeld et al., 2000), research on balance (e.g., Almeida & Kogut, 1999; Berry & Broadbent, 1984; Galbraith, 1990) suggests that rotating people across work groups can facilitate knowledge transfer in organizations (for a review, see Argote & Ingram, 2000). This conclusion is also in harmony with the notion that turnover can increase, not decrease, organizational effectiveness due to the greater innovation potential in mobile than in immobile organizations (Dalton & Todor, 1979; Price, 1977; Staw, 1980).

HOW MEMBERSHIP CHANGE PROMOTES GROUP CREATIVITY

In the previous section, we introduced two competing perspectives regarding how membership change affects several important aspects of group functioning. In this section, we now specifically examine how membership change affects group creativity and introduce an empirical testing of our research hypotheses.

Impact of Membership Change on Group Creativity

According to the notion that membership change disrupts group functioning, one might expect that membership change would only hinder groups'
creativity. As illustrated by the stimulation perspective, however, there is
reason to expect that membership change can actually be beneficial for
groups. Drawing on previous theoretical analyses of how membership
change affects the dynamics within groups, we propose what we might call a
stimulation hypothesis, and we argue that membership change can enhance the creativity of groups. Our prediction is based on the following
three reasons.

First, groups that experience membership change are typically more focused on getting the job done than those that do not experience such
change (Ziller, 1965). That is, membership change can promote the level
of task orientation in a group. Moreover, when the group membership is
transitory, establishing a rigid status system in a group is neither useful nor
desirable. For this reason, criticisms arising from status striving are often
minimized (Stein, 1953; Ziller, Behringer, & Goodchilds, 1962). To the extent that high levels of task orientation (cf. West, 1996) and lack of evaluation apprehension (cf. Osborn, 1957) promote creative thinking in groups,
membership change should have a positive impact on group creativity.

Second, membership change can diversify groups' knowledge base via
the infusion of new perspectives and information. This greater diversity in
knowledge and information, in turn, can increase cognitive stimulation
during idea generation (Milliken et al., 2003; Moreland et al., 1996; Paulus
et al., 2000). Thus, membership change should be beneficial for group creativity insofar as it increases diversity in groups' knowledge base and diversity facilitates creativity (cf. Levine & Choi, 2004).

Third, membership change can elicit social processes that are conducive
to creativity. This can happen through the process by which the presence of
newcomers motivates old timers to change the structure or process of the
group in the service of better attaining group goals (Moreland & Levine,
1982). Moreover, while "showing the ropes" or transmitting task-related
knowledge to newcomers, old timers reflect on how the work is being done
within the group (Feldman, 1994; Levine & Moreland, 1991; Sutton &
Louis, 1987). This enhanced reflexivity can result in a variety of activities
that can promote group creativity, such as redistribution of knowledge,
eliminating obstacles in information sharing, obtaining resources needed,
redesigning of the task, and implementing new and improved methods to
perform the task. This line of reasoning is also consistent with the notion
that groups whose members have been working together for a long time are
not likely to be creative because increased longevity can lead to likeminded-
ness among members (Katz, 1982), and groups fall prey to the common

knowledge bias as they gain too much experience working together as a group (Kim, 1997).

Empirical Testing

To our knowledge, the only empirical test for the proposition that membership change can enhance group creativity has been offered by Ziller et al. (1962). In this study, all groups first performed a dot-estimation task. Before beginning a second group task, which involved generating cartoon captions, open groups experienced one of the following three kinds of membership change: addition, subtraction, or replacement of a group member. In contrast, closed groups retained the same members for the task. Results indicate that group creativity, measured by the number of captions generated and the humor of these captions, was higher in open groups than in closed groups. Although intriguing, results of this study need to be interpreted with caution. First of all, it is not clear whether participants in open groups were more creative than those in closed groups because of the membership change as the study failed to obtain the baseline creativity prior to the membership change. Moreover, membership change in this study involved adding a new person to an existing group, subtracting a member from the group, or replacing members between groups. Thus, groups in the open group condition differed in terms of the group size and the kinds of membership change they experienced. Due to this confounding, it is difficult to assess the unique effect of membership change on group creativity.

Another potentially relevant study was conducted by Gruenfeld et al. (2000), in which they examined how rotating members across groups affected knowledge transfer between groups. Our studies differ from Gruenfeld et al. in several important ways. First, the Gruenfeld et al. study adopted a temporary member rotation paradigm, in which itinerant members visited new groups and then came back to their groups of origin. Second, these researchers found that college students' classwork contained more ideas after itinerant members returned to their original groups than prior to or during the period of membership change. Because there was no control condition, however, it is difficult to assess whether the obtained results were solely due to membership change. Moreover, their findings involve the number of ideas used in individual work (i.e., while group members worked independently), not a joint outcome produced by groups.

Recently, we modified the Ziller et al. (1962) open versus closed group paradigm and investigated the impact of membership change on group creativity (Choi & Thompson, 2003). The membership change in our research involved randomly replacing one group member with a newcomer who had the same amount and type of task experience as the person he or she was replacing. Using this paradigm, we examined the creativity of open groups and closed groups in two studies.

Our first study involved 20 three-person groups assigned to either an open group condition or a closed group condition. We arranged each experimental session such that multiple groups performed simultaneously in separate places. All groups first performed an idea-generation task (referred to as Part 1), during which they generated alternative ways of classifying 12 fruit items such as grapes and apple (cf. Crowe & Higgins, 1993). We then introduced membership change in the open group condition by randomly switching one member between groups. Thus, each group in this condition had one newcomer and two old timers after Part 1. Following the membership change, groups performed a second idea-generation task (referred to as Part 2), during which they generated alternative ways to classify 12 vegetable items such as peas and spinach. In contrast, participants in the closed group condition retained the same three members and performed Part 2. We chose a task that is highly unusual yet fun for most people because it is conducive to divergent thinking (cf. Guilford, 1967). Group creativity was measured in terms of the number of unique ideas (i.e., fluency) and the number of conceptual categories represented in ideas (i.e., flexibility; cf. Guilford, 1967; Kelly & Karau, 1993; Paulus & Yang, 2000). The intercoder reliability was high for both measures. To assess how membership change affected group creativity, we used Part 1 measures as proxies of baseline creativity and controlled these measures in our analyses. Our analyses indicate that, as expected, open groups generated significantly more unique ideas (i.e., higher fluency) and more conceptually different kinds of ideas (i.e., higher flexibility) than did closed groups.

We conducted a second study to further illuminate the effects of membership change on group creativity. This study involved 33 three-person groups and had two specific goals. Recall that groups in our first study generated ideas for the two objects that were quite similar during the two group tasks (fruits and vegetables). Had groups generated ideas for the objects that were quite different from each other during the two tasks, the observed difference between open groups and closed groups might have been smaller than we found because the knowledge and task experience of newcomers may not be readily applicable in their new groups. Thus, we wanted to examine whether the similarity in ideation objects prior to and after membership change matters. We also wanted to understand the underlying mechanisms of the group openness effect by examining the amount and kind of contributions made by newcomers and old timers after membership change.[2]

---

[2]We use the term *old timers* to refer to those who were not replaced throughout the experiment.

The creativity task in our second study involved two parts. Part 1 was identical to the vegetables task used in the first study. During the second part of the task (Part 2), participants generated as many possible uses as they could for a cardboard box. We used the same procedure and dependent variables as the first study. To identify the source of ideas generated within each group, each participant was identified by a color-coded tag, and ideas were recorded according to who said what. Interrater reliability for our dependent measures were all high. Like the first study, we analyzed Part 2 measures while controlling for Part 1 measures. Results indicate that, as in Experiment 1, both fluency and flexibility were significantly higher in the open group condition than in the closed group condition. This suggests that our findings in the first study may not be attributable to the similarity in the ideation object prior to and after membership change.

Another goal of our second study was to examine the nature of contributions made by newcomers and old timers after membership change. We addressed this question in two ways. We first examined the contribution of newcomers by assessing the impact of newcomer quality, reasoning that newcomers who scored high on fluency and flexibility on Part 1 were more creative than those who scored low on these measures, and therefore would have a more positive impact on the groups they joined. To test this idea, we developed an index of newcomer quality based on their creativity during Part 1. We then obtained partial correlations between newcomers' Part 1 creativity and receiving groups' Part 2 creativity, holding constant receiving groups' Part 1 creativity. Here, *receiving* groups refer to the groups that newcomers joined. Consistent with our expectation, the partial correlations indicated that the higher the newcomer's Part 1 fluency, the higher the receiving group's Part 2 fluency. We found the same pattern of results for flexibility, suggesting that the increase in creativity was due in part to his or her creativity per se, not simply that the newcomer was new.

Our next question was whether there were any changes in the creativity of old timers in open groups after newcomer entry and, if so, what it was like compared to those in closed groups. To answer this question, we computed average fluency and average flexibility for the two old timers within each group in the open group condition. We also computed average fluency and flexibility for the three members within each group in the closed group condition. We then computed difference scores by subtracting Part 1 measures from Part 2 measures. Analysis on the difference scores indicated that fluency increased from Part 1 to Part 2 in both conditions, but the increase was greater in the open group condition than in the closed group condition. We found the same pattern of results for flexibility, suggesting that it was an increase in the number and diversity of ideas that enhanced performance. Notice that the increase in the creativity of closed groups from Part 1 to Part 2 could be the result of learning. If so, then the finding that fluency and flexibility of old timers increased more in open groups than in closed groups suggests that membership change had an impact on groups over and above the learning effect.

Overall, results from our studies suggest that membership change can promote group creativity. Specifically, we found evidence that newcomer quality matters because it was linked to the creativity of open groups after membership change. What is more intriguing to us is the result regarding changes in old timers after membership change. To our knowledge, it is the first empirical evidence demonstrating that membership change can enhance the creativity of old timers. Although more work is needed to further illuminate the underlying mechanisms of the group openness effect, our initial studies suggest that work groups can benefit from strategic uses of membership change where it is feasible and appropriate to do so. Stability in group membership would seem to be best for the business environment where there is little need for innovation. In other organizations where there is a constant need to produce innovations, membership change can be planned strategically to boost group creativity.

DISCUSSION

We began this chapter by highlighting the renewed interest in group creativity in organizations. We suggested that many organizational attempts to rekindle or instigate creative ideation are focused on structural as opposed to personnel changes. We suggested that reorganization and restaffing are often negatively perceived by managers and those who are affected. Indeed there is some basis of truth here as countless investigations of organizational downsizing and organizational mergers point to heightened conflict and tension among those affected. In this chapter, we attempted to look at the bright side of group reorganization and restaffing. We examined a specific type of reorganization—membership change—and its effects on group creativity. The relevant literature suggested a number of cognitive and behavioral factors, including heightened focus on task processes that might conspire to enhance creativity. In our laboratory investigations, we found causal evidence that membership change enhances the number of creative ideas generated by groups as well as the complexity and variance of these ideas—two of the most commonly used measures of group creativity.

Our results as well as arguments favoring the stimulating effects of membership change must be interpreted with a certain amount of theoretical and practical caution. First, the focus of our research is on groups' ability to generate new ideas as a function of membership change. Although there is little doubt that developing new ideas is an important part of group creativity, whether membership change necessarily leads to successful innovation in organizations remains unanswered (see West et al., chap. 7, this volume).

A related issue is the amount of time group members work together after membership change. Groups in our studies worked on the task for a relatively short period of time after the membership change. Thus, it is not clear whether membership change has a long-lasting positive impact on group creativity.

Second, the underlying mechanisms of the group openness effect need to be further illuminated. On the one hand, our results regarding the impact of newcomer quality suggest that membership change can enhance group creativity via the cognitive stimulations fueled by creative newcomers. On the other hand, our finding that the creativity of old timers increased after membership change suggests that, at least to some extent, the presence of a newcomer can be socially stimulating and have a motivating effect on idea-generation groups. Conceptually differentiating the social and cognitive stimulation effect can help us better understand why open groups were more creative than closed groups in our studies.

Third, the impact of membership change on group creativity can depend on the characteristics of the group as well as the people involved in the change. Our studies identified one such characteristic—namely, the creativity of newcomers and old timers prior to membership change. There are, of course, many other factors that can affect the link between membership change and group creativity. For example, the ability of newcomers and old timers to collaborate and coordinate would be important because without these skills groups would not be able to enjoy the potential benefits of membership change. In addition, group members' ability to adjust their roles during the course of membership change can be crucial because it is often linked to improved group performance (cf. LePine, 2003). Group norms that support changes and experimentation of new ideas (cf. George & Zhou, 2001; Levine et al., 2003; West, 1996) can also play an important role because groups that are open to new experiences would be more receptive to the ideas brought by newcomers.

Finally, our results must not somehow grant team and organizational leaders free license to dismantle teams or to create endless team musical chairs. We suggest that at least four considerations should be weighed when considering recomposition (cf. Arrow & McGrath, 1995; Levine et al., 2003): the timing of membership change (e.g., when should recomposition occur—in early or later stages of group development?), the frequency of membership change (e.g., how often—once per year, once per quarter?), the content of membership change (e.g., swapping similarly skilled people or people with fundamentally different training?), and the expectations that the group has (e.g., is membership change under the group's control and planned vs. imposed by the organization and unpredictable?). Obviously, frequent changes in group membership in early stages of group development are simply too disruptive. Similarly, changes in group membership in the middle of a task, rather than at a natural break point in the task, would disrupt the group process and hinder group creativity (cf. Gersick & Hackman, 1990). Moreover, membership change can cause more harm than good if the change is not under the group's control and largely unpredictable. Swapping similarly skilled people may not be terribly useful either because it is not likely to diversify the group's knowledge base. These thorny issues are often neatly sidestepped in the starkness of the laboratory, but they are obviously front-and-center stage in real organizations. Future studies need to address these issues in both laboratory and field settings.

A related issue centers on indexes of group functioning. It is abundantly clear that one of the sharpest points of friction results from the microfocus of the researcher and the macrofocus of the manager. Simply stated, our results might be able to convince a team manager that membership change might very well in fact enhance creativity. For a product development team in a company, this might be good news. However, managers have a set of other, perhaps equally relevant, concerns about the functioning of their teams. If restaffing results in greater interpersonal conflict, as opposed to cognitive conflict (cf. Jehn, 1995), this might mean a significant increase in the number of hours that managers may need to invest in conflict resolution. Likewise, if membership change results in a great deal of coordination loss in teams, managers must first deal with this even before considering how the team might benefit from the change.

In conclusion, understanding the impact of membership change in groups is important not only because it is inevitable in most work groups, but it is often linked to improved performance and creativity. For the most part, introducing new talent to the group can ensure that the group remains fresh. It can also create an environment for healthy cognitive conflicts in work groups. Too often this positive side of membership change is neglected, and teams and organizations alike show strong opposition to such change. In our view, strategic uses of membership change can help, not hurt, groups by keeping them diverse, thereby increasing the chance to avoid the self-destructing cycle of group homogeneity. Although more work is needed to further illuminate the impact of membership change on group creativity, findings from our initial studies are quite encouraging and invite a special research concern. We hope this chapter provides a useful framework to tap into the bright side of membership change and attract more research in this area.

ACKNOWLEDGMENTS

We thank Paul Paulus and two anonymous reviewers for their helpful comments on an earlier version of this chapter.

REFERENCES

Almeida, P., & Kogut, B. (1999). Localization of knowledge and the mobility of engineers in regional networks. *Management Science, 47*, 905–917.

Ancona, D. G., & Caldwell, D. F. (1992). Demography and design: Predictors of new product team performance. *Organization Science, 3*(3), 321–341.

Ancona, D. G., & Caldwell, D. F. (1998). Rethinking team composition from the outside in. In M. Neale & E. Mannix (Eds.), *Research on managing groups and teams* (Vol. 1, pp. 21–38). Stamford, CT: JAI.

Argote, L. (1999). *Learning: Creating, retaining and transferring knowledge.* Kluwer Academic.

Argote, L., & Ingram, P. (2000). Knowledge transfer: A basis for competitive advantage in firms. *Organizational Behavior and Human Decision Processes, 82*(1), 150–169.

Argote, L., Insko, C. A., Yovetich, N., & Romero, A. A. (1995). Group learning curves: The effects of turnover and task complexity on group performance. *Journal of Applied Social Psychology, 25*, 512–529.

Argote, L., & Kane, A. (2003). Learning from direct and indirect organizations: The effects of experience content, timing, and distribution. In P. Paulus & B. Nijstad (Eds.), *Group creativity* (pp. 277–303). New York: Oxford University Press.

Arrow, H., & McGrath, J. E. (1993). Membership matters: How member change and continuity affect group structure, process, and performance. *Small Group Research, 24*, 334–361.

Arrow, H., & McGrath, J. E. (1995). Membership dynamics in groups at work: A theoretical framework. In B. M. Staw & L. L. Cummings (Eds.), *Research in organizational behavior* (pp. 373–411). Greenwich, CT: JAI.

Austin, J. R. (2003). Transactive memory in organizational groups: The effects of content, consensus, specialization, and accuracy on group performance. *Journal of Applied Psychology, 88*, 866–878.

Bauer, T. N., Morrison, E. W., & Callister, R. R. (1998). Organizational socialization: A review and directions for future research. *Research in Personnel and Human Resource Management, 16*, 149–214.

Berry, D. C., & Broadbent, D. E. (1984). On the relationship between task performance and associated verbalizable knowledge. *Quarterly Journal of Experimental Psychology, 36A*, 209–231.

Brawley, L. R., Carron, A. V., & Widmeyer, W. N. (1988). Exploring the relationship between cohesion and group resistance to disruption. *Journal of Sport and Exercise Psychology, 10*, 199–213.

Brown, J. (2002, March 18). Prada gets personal. *BusinessWeek*, p. EB8.

Campbell, D. (1958). Common fate, similarity, and other indices of the status of aggregates of persons as social entities. *Behavioral Science, 3*, 14–25.

Choi, H.-S., & Levine, J. M. (2004). Minority influence in work teams: Impact of newcomers. *Journal of Experimental Social Psychology, 40*, 273–280.

Choi, H.-S., & Thompson, L. (2003). *Old wine in a new bottle: Brainstorming in open and closed groups.* Working paper, Kellogg School of Management.

Crowe, E., & Higgins, E. T. (1997). Regulatory focus and strategic inclinations: Promotion and prevention in decision-making. *Organizational Behavior and Human Decision Processes, 69*, 117–132.

Dalton, D. R., & Todor, W. D. (1979). Turnover turned over: An expanded and positive perspective. *Academy of Management Review, 4*, 225–235.

Devadas, R., & Argote, L. (1995, May). *Collective learning and forgetting: The effects of turnover and group structure.* Paper presented at the annual meeting of the Midwestern Psychological Association, Chicago, IL.

Feldman, D. C. (1994). Who's socializing whom? The impact of socializing newcomers on insiders, work groups, and organizations. *Human Resource Management Review, 4*, 213–233.

Galbraith, C. S. (1990). Transferring core manufacturing technologies in high technology firms. *California Management Review, 32*(4), 56–70.

George, J. M., & Zhou, J. (2001). When openness to experience and conscientiousness are related to creative behavior: An interactional approach. *Journal of Applied Psychology, 86,* 513–524.

Gersick, C. J. G., & Hackman, J. R. (1990). Habitual routines in task-performing groups. *Organizational Behavior and Human Decision Processes, 47,* 65–97.

Goodman, P. S., & Leyden, D. P. (1991). Familiarity and group productivity. *Journal of Applied Psychology, 76*(4), 578–586.

Gruenfeld, D. H., & Fan, E. T. (1999). What newcomers see and what oldtimers say: Discontinuities in knowledge exchange. In L. Thompson, J. M. Levine, & D. M. Messick (Eds.), *Shared cognition in organizations: The management of knowledge* (pp. 245–266). Mahwah, NJ: Lawrence Erlbaum Associates.

Gruenfeld, D. H., Martorana, P. V., & Fan, E. (2000). What do groups learn from their worldliest members?: Direct and indirect influence in dynamic teams. *Organizational Behavior and Human Decision Processes, 82,* 45–59.

Guilford, J. P. (1967). The nature of human intelligence. *Intelligence, 1,* 274–280.

Guzzo, R. A., & Dickson, M. W. (1996). Teams in organizations: Recent research on performance and effectiveness. *Annual Review of Psychology, 47,* 307–338.

Hackman, J. R. (1987). The design of work teams. In J. Lorsch (Ed.), *Handbook of organizational behavior.* Englewood Cliffs, NJ: Prentice-Hall.

Jackson, S. E., Brett, J. F., Sessa, D. M., Cooper, D. M., Julin, J. A., & Peyronnin, K. (1991). Some differences make a difference: Individual dissimilarity and group heterogeneity as correlates of recruitment, promotions, and turnover. *Journal of Applied Psychology, 76,* 675–689.

Jackson, S. E., May, K. E., & Whitney, K. (1995). Understanding the dynamics of diversity in decision-making teams. In R. A. Guzzo & E. Salas (Eds.), *Team effectiveness and decision making in organizations* (pp. 383–396). San Francisco: Jossey-Bass.

Jehn, K. (1995). A multimethod examination of the benefits and detriments of intragroup conflict. *Administrative Science Quarterly, 40,* 256–282.

Kao, J. (1996). *Jamming: The art and discipline of corporate creativity.* New York: HarperBusiness.

Katz, R. (1982). The effects of group longevity on project communication and performance. *Administrative Science Quarterly, 22,* 81–104.

Kelley, T. (2001). *The art of innovation: Lessons in creativity from IDEO, America's leading design firm.* New York: Doubleday.

Kelly, J. R. (1988). Entrainment in individual and group performance. In J. E. McGrath (Ed.), *The social psychology of time: New perspectives* (pp. 89–110). Newbury Park, CA: Sage.

Kelly, J. R., & Karau, S. (1993). Entrainment of creativity in small groups. *Small Group Research, 24,* 179–198.

Kim, P. H. (1997). When what you know can hurt you: A study of experiential effects on group discussion and performance. *Organizational Behavior and Human Decision Processes, 69,* 165–177.

Klimoski, R. J., & Mohammed, S. (1994). Team mental models: Construct or metaphor? *Journal of Management, 20*(2), 403–437.

LePine, J. A. (2003). Team adaptation and postchange performance: Effects of team composition in terms of members' cognitive ability and personality. *Journal of Applied Psychology, 88,* 27–39.

Levine, J. M., & Choi, H.-S. (2004). Impact of personnel turnover on team performance and cognition. In E. Salas & S. M. Fiore (Eds.), *Team cognition: Process and performance at the inter/intra individual level* (pp. 163–176). Washington, DC: American Psychological Association.

Levine, J. M., Choi, H.-S., & Moreland, R. L. (2003). Newcomer innovation in work teams. In P. Paulus & B. Nijstad (Eds.), *Group creativity* (pp. 202–224). New York: Oxford University Press.

Levine, J. M., & Moreland, R. L. (1985). Innovation and socialization in small groups. In S. Moscovici, G. Mugny, & E. van Avermaet (Eds.), *Perspectives on minority influence* (pp. 143–169). Cambridge, England: Cambridge University Press.

Levine, J. M., & Moreland, R. L. (1991). Culture and socialization in work groups. In L. B. Resnick, J. M. Levine, & S. D. Teasdale (Eds.), *Perspectives on socially shared cognition* (pp. 257–279). Washington, DC: American Psychological Association.

Levine, J. M., & Moreland, R. L. (1994). Group socialization: Theory and research. In W. Stroebe & M. Hewstone (Eds.), *European review of social psychology* (Vol. 5, pp. 305–336). Chichester, UK: Wiley.

Levine, J. M., & Moreland, R. L. (1998). Small groups. In D. Gilbert, S. Fiske, & G. Lindzey (Eds.), *Handbook of social psychology* (4th ed., Vol. 2, pp. 415–469). Boston: McGraw-Hill.

Liang, D. W., Moreland, R. L., & Argote, L. (1995). Group versus individual training and group performance: The mediating role of transactive memory. *Personality and Social Psychology Bulletin, 21*, 384–393.

Mathiyalakan, S. (2002). A methodology for controlled empirical investigation of membership continuity and change in GDSS groups. *Decision Support Systems, 32*(3), 279–295.

McGrath, J. E. (1998). A view of group composition through a group-theoretic lens. In M. Neale, E. Mannix, & D. Gruenfeld (Eds.), *Research on managing groups and teams: Composition* (Vol. 1, pp. 255–272). Greenwich, CT: JAI.

McGrath, J. E., & Kelly, J. R. (1986). *Time and human interaction: Toward a social psychology of time*. New York: Guilford.

Milliken, F. J., Bartel, C. A., & Kurtzberg, T. R. (2003). Diversity and creativity in workgroups: A dynamic perspective on the affective and cognitive processes that link diversity and performance. In P. B. Paulus & B. A. Nijstad (Eds.), *Group creativity: Innovation through collaboration* (pp. 32–62). New York: Oxford University Press.

Mohrman, S. A., Cohen, S. G., & Mohrman, A. M. (1995). *Designing team-based organizations: New forms for knowledge work*. San Francisco: Jossey-Bass.

Monahan, T. (2002). *The do it yourself lobotomy: Open your mind to greater creative thinking*. New York: Wiley.

Moreland, R. L. (1985). Social categorization and the assimilation of "new" group members. *Journal of Personality and Social Psychology, 48*, 1173–1190.

Moreland, R. L. (1999). Transactive memory: Learning who knows what in work groups and organizations. In L. Thompson, J. Levine, & D. Messick (Eds.), *Shared cognition in organizations: The management of knowledge* (pp. 3–31). Mahwah, NJ: Lawrence Erlbaum Associates.

Moreland, R. L., Argote, L., & Krishnan, R. (1998). Training people to work in groups. In R. S. Tindale & Colleagues (Eds.), *Theory and research on small groups* (pp. 37–60). New York: Plenum.

Moreland, R. L., & Levine, J. M. (1982). Socialization in small groups: Temporal changes in individual–group relations. In L. Berkowitz (Ed.), *Advances in experimental social psychology* (Vol. 15, pp. 137–192). New York: Academic Press.

Moreland, R. L., & Levine, J. M. (1989). Newcomers and oldtimers in small groups. In P. Paulus (Ed.), *Psychology of group influence* (2nd ed., pp. 143–186). Hillsdale, NJ: Lawrence Erlbaum Associates.

Moreland, R. L., & Levine, J. M. (1992). The composition of small groups. In E. Lawler, B. Markovsky, C. Ridgeway, & H. Walker (Eds.), *Advances in group processes* (Vol. 9, pp. 237–280). Greenwich, CT: JAI.

Moreland, R. L., & Levine, J. M. (2003). Group composition: Explaining similarities and differences among group members. In M. A. Hogg & J. Cooper (Eds.), *Sage handbook of social psychology* (pp. 367–380). London: Sage.

Moreland, R. L., Levine, J. M., & Wingert, M. L. (1996). Creating the ideal group: Composition effects at work. In J. Davis & E. Witte (Eds.), *Understanding group behavior* (Vol. 2, pp. 11–35). Mahwah, NJ: Lawrence Erlbaum Associates.

Moscovici, S. (1985). Social influence and conformity. In G. Lindzey & E. Aronson (Eds.), *Handbook of social psychology* (3rd ed., Vol. 2, pp. 347–412). New York: Random House.

Moscovici, S., Mucchi-Faina, A., & Maass, A. (Eds.). (1994). *Minority influence*. Chicago: Nelson-Hall.

Naylor, J. C., & Briggs, G. E. (1965). Team-training effectiveness under various conditions. *Journal of Applied Psychology, 49,* 223–229.

Neale, M., Mannix, E., & Gruenfeld, D. (Eds.). (1998). *Research on managing groups and teams: Composition* (Vol. 1). Greenwich, CT: JAI.

Nemeth, C. J. (1992). Minority dissent as a stimulant to group performance. In S. P. Worchel, W. Wood, & J. L. Simpson (Eds.), *Productivity and process in groups* (pp. 95–111). Newbury Park, CA: Sage.

Nemeth, C. J., & Owens, P. D. (1996). Making groups more effective: The value of minority dissent. In M. West (Ed.), *Handbook of work group psychology* (pp. 125–141). England: Wiley.

Osborn, A. F. (1957). *Applied imagination* (2nd ed.). New York: Scribner.

Paulus, P. B., Larey, T. S., & Dzindolet, M. T. (2001). Creativity in groups and teams. In M. Turner (Ed.), *Groups at work: Theory and research* (pp. 319–338). Mahwah, NJ: Lawrence Erlbaum Associates.

Paulus, P. B., & Yang, H. C. (2000). Idea generation in groups: A basis for creativity in organizations. *Organizational Behavior and Human Decision Processes, 82,* 76–87.

Price, J. (1977). *The study of turnover.* Ames, IA: Iowa State University.

Rogelberg, S. G., Barnes-Farrell, J. L., & Lowe, C. A. (1992). The stepladder technique: An alternative group structure facilitating effective group decision making. *Journal of Applied Psychology, 77*(5), 730–737.

Rogelberg, S. G., & O'Connor, M. S. (1998). Extending the stepladder technique: An examination of self-paced stepladder groups. *Group Dynamics: Theory, Research, and Practice, 2*(2), 82–91.

Rogelberg, S. G., O'Connor, M. S., & Sederburg, M. (2002). Using the stepladder technique to facilitate the performance of audioconferencing groups. *Journal of Applied Psychology, 87,* 994–1000.

Rogers, M. S., Ford, J. D., & Tassone, J. A. (1961). The effects of personnel replacement on an information-processing crew. *Journal of Applied Psychology, 45,* 91–96.

Salas, E., & Cannon-Bowers, J. A. (2001). Special issue preface. *Journal of Organizational Behavior, 22,* 87–88.

Schippers, M. C., Den Hartog, D. N., Koopman, P. L., & Wienk, J. A. (2003). Diversity and team outcome: The moderating effects of outcome interdependence and group longevity and the mediating effect of reflexivity. *Journal of Organizational Behavior, 24,* 779–802.

Staw, B. M. (1980). Rationality and justification in organizational life. In B. M. Staw & L. L. Cummings (Eds.), *Research in organizational behavior* (Vol. 2, pp. 45–80). Greenwich, CT: JAI.

Stein, M. (1953). Creativity and culture. *Journal of Psychology, 36,* 311–322.

Sundstrom, E. (1999). *Supporting work team effectiveness: Best management practices for fostering high performance.* San Francisco: Jossey-Bass.

Sutton, R. I. (2002). *Weird ideas that work: 11½ ideas for promoting, managing and sustaining motivation.* New York: The Free Press.

Sutton, R. I., & Louis, M. R. (1987). How selecting and socializing newcomers influences insiders. *Human Resource Management, 26,* 347–362.

Swift, T. A., & West, M. A. (1998). *Reflexivity and group process: Research and practice.* Unpublished manuscript, University of Sheffield.

Szulanski, G. (1996). Exploring internal stickiness: Impediments to the transfer of best practice within the firm. *Strategic Management Journal, 17,* 27–43.

Thompson, L. (2003). Improving the creativity of organizational work groups. *Academy of Management Executive, 17*(1), 96–109.

Thompson, L., & Fine, G. A. (1999). Socially shared cognition, affect and behavior: A review and integration. *Personality and Social Psychology Review, 3,* 278–302.

Torrance, E. P. (1955). Some consequences of power differences on decision making in permanent and temporary three-man groups. In A. P. Hare, E. F. Borgatta, & R. F. Bales (Eds.), *Small groups* (pp. 482–492). New York: Knopf.

Trow, D. B. (1960). Membership succession and team performance. *Human Relations, 13,* 259–269.

Wanous, J. P., & Colella, A. (1989). Organizational entry research: Current status and future directions. In G. R. Ferris & K. M. Rowland (Eds.), *Research in personnel and human research management* (Vol. 7, pp. 59–120). Greenwich, CT: JAI.

Watson, W. E., Kumar, K., & Michaelson, L. K. (1993). Cultural diversity's impact on interaction process and performance: Comparing homogeneous and diverse task groups. *Academy of Management Journal, 36*(3), 590–602.

Weiss, H. M., & Ilgen, D. R. (1985). Routinized behavior in organizations. *Journal of Behavioral Economics, 14,* 57–67.

West, M. A. (1996). Reflexivity and work group effectiveness: A conceptual integration. In M. A. West (Ed.), *Handbook of workgroup psychology* (pp. 555–579). Chichester: Wiley.

West, M. A. (2000). Reflexivity, revolution and innovation in work teams. In M. M. Beyerlein, D. A. Johnson, & S. T. Beyerlein (Eds.), *Product development teams* (Vol. 5, pp. 1–29). Stamford, CT: JAI.

Williams, K. Y., & O'Reilly, C. A. (1998). Demography and diversity in organizations: A review of 40 years of research. In B. Staw & R. Sutton (Eds.), *Research in organizational behavior* (Vol. 20, pp. 77–140). Greenwich, CT: JAI.

Ziller, R. C. (1965). Toward a theory of open and closed groups. *Psychological Bulletin, 65,* 164–182.

Ziller, R. C., Behringer, R. D., & Goodchilds, J. D. (1962). Group creativity under conditions of success or failure and variations in group stability. *Journal of Applied Psychology, 46,* 43–49.

Chapter **6**

Explaining Psychological Safety in Innovation Teams: Organizational Culture, Team Dynamics, or Personality?

Amy C. Edmondson
Josephine P. Mogelof
Harvard University

An organization's ability to innovate—whether to develop new products, implement new technologies, or formulate new strategies—is critical to success in a changing world. In contrast to activities that support execution, activities supporting innovation involve risk, uncertainty, and even failure along the way to success. Team members are often reluctant to offer novel contributions for fear of being wrong (Edmondson, 1999) or for fear of slowing team progress and creating frustration (Ford & Sullivan, 2004). One of the core challenges of innovation, therefore, is coping with the increased risk of failure that the creative process entails. Past research has identified an interpersonal climate characterized by psychological safety as conducive to interpersonal risk taking and hence to creativity and innovation in teams (Edmondson, 2002; West, 1990), yet we know less about factors that give rise to psychological safety.

This chapter extends past work on team learning and innovation by systematically considering the antecedents of psychological safety in innovation teams. The results increase our understanding of what factors enable people to experience a sense of psychological safety at work and thereby also shed light on antecedents of organizational innovation.

WHY STUDY PSYCHOLOGICAL SAFETY IN INNOVATION TEAMS?

Increasingly, organizations use teams to accomplish their innovation goals (Lewis et al., 2002; Wheelwright & Clark, 1995). Innovation teams—project teams in organizations put together to develop new products or implement

109

substantial change—face considerable uncertainty. Team members must embrace the creative process of taking risks, experimenting, and frequently experiencing failure while working closely together with each other, navigating differences in discipline, experience, status, and other factors. This navigation of differences takes both interpersonal skill and an environment of psychological safety.

Psychological safety describes taken-for-granted beliefs that others will respond positively when one exposes one's thoughts, such as by asking a question, seeking feedback, reporting a mistake, or proposing a new idea (Edmondson, 1999). It is a psychological state that has consequences for how members of innovation teams behave. Effective action in innovation teams necessarily involves behaviors for which outcomes are unpredictable, including asking questions, seeking honest feedback about a new idea, and experimenting. Although these activities are integral to innovation, engaging in them is risky for individuals who may be seen as ignorant, disruptive, or even incompetent by others as a result (Edmondson, 2003a). Most people feel a need to manage this risk to minimize harm to their image. The experience of psychological safety can allow team members to relax their guard and engage openly in the behaviors that underlie learning and innovation.

In psychologically safe environments, people believe that if they make a mistake or ask a naive question, others will not penalize or think less of them for it. Psychological safety differs from other constructs that may be associated with creativity, such as efficacy (Bandura, 1982), trust (Kramer, 1999), and intrinsic motivation (Amabile, 2001). Whereas efficacy is the belief that taking action will produce a desirable effect, trust is the belief that others' actions will be favorable to one's interests, and intrinsic motivation is the belief that engaging in a task will be inherently rewarding; psychological safety is the belief that taking action will not lead to one's own denigration or humiliation. Thus, although other factors also promote creativity and innovation in organizations, psychological safety is seen to have a unique mediating function (see Edmondson, 2004, for more detail).

The construct of psychological safety dates back to early, classic research on organizational change by Schein and Bennis (1965), who discussed the need for psychological safety to help people cope with significant change. Schein (1985) argued that psychological safety helps people confront data that disconfirm their expectations or hopes—virtually inevitable in the context of an innovation team—without defensiveness. Psychological safety does not refer to a cozy environment in which people are close friends, nor does it suggest an absence of pressure or problems. The construct is distinct from group cohesiveness, which reduces willingness to disagree and challenge others' views (Janis, 1982). Psychological safety instead describes a climate in which the focus can be on productive discussion that enables early prevention of problems and the accomplishment of shared goals because people are less likely to focus on self-protection (see Edmondson, 1999, for more detail on the construct and its history). It is thus important to note that psychological safety does not reduce conflict in teams, but rather allows it to be managed more productively than when psychological safety is not present (Barsade et al., 2001).

Teams lacking psychological safety are less likely to engage in the behavioral hallmarks of creativity: Members are less likely to speak up to suggest novel ideas, criticize others' ideas, challenge the status quo, ask naive questions, or admit mistakes for fear of ridicule or more subtle forms of interpersonal rejection. Psychological safety in teams thus enables creativity and innovation by facilitating the interpersonal risks inherent in the innovation process (West, 1990).

Although effects of psychological safety on learning, performance, productive handling of conflict, and experimentation have been discussed in the organizational literature (Barsade et al., 2001; Edmondson, 1996, 1999, 2002, 2003b; Frese & Baer, 2003; Lee et al., 2004), less work has investigated drivers of individuals' perceptions of psychological safety. In particular, conditions affecting psychological safety in innovation teams are not well understood.

Some researchers have examined psychological safety as a feature of organizational culture (Schein, 1985), others as a team characteristic shaped by team leader behavior (Edmondson, 1996, 2003b), and still others as an individual difference. For instance, Tynan (2005) developed and validated an individual difference measure of face threat sensitivity and showed its negative relationship with upward communication in a hierarchy. Schlenker and Leary (1982) found that some individuals have a dispositional tendency toward feeling anxious about social interactions. These individuals doubt their ability to make a positive impression on others (Leary & Kowalski, 1995; Schlenker & Leary, 1982), leading to social withdrawal (Schlenker & Leary, 1982), inhibition and avoidance (Leary & Atherton, 1986; Leary, Atherton, Hill, & Hur, 1986), and passiveness in one-on-one interactions (Leary, Knight, & Johnson, 1987).

The aim of this chapter is to show that an individual's experience of psychological safety in an innovation team is affected by factors at multiple levels of analysis, including organizational culture, team leader behavior, team member interactions, and individual differences in personality. First, we develop theoretical arguments for why this should be the case. We then examine the effects of multilevel factors simultaneously by analyzing longitudinal data from 26 innovation teams in seven companies. Finally, we discuss what we have learned from these analyses and suggest implications for future research and management practice.

PSYCHOLOGICAL SAFETY IN THE WORKPLACE

In this section, we develop a theoretical model that posits factors at multiple levels of analysis as influences on the psychological safety experienced by individuals working on organizational innovation projects. We argue that these multilevel influences imply that psychological safety will vary across organizations, as well as across groups or teams within organizations.

The Multilevel Nature of Influences on Psychological Safety

Understanding the experience of psychological safety at work requires theoretical and empirical justification for the level of analysis at which the construct resides. We thus start by exploring whether psychological safety at work is an experience that characterizes the individual (shaped by a priori differences in personality), the face-to-face working group (shaped by interpersonal experiences and shared mental models that accumulate over time), or the broader organization (shaped by corporate culture).

At first this seems an unnecessary diversion. Psychological safety is an intrapsychic state; surely it lives in the hearts and minds of individual employees. Yet theory and past research suggest that psychological safety differs significantly across work groups—even for groups with highly diverse members or in strong organizational cultures (e.g., Edmondson, 1996, 1999). If members of a team have shared beliefs about the psychological safety of their work environment, and other teams have different shared beliefs, then the construct can be said to describe groups, not individuals (Edmondson, 2004).

At the same time, research finding stable individual differences in sensitivity to face threat or social interaction anxiety suggests that some people have thicker skin than others. Thus, they may feel inherently psychologically safer than others, finding it easier to speak up in any environment relative to their thinner-skinned counterparts. Social interaction anxiety can lead to disengagement, and lowered input into group-based activities, with negative implications for group performance, and perhaps limit the kind of risk taking experience that supports the development of psychological safety in a team. For instance, groups composed of half or more socially anxious individuals performed worse on brainstorming activities than those groups composed of individuals who were not socially anxious (Camacho & Paulus, 1995), illustrating how an individual difference can translate into group attributes and outcomes.

Not only do individuals differ in ways that should affect their experienced psychological safety, organizations may also vary in interpersonal climate. Theories of corporate culture imply that organizations can have signature levels of psychological safety (e.g., Schein, 1985). The popular management press is replete with stories of organizations in which speaking up is believed to be nearly impossible by employees (e.g., Ryan & Oestrich, 1988), as well as those in which employee voice and participation are celebrated (e.g., Collins & Porras, 1994).

The prior theoretical argument, which implies that psychological safety could vary on all three levels of analysis simultaneously, has not previously been tested. Research has not measured variance in psychological safety across groups and organizations in the same empirical study nor has it included the contribution of individual differences. In addition to differences across levels, we might anticipate differences across time. For example, the level of psychological safety an innovation team member feels might vary over the course of a project. The study reported in this chapter thus includes variables measured longitudinally at all three levels of analysis, as described next, and finds preliminary support for a multilevel model, in which contributions to psychological safety exist at individual, group, and organizational levels of analysis at varying times.

Organizational Level Influences

Corporate cultures have been shown to vary dramatically across companies, and such attributes as deference to authority, outspokenness, and participation are central markers of an organization's culture (Collins & Porras, 1994; Deal & Kennedy, 1982; De Pree, 1987; Peters & Waterman, 1982). An extensive literature on organizational culture examines how norms, values, and beliefs arise in organizations to reduce the anxiety people feel confronting ambiguity and uncertainty (Schein, 1985). Anxiety can arise when individuals cope with the uncertainty of innovation, for example, and an organization's culture may exacerbate or mitigate this psychological state.

In particular, words and actions of high-level managers in an organization—especially those that indicate their supportiveness, openness, and tolerance for error—should affect others' beliefs about acceptability of open discussion of threatening issues (Detert, 2003). Apocryphal stories prevalent in many organizations capture the ways in which senior management can powerfully influence views of psychological safety in the organization as a whole. One such story involves Tom Watson, Jr., at IBM and a field executive responsible for a $10 million mistake. Called into the chairman's office, the executive was understandably anxious. As retold by Carroll (1993), "Watson asked, 'Do you know why I've asked you here?' The man replied, 'I assume I'm here so you can fire me.' Watson looked surprised. 'Fire you?' he asked 'Of course not. I just spent $10 million educating you.' He then reassured the executive and suggested he keep taking chances" (p. 51).

True or merely myth, such stories have lasting organizational effects. The sent message is that error is inevitable and the point is to learn, share the learning, and try again. As espoused by Watson, "You really aren't committed to innovation unless you're willing to fail. . . . The fastest way to succeed is to double your failure rate" (Farson & Keyes, 2002, p. 64).

In addition to senior management actions, organizational structures can diminish or increase barriers between individuals and groups. When cross-functional relationships among peers are encouraged and enabled by organizational norms and structures, this should increase the general climate of psychological safety. With more experience interacting with others who have different views and expertise and who face different pressures, organization members will become more familiar and comfortable with diverse perspectives. This broader view of the organization's activities is likely to make it easier for people to understand others' work and to feel comfortable communicating their own ideas and goals, such as when seeking help or input. In this way, stronger interpersonal ties can increase the sharing of information (Hansen, 1999) and promote a sense of psychological safety. In contrast, when organizational "silos" present divisive barriers to communication, peer relationships across departments or functions are likely to be characterized by weaker ties, lower willingness to share information, and less psychological safety. In summary, organizational characteristics are likely to affect individuals' perceptions of psychological safety, leading to differences across firms.

Proposition 1a: Psychological safety will show significant differences across organizations.

More specifically, when members of innovation teams perceive top management in their organization as supportive of innovation and believe that collaboration among peers is supported by the organization, they are likely to experience their work environment as having greater psychological safety.

Proposition 1b: An organizational climate for innovation will increase the psychological safety experienced by members of innovation teams.

Group-Level Influences

In addition to organizational effects, within a given company we expect individuals working closely together on a project to develop shared perceptions of how safe their environment is for speaking up about difficult issues. Cues in the environment about speaking up and shared perceptions of proximal or local authority figures, such as supervisors and team leaders, will contribute to shared beliefs about psychological safety. It is also possible that the documented tendency to fail to discuss relevant information in groups—not due to interpersonal fear, but to air time limits and failure to recognize the salience of privately held information (e.g., Stasser, 1999; Stasser & Titus, 1985)—can affect psychological safety indirectly. When relevant information fails to surface, group members may infer that it is not safe to discuss certain things.

In summary, psychological safety describes beliefs about interpersonal interaction, and these are likely shaped by the history of interactions in a team. To illustrate, teammates of a nurse who reported being "made to feel like a 2-year-old" when reporting a drug error independently reported similar feelings of discomfort about speaking up—for example, commenting that "nurses are blamed for mistakes" and "[if you make a mistake here,] doctors bite your head off." These nurses, either from personal or vicarious experience, came to the common conclusion that, on their team, reporting mistakes was interpersonally penalized (Edmondson, 1996). When relationships within a work group are characterized by trust and respect, individuals are likely to believe they will be given the benefit of the doubt, contributing to a sense of psychological safety (Edmondson, 2003a).

Our focus on team member interactions builds on previous research on innovation teams where different members often have equal status, deep expertise in different disciplines, and must work hard to overcome these differences (Dougherty, 1992). Given the communication challenges in innovation teams and the importance of psychological safety for enabling open learning-oriented conversation (Edmondson, 1999), the team level of analysis is especially likely to show variance in an empirical study.

Proposition 2a: Different teams within the same organization will have different levels of psychological safety.

The quality of interpersonal interactions within a team is particularly salient in establishing psychological safety (Edmondson, 1999), and thus should be associated with the variance anticipated by Proposition 2a. Over the course of a project, day-to-day team member interactions should influence the extent to which members of a team feel others are accepting of and respectful of disagreements, criticism, or new ideas.

Proposition 2b: Positive team member interactions promote psychological safety.

Past research also suggests that interactions with team leaders, who have greater positional power and status than other members, powerfully influence psychological safety (Edmondson, 1996). For example, team leader coaching by surgeons was important for creating psychological safety in a recent study of operating room teams (Edmondson, 2003b).

Proposition 2c: Positive team leader interactions with the team promote psychological safety.

We also suggest that initial team member interactions will have an important and lasting effect on psychological safety in an innovation team. In contrast, once beliefs about the team's psychological safety are created, later interactions may have a limited impact on interpersonal climate due, in part, to the tendency of individuals to seek and pay attention to data that confirm initial impressions (Nisbett & Ross, 1980).

Proposition 2d: The influence of positive project team member interactions on psychological safety will dissipate over time.

In addition to interpersonal dynamics in a team, the supportiveness of team structures (Hackman, 1987) may affect psychological safety experienced by innovation team members. Supportive structures include a well-defined team task, clearly articulated team goals, and sufficient information and resources to get the job done. Structures that enable a team to get its work done decrease the degree to which members find themselves facing anxiety and ambiguity, and increase the chances that team members will have positive views about the chances of success and will work together effectively. Together these factors should decrease chances of negative events that are interpreted as violations of camaraderie and teamwork, creating a general atmosphere of success that may promote psychological safety.

The availability of resources and organizational support for an innovation team should also increase the team's ability to get work done and increase members' sense of psychological safety. When resources are plentiful, there should be less anxiety and concern about competing with others for scarce funds, opportunities, or access. Further, as projects approach deadlines, a lack of resources may become increasingly salient such that the effect of resources on psychological safety is stronger over time.

Proposition 2e: Having sufficient resources with which to carry out a project will promote psychological safety, and this effect will increase over time.

Next, we suggest that goal clarity is likely to be more important for psychological safety later in an innovation team's tenure than it would be earlier. Immediately following a team's creation, members would not be expected to have full clarity about their shared aims. However, as time passes and project deadlines approach, clarity about the team's goal should become more important in sharing a sense of psychological safety. A team member's confidence that he or she knows not only the team's overall aims, but also his or her tasks for helping to accomplish them, should make it easier to speak up with questions, challenges, and concerns, thereby reinforcing a climate of psychological safety. Project teams at times may reconsider team goals or processes (Gersick, 1988). We argue that as final deadlines approach in innovation teams, the increased time pressure experienced by team members will lead such questioning and reconsideration to be more threatening than it would be early in a project. We thus suggest that a positive relationship between clear goals and psychological safety should increase over time for innovation teams. That is, a clear goal is associated with psychological safety in general, but is more important as deadlines approach.

Proposition 2f: Team goal clarity will promote psychological safety in an innovation team, and the strength of the relationship will increase over time.

Individual-Level Influences

As noted earlier, individual differences may also affect team members' experiences of psychological safety. In addition to differences in social anxiety and threat sensitivity, individuals differ in the extent to which they are focused on learning versus performing (Dweck & Leggett, 1988; Elliott & Dweck, 1988). Some individuals vigorously pursue opportunities to learn and grow, whereas others seek validation (Dykman, 1998; Pichanick, 2003). When individuals are more concerned with how others evaluate them than with opportunities for learning, they are likely to feel less psychologically safe than those who are not as concerned, and they may refrain from asking questions, experimenting with ideas, or seeking help. Individuals with thin skin may be less tolerant of criticism and may go out of their way to avoid it, simultaneously compromising learning opportunities that could lead to important innovations.

Because they are frequently studied and recognized across fields, we use the framework of the "Big Five" personality factors to develop specific predictions about psychological safety at work. Further, using measures such as social interaction anxiety or face threat sensitivity to predict psychological safety in work interactions might run the risk of tautology. In contrast, three of the five well-known personality factors—neuroticism, extraversion, and openness—may have theoretical relationships with psychological safety and interpersonal risk taking without being nearly identical constructs (Costa & McCrae, 1992).

First, individuals with high levels of neuroticism tend to experience persistent negative affect, including feelings of anxiety, inferiority, and shame. Pervasive concerns such as these could lead individuals to be suspicious of others' motives and to construe their work environments as hostile and unwelcoming. Second, extraverts tend to be outgoing and assertive in their interactions with others—traits that may result in speaking up regardless of the interpersonal climate. Third, individuals characterized by openness tend to exhibit a natural curiosity about the world. Being open to new ideas and different ways of doing things may increase the likelihood that individuals would feel safe taking risks and exposing their vulnerabilities in a work environment.

We thus expect that individual differences in neuroticism, extraversion, and openness influence individuals' experience of psychological safety at work. Further, we suggest that these personality differences should be more important in determining psychological safety earlier in the course of a team's life than later; as team members gain experience working together, team influences will become stronger, potentially overwhelming initial individual differences. After a project has had a chance to get going, personality influences may be less salient and less influential than organizational and group factors that play out on a daily basis.

Proposition 3a: Neuroticism will be negatively associated with psychological safety experienced by members of innovation teams, especially early in the team's tenure.

Proposition 3b: Extraversion will be positively associated with psychological safety experienced by members of innovation teams, especially early in the team's tenure.

Proposition 3c: Openness will be positively associated with psychological safety experienced by members of innovation teams, especially early in the team's tenure.

Summary

We posit multiple simultaneous influences on psychological safety in innovation teams. Specifically, those teams with supportive organizational climates, adequate resources, supportive team interactions, and high levels of goal clarity will have higher levels of psychological safety than teams that do not. Although we also predict that psychological safety will be negatively associated with neuroticism and positively associated with extraversion and openness, we anticipate organizational and team influences to get stronger over time, as a project unfolds, and individual differences to become less predictive of psychological safety, over time. Figure 6.1 depicts the predicted influences on psychological safety over time. In the next section, we describe a field study in which support for these relationships can be examined.

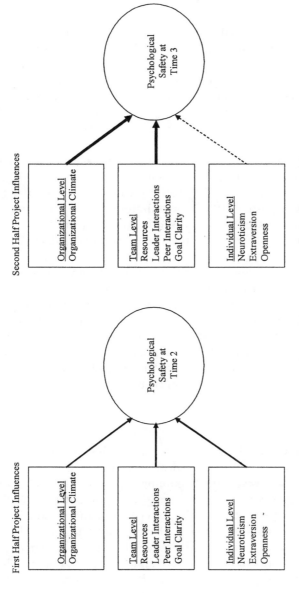

FIG. 6.1.   Predicted multiple-level influences on psychological safety over time.

119

METHOD

Participants

We obtained longitudinal data on 26 innovation teams from a study of team events and motivation (Amabile et al., 2004). Survey measures of psychological safety were obtained in the beginning, middle, and end of team projects or significant project phases, allowing us to compare earlier and later measures of the same construct to see how it might change over time in innovation teams. These data also provide better indications of causal relationships than could be obtained from survey data collected at a single point in time.

Additional individual, team, and organizational data were obtained electronically on a daily basis from members of the teams throughout the course of a major project. The teams were drawn from seven organizations within three industries (three organizations were in technology, two in chemicals/pharmaceuticals, and two in consumer products). In total, 238 individuals participated in the study. Data collection occurred between May 1996 and April 1998.

Each team was followed from the first day of a project (or major project phase) to the last. Project periods covered by the study ranged from 6 weeks to 10 months. Most participating teams' projects involved the development of new products or new processes. Teams that participated consisted of 3 to 20 members, and all or most dedicated at least 50% to a particular time-bound project with specific outcome objectives. Response rates were 75% for the daily questionnaire and 87%, 75%, and 66% for the paper surveys at beginning, middle, and end, respectively.

Measures

The first author had input regarding the wording of survey items and contributed items to assess psychological safety. For each team, the dependent variables were assessed at the beginning, midpoint, and end of the project, and the independent variables were assessed on a daily basis throughout the course of the study with the exception of the personality measures; these data were collected once at the beginning of the study.

A short e-mail questionnaire was sent to team members to assess their perceptions of organizational, team, and work factors on a daily basis. We anticipated that individuals would tend to be consistent over time in their responses. To test this, we used one-way analyses of variance (ANOVAs) to check whether individuals' daily responses were more similar across time (within individual) than between individuals and found that this was the case. Using individuals as the independent variable and daily questionnaire variables as dependent variables, we found that significant differences existed between individuals. We then averaged the daily measures to produce aggregate measures of individuals' responses; specifically, we chose to create an average of each individual's daily response data for both the first and second half of each project. Thus, we have measures of psychological safety at three time points and two temporal measures of each independent variable (with the exception of the personality variables), one reflecting the first half and one the second half of each project.

Measures of organizational characteristics included organizational climate for innovation as described next. Group and work influences included resources, interpersonal interactions, and goal clarity. Individual influences included neuroticism, extraversion, and openness.

Psychological Safety (at Times 1, 2, and 3). New scales for the dependent variables were constructed from items from the Keys, a survey assessing organizational climate for creativity (Amabile et al., 1996). The resulting scale consisted of five items: "There is free and open communication within my work group," "People in my work group are open to new ideas," "My supervisor is open to new ideas," "There is a feeling of trust among the people I work with most closely," and "Within my work group, we challenge each other's ideas in a constructive way." Items were rated on a 4-point scale from *never or almost never* to *always or almost always*. The scales had an internal consistency reliability of .79, .78, and .84 for the measures at project beginning (psychological safety 1), midpoint (psychological safety 2), and end (psychological safety 3), respectively.

Organizational Climate for Innovation (1, 2). The daily measure of organizational climate included two items assessing the extent to which participants perceived high-level management encouragement of team creativity and collaborative idea flow across the organization concerning their projects. These items were intended to assess the organizational climate for innovation and were highly correlated with each other, such that the resulting scale had internal consistency reliabilities of .74 for the first half of team projects and .84 for the second half.

Resources (1, 2). A single item assessed whether individuals perceived sufficient resources to be available for their work. The use of single-item measures has been shown to be particularly effective in assessing constructs that are sufficiently narrow or unambiguous (Wanous et al., 1997).

Team Interactions (1, 2). Four items assessed interactions among team members and their leaders on a daily basis. We had expected to distinguish between interactions among peers and those between team members and leaders using two variables. In these data, however, team members rated both in similar ways in their daily responses, in part because the leaders were also considered members of the teams—and, as the data suggested, were less likely to be seen as supervisory authorities. The daily items asked individuals to rate the extent to which they perceived "supportive interactions within the team," "encouragement and support from the project supervisor," and "positive interactions between the team and the supervisor," and all were highly correlated. The internal consistency reliability for the team interactions measure was .92 for the first half of team projects and .91 for the second half.

Goal Clarity (1, 2).   A single item assessed the extent to which individuals felt they had clarity regarding the goals of the project. This item was assessed on a daily basis.

Individual Differences.   Participants' neuroticism, extraversion, and openness were measured in the beginning of the study using the NEO Personality Inventory (Costa & McCrae, 1992). The response rate for this measure was 90%.

Analyses

First, we conducted ANOVAs to test whether individuals' daily responses should be aggregated across time to provide meaningful individual-level measures of certain team properties. Second, we conducted ANOVAs to test whether significant variance in psychological safety was found at the team or organizational level or both. We then used multivariate general linear model (GLM) analyses of psychological safety at the project midpoint and completion (Times 2 and 3), with psychological safety 2 or 3 as the dependent variable. For each time period, the predictors were the corresponding temporally antecedent variables that assessed organizational climate, resources, team interactions, goal clarity, and individual differences in personality.

RESULTS

Variance in Psychological Safety

Across all 26 teams, the means of psychological safety at the beginning, midpoint, and end of projects were 3.06, 3.07, and 3.01, respectively, on a 5-point scale. Most teams experienced little change in psychological safety over the course of their projects: The mean difference between psychological safety 1 and psychological safety 2 was $-.04$ ($SD = .20$); the mean difference between psychological safety 2 and psychological safety 3 was $-.07$ ($SD = .16$).

At the beginning of each project, psychological safety varied significantly at both the team and organizational levels. Because about half of the teams had experience working together at the start of the study, psychological safety may have been partly established in some, but not all teams measured. At the midpoint, teams within the same organization had become more similar, such that psychological safety still differed significantly across organizations, but not across teams within organizations. At the end of each project, there were again differences in psychological safety across both teams and companies (Tables 6.1, 6.2, and 6.3 show these differences in psychological safety over project duration).

These data provide consistent support for Proposition 1a, that psychological safety differs across organizations, and inconsistent support for Proposition 2a, that psychological safety varies across teams within organizations. Although psychological safety did vary across teams at the beginning and end of projects, at project midpoints, teams within the same organ-

TABLE 6.1
Company and Team Variance in Psychological Safety at Time 1

Source	Sum of Squares	df	Mean Square	F	p <
Corrected model	22.13	25	0.89	4.28	.001
Intercept	1,586.32	1	1,586.32	7,664.50	.001
Company	9.25	6	1.54	7.45	.001
Team (company)	12.02	19	0.63	3.06	.001
Error	38.29	185	0.21		
Total	2,037.30	211			
Corrected total	60.42	210			

Note. $R^2 = .37$ (adjusted $R^2 = .28$).

TABLE 6.2
Company and Team Variance in Psychological Safety at Time 2

Source	Sum of Squares	df	Mean Square	F	p <
Corrected model	12.47	24	0.52	2.38	.001
Intercept	1,368.95	1	1,368.95	6,265.01	.001
Company	7.54	6	1.26	5.75	.001
Team (company)	3.84	18	0.21	0.98	.50
Error	33.43	153	0.22		
Total	1,728.08	178			
Corrected total	45.90	177			

Note. $R^2 = .27$ (adjusted $R^2 = .16$).

TABLE 6.3
Company and Team Variance in Psychological Safety at Time 3

Source	Sum of Squares	df	Mean Square	F	p <
Corrected model	19.36	25	0.77	3.24	.001
Intercept	1,122.90	1	1,122.90	4,691.30	.001
Company	9.27	6	1.54	6.45	.001
Team (company)	8.40	19	0.44	1.85	.05
Error	32.07	134	0.24		
Total	1,496.24	160			
Corrected total	51.44	159			

Note. $R^2 = .38$ (adjusted $R^2 = .26$).

ization were not significantly different. We explore possible interpretations of these findings in the discussion section.

Predicting Psychological Safety in Teams at Project Midpoint and End

The relations among all the dependent and independent variables are shown in Table 6.4. Psychological safety at all time points is moderately related to almost all of the independent variables.

We conducted multivariate general linear model analyses predicting psychological safety at the project midpoint and end (Times 2 and 3) using the temporally antecedent organizational climate, resources, team interactions, goal clarity, and individual differences in personality as predictors. Analyses were conducted with individuals nested in teams and teams nested in companies.

Results show that neither extraversion (Proposition 3b) nor antecedent perceptions of organizational climate (Proposition 1b), nor resources (Proposition 2e) were significant predictors of psychological safety; this finding was consistent at both project midpoint and end, and therefore we excluded these predictors from the final models. Significant predictors of midpoint psychological safety (psychological safety 2) were company, team interactions, neuroticism, and openness. Significant predictors of psychological safety at project end included both company and team (i.e., simply being members of a given team or company accounted for significant variance in psychological safety) and temporally antecedent perceptions of interpersonal interactions and goal clarity (both in the predicted positive direction). Also as predicted, neuroticism was negatively associated with psychological safety 3. Tables 6.5 and 6.6 show these models.

Although goal clarity was not a significant predictor of psychological safety at Time 2, Proposition 2f was partially supported in that goal clarity

TABLE 6.4

Correlations Among Psychological Safety and Independent Variables

	1	2	3	4	5	6	7	8	9	10	11	12	13
1. PS 1													
2. PS 2	.68**												
3. PS 3	.63**	.78**											
4. Org Clim 1	.36**	.35**	.92**										
5. Org Clim 2	.36**	.35**	.33**	.82**									
6. Resources 1	.25**	.27**	.31**	.26**	.26**								
7. Resources 2	.13†	.19*	.23**	.13*	.22**	.78**							
8. Team Inter 1	.50**	.48**	.51**	.65**	.55**	.33**	.20**						
9. Team Inter 2	.44**	.47**	.54**	.58**	.59**	.32**	.23**	.81**					
10. Goal Clar 1	.31**	.25**	.30**	.44**	.44**	.32**	.17*	.47**	.42**				
11. Goal Clar 2	.25**	.27**	.32**	.41**	.50**	.31**	.29**	.34**	.47**	.81**			
12. Neuroticism	-.17*	-.25**	-.35**	-.08	-.13†	-.11†	-.04	-.08	-.17*	-.13*	-.14*		
13. Extraversion	.10	.19*	.17*	.15*	.17*	-.04	-.08	.15*	.19*	.14*	.13†	-.46**	
14. Openness	-.01	-.05	.13	.10	.10	-.02	-.05	.04	.02	.07	.05	-.19**	.29**

†$p < .10.$ *$p < .05.$ **$p < .01.$

TABLE 6.5
General Linear Model of Psychological Safety at Project Midpoint

Source	Sum of Squares	df	Mean Square	F	p <
Corrected model	19.65	28	0.70	3.97	.001
Intercept	17.47	1	17.47	98.90	.001
Company	4.20	6	0.70	3.96	.001
Team (company)	2.47	18	0.14	0.78	.75
Team interactions	2.03	1	2.03	11.50	.001
Goal clarity	0.14	1	0.14	0.78	.40
Neuroticism	2.27	1	2.27	12.85	.001
Openness	0.62	1	0.62	3.53	.06
Error	25.96	147	0.18		
Total	1,704.88	176			

Note. $R^2 = .43$ (adjusted $R^2 = .32$).

TABLE 6.6
General Linear Model of Psychological Safety at Project End

Source	Sum of Squares	df	Mean Square	F	p <
Corrected model	30.06	29	1.04	6.57	.001
Intercept	8.16	1	8.16	51.65	.001
Company	4.78	6	0.80	5.05	.001
Team (company)	6.69	19	0.35	2.23	.001
Team interactions	1.36	1	1.36	8.59	.001
Goal clarity	1.65	1	1.65	10.44	.001
Neuroticism	2.75	1	2.75	17.40	.001
Openness	0.22	1	0.22	1.41	.25
Error	20.21	128	0.16		
Total	1,480.68	158			

Note. $R^2 = .60$ (adjusted $R^2 = .51$).

was a significant predictor at Time 3, suggesting goal clarity became increasingly more important over the course of the project. Next, the propositions regarding team interactions (2b, 2c, and 2d) were partially supported as follows. Because the items assessing team leader and member interactions were highly correlated, discriminant validity between the two measures did not exist, and so we combined them to create a measure of the positivity of team interactions. We then found that positive team interactions were significant predictors of psychological safety at Times 2 and 3.

Contrary to the expectation that the role of individual differences would diminish over time, neuroticism (Proposition 3a) was a significant predictor of psychological safety at Times 2 and 3. As predicted, openness (Proposition 3c) was a significant predictor of psychological safety at Time 2 but not at Time 3. Figure 6.2 depicts these findings together.

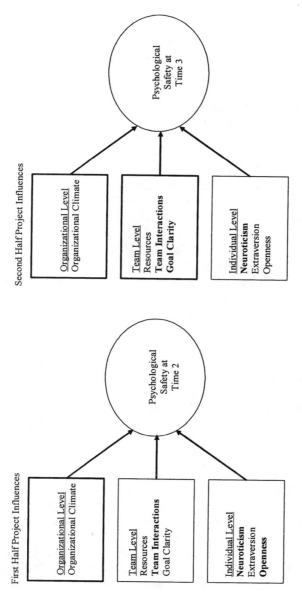

FIG. 6.2. Multiple-level predictors of psychological safety across time.

127

DISCUSSION

The findings in this study support the overarching premise that psychological safety in innovation teams is influenced by factors at multiple levels of analysis. Previous research has emphasized the importance of psychological safety—to allow the freedom to imagine alternative possibilities and to take risks—but has not systematically investigated antecedents of this psychological state. This chapter does so with an unusually comprehensive data set drawn not only from multiple teams, but also from multiple companies and industries, while including longitudinal data that enable examination of relationships between the same constructs at different points in time.

A number of studies have found group-level differences in psychological safety (e.g., Edmondson, 1996, 1999, 2003a, 2003b). An unstated implication of this past work was that personality was not important because social processes were the major influence on this psychological state, effectively swamping individual differences. This chapter challenges this view by showing that individual differences exert an independent influence on perceptions of psychological safety in innovation teams.

At the same time, most of the individual differences were uncorrelated with group and organizational factors (as shown in Table 6.4), implying that, despite personality differences that predispose individual team members to feel more or less psychologically safe in the teams in which they work, other influences powerfully shape the average level of psychological safety felt by members of a team. Given that influential variables, such as goal clarity and team interactions, are more conducive to change via managerial intervention than personality, the finding that differences across teams are not dominantly shaped by the personality composition of those teams is reassuring for the aims of practice.

This study was consistent with previous work in finding group-level differences in psychological safety, and it provides new empirical evidence consistent with the proposition that organizations differ in psychological safety at the same time. Previous work suggested that organizational cultures would have a main effect on psychological safety without explicitly testing this proposition with data from multiple teams and organizations at the same time. Although the group-level differences were only significant at the beginning and end of the team projects, not at the midpoints, further research is needed to know whether this is a meaningful and replicable result. It is possible that when teams are first formed, members are particularly attuned to the interpersonal climate of the team; as teams get underway, project management routines imposed by the organization lead to greater similarity across teams in how members experience the workplace. Subsequently, divergence may reemerge as projects begin to experience discrepant events and focus on proximal impediments to project execution particularly from the midpoint onward.

Finally, although previous work has emphasized the role of team leaders in creating psychological safety (Edmondson, 1996, 2003a, 2003b), this study was unable to find support for this relationship. In contrast to predictions, effects of leader behavior could not be disentangled from effects of team member interactions. Thus, team interpersonal interactions emerged as a single influence; members' perceptions of team member and team leader interactions were so highly correlated that they formed a single construct, which we referred to as positivity of team member interactions.

Temporal Dynamics

A central contribution of this study is its inclusion of data that span the innovation team lifetime. This allowed us to detect changes in relationships between variables at different points in time. Some of these were predicted and make logical sense, some of them are more difficult to understand, and clearly some may be noise or artifacts of data collection. It is also possible that the perceptions of respondents, surveyed multiple times, shifted in ways that do not accurately capture the actual underlying processes in these teams. We explore these issues further in discussing the study's limitations.

As noted previously, psychological safety remained relatively stable in teams across time. Despite this consistency, factors predicting psychological safety at the middle and end of a team project differed. These findings run somewhat counter to what both research and intuition suggest about how teams should approach their work. First, it is a commonly held notion that team members should agree on team goals from the outset. Further, teams that focus on process and procedures to the detriment of goals may perform less well than those that emphasize goals (Woolley, 2003). However, recent empirical evidence that teams which actively reflect on both goals and processes (*team reflexivity*) outperform those that do not (Schippers, 2003) suggests that flexibility and mindful attention to goals may be more important than early agreement.

We argued earlier that goal clarity would foster a sense of psychological safety because a clear and agreed-on goal would remove a potential source of anxiety in a team. We found that this was the case, but only at later project stages, suggesting that it may be less threatening (and hence easier to discuss) a lack of goal clarity at the outset of a team's work than later in its tenure. In particular, as deadlines approach, a lack of goal clarity may be particularly threatening, harming psychological safety. This possibility is consistent with Gersick's midpoint theory, which posits that much of the important interdependent work accomplished by a time-limited team begins with a midpoint crisis or reevaluation. We build on these ideas by suggesting that a clear sense of team goals is important for psychological safety later, but not earlier, in a team project.

In addition, it may often be the case that at first meetings teams pay lip service to creating an atmosphere of open and supportive communication, but that little is done to ensure that such interactions occur in the course of carrying out a challenging project (West, 1990). We found that positive team interactions were a significant predictor of psychological safety both earlier and later in a project team. This finding suggests that teams would do well to place a consistent focus on the nature of their interactions not just early on, but at all stages of their work.

Finally, these findings have consequences for research on teams that often relies on survey data collected at single points in time. This study shows that *when* survey data are collected influences—for some relationships powerfully—the results obtained. We showed that the strength of influences on a given construct such as psychological safety can fluctuate over time. Clearly these results need to be replicated to increase our confidence in them; nonetheless, these preliminary findings constitute an important contribution to our understanding of the temporal dynamics of the antecedents of psychological safety.

Unexpected Results

Although, as expected, most organizational and team influences measured in this study emerged as significant predictors of psychological safety over time, several study hypotheses were not supported by these data. Notably, different teams within the different companies did not differ in psychological safety at project midpoints, and neither organizational climate, team resources, nor extraversion were significant predictors of psychological safety.

Extraversion may not have been related to psychological safety because it may be the case that extraverts' perceptions of whether an environment is psychologically safe do not differ significantly from introverts, whereas their behavior, which we did not measure, does differ. If we had measured *speaking up* instead of psychological safety (as in Detert, 2003; Edmondson, 2003b), we perhaps would have detected a relationship between extraversion and this behavioral manifestation of psychological safety.[1]

---

[1]Note that this is not the same disclaimer as saying survey measures are not necessarily good indexes of actual behavior. Rather we argue that the intrapsychic state of psychological safety is not the same construct (despite being related theoretically) as the behavior of speaking up, and that speaking up behavior is likely to be more strongly related to extraversion than is psychological safety.

We expected that a lack of resources would be associated with lower psychological safety—that is, with team members being more concerned about risk-taking behavior—but this was not the case. This may be due to the need for a moderator to better understand this relationship. Closer examination of the data suggests that some teams lacked both resources and psychological safety, whereas others' lack of resources seemed to trigger creative solutions and a sense of openness and psychological safety. It is possible that in some teams a lack of resources creates a productive sense of urgency that frees members up to experiment and try new ways of doing things. Yet we lack understanding of what makes such a response more likely. Research should explore this relationship further to investigate the conditions under which scarce resources impede versus facilitate psychological safety.

Finally, we found that an organizational climate for innovation did not significantly predict individuals' perception of psychological safety. Perhaps in some organizations, support for innovation may be accompanied with an intense demand for quick or lucrative results—the result of which could be a mixed message for teams with regard to how safe it is to ask questions, take time to experiment, and focus on learning (e.g., see Lee et al., 2004). Again, further research is needed to evaluate what organizational factors support psychological safety and innovation.

Limitations

Although considerable effort was involved in the collection of extensive, longitudinal data, concerns about common method remain. General positive or negative affect could create stronger correlations across variables than is warranted by relationships between the underlying constructs. On the one hand, our strategy for aggregation of data led to more robust measures than data collected from individuals at a single point of time would produce. On the other hand, the data are survey data that are subject to usual concerns about imprecision and affective halos. For example, the daily electronic surveys failed to show discriminant validity with respect to phenomena such as peer interactions versus leader–member interactions. This may be because leaders in all 26 teams were so integrated into the teams that they were not perceived as being distinct from other team members. In general, our data suffer from being respondents' perceptions, which are not independently validated with behavioral measures.

Similarly, aggregation from daily scores to individual-level measures of a given construct for the period covering the first or second half of a project's duration produced robust measures, but also ones in which much data are necessarily lost. The particular aggregation strategy that we developed was chosen after extensive contemplation of possibilities. It is possible that alternative approaches to aggregation or analysis of individual daily survey data without aggregation would be preferable, but this approach was chosen for parsimony and clarity.

We lack data on specific organizational variables that might explain differences in psychological safety. That is, although organizational climate did not predict psychological safety, psychological safety did differ significantly across organizations; other factors are needed to explain these differences. Similarly, the significant differences found across teams were not fully explained by goal clarity and team interactions.

In summary, although our abundant data produced limited marginal value for answering certain questions, they do provide support for the premise that multiple influences—specific, meaningful organizational, team, and personality influences—affect psychological safety in innovation teams.

Implications for Research

One implication of the findings reported in this chapter is that the design of survey studies of innovation teams must pay particular attention to timing, specifically to when in a team's project life data are to be collected. First, we can better understand the antecedents and consequences of a construct when we have measured these relationships at different points in time. Second, and more specifically, these findings suggest that causes of psychological safety in innovation teams vary somewhat from the beginning to the end of a project.

To build on the observed associations between variables reported here, further research is needed to better understand how to create psychological safety and how to enhance a team's ability to innovate. In particular, to complement the extensive quantitative data collected in this study, qualitative case studies of a small number of innovation teams would help shed light on the leadership and interpersonal processes through which psychological safety is created.

We combined individuals' daily responses into measures of first and second half of the project to create robust measures of team interaction and other variables that were temporally antecedent to the dependent variables collected at project midpoints and end points. Although the multiple data points aggregated to produce each team measure may increase our confidence in the measures, they also may represent limited marginal returns to a large investment in terms of research expenses and participant time. We thus suggest that such quantitative longitudinal data collected periodically, such as once a week or month, rather than daily might provide the strengths of longitudinal data with less effort and expense.

Implications for Practice

We argued and found empirical support for the idea that an individual's experience of psychological safety at work is affected by personality, group, and organizational attributes. This implies that many managerial roads lead to the desired climate of psychological safety for innovation. Organizations can do much to create environments that foster innovation, and finding ways to promote psychological safety throughout an organization presents an important avenue for intervention-oriented research. With respect to individual differences that may affect psychological safety, an awareness that these influences can differentially affect team members could provide additional information that helps leaders and teams work better together.

The pattern of results does, however, reinforce the dominance of group-level influences (e.g., Edmondson, 1999, 2002). Although organizational and individual differences may play an important role, day-to-day interactions among peers and supervisors have the potential to make a critical and substantial difference in psychological safety even after accounting for these other influences. Creating and sustaining a psychologically safe environment is largely an outcome of team members' own behaviors—through norms they set regarding risk-taking and learning behaviors. An effort to be explicit about goals and what is and is not yet clear at the outset, and especially in later stages of a project, can enable open and productive discussion of concerns, questions, and aspirations in an innovation team. Knowing that negative team interactions and a lack of goal clarity can reduce psychological safety as team projects unfold over time may encourage team leaders and members to discuss these important issues early and often.

CONCLUSION

The road to innovation is fraught with obstacles. Innovation teams manage numerous risks, uncertainties, and failures along the way to creating new and exciting results. Psychological safety is a key factor in helping such teams and their members to take the interpersonal risks, conduct the experiments, and learn from the mistakes integral to this creative process. This chapter takes an important step in building understanding of how this psychological state is created in innovation teams. We argue and show that psychological safety is malleable, dynamic, and subject to multiple influences. Our results thus suggest that innovation teams seeking to encourage risk taking among members can achieve the desirable outcome of a state of psychological safety in more than one way.

The aim of this chapter was to directly address the question of what influences psychological safety in innovation teams. Our review of related literature, together with our new theoretical arguments about factors that might contribute to psychological safety in project teams, precluded arriving at a simple answer—a single cause or explanation of this psychological state. Instead we offer a multilevel, multivariable model that suggests psychological safety in the workplace is complexly and multiply determined. At the same time, drawing inferences from the patterns of variance, we can conclude that the power to change the team's climate for innovation lies primarily in the hands of those working together in the team. Ultimately, the day-to-day interactions of team members are the critical determinants of perceptions of how safe it is to take the risks of innovation.

REFERENCES

Amabile, T. M. (2001). Beyond talent: John Irving and the passionate craft of creativity. *American Psychologist, 56*(4), 333–336.

Amabile, T. M., Conti, R., Coon, H., Lazenby, J., & Herron, M. (1996). Assessing the work environment for creativity. *Academy of Management Journal, 39*, 1154–1184.

Amabile, T. M., Schatzel, E. A., Moneta, G. B., & Kramer, S. J. (2004). Leader behaviors and the work environment for creativity: Perceived leader support. *The Leadership Quarterly, 15*(1), 5–32.

Bandura, A. (1982). Self-efficacy mechanism in human agency. *American Psychologist, 37,* 22–147.

Barsade, S. G., Gibson, D. E., et al. (2001). *To be angry or not to be angry in groups: Examining the question.* Washington, DC: Academy of Management.

Camacho, L. M., & Paulus, P. B. (1995). The role of social anxiousness in group brainstorming. *Journal of Personality and Social Psychology, 68*(6), 1071–1080.

Carroll, P. (1993). *Big blues.* New York: Crown.

Collins, J. C., & Porras, J. I. (1994). *Built to last.* New York: HarperCollins.

Costa, P. T., & McCrae, R. R. (1992). *Revised NEO Personality Inventory (NEO PI-R) and NEO Five-Factor Inventory (NEO-FFI) professional manual.* Odessa, FL: Psychological Assessment Resources.

De Pree, M. (1987). *Leadership is an art.* East Lansing, MI: Michigan State University Press.

Deal, T. E., & Kennedy, A. A. (1982). *Corporate cultures: The rites and rituals of corporate life.* Reading, MA: Addison-Wesley.

Detert, J. R. (2003). *To speak or not to speak: The multi-level influences on voice and silence in organizations.* Unpublished doctoral dissertation, Harvard University.

Dougherty, D. (1992). Interpretive barriers to successful product innovation in large firms. *Organization Science, 3*(2), 179–202.

Dweck, C. S., & Leggett, E. L. (1988). A social-cognitive approach to motivation and personality. *Psychological Review, 95,* 256–273.

Dykman, B. (1998). Integrating cognitive and motivational factors in depression: Initial tests of a goal-orientation approach. *Journal of Personality & Social Psychology, 74,* 139–158.

Edmondson, A. C. (1996). Learning from mistakes is easier said than done: Group and organizational influences on the detection and correction of human error. *Journal of Applied Behavioral Sciences, 32*(1), 5–32.

Edmondson, A. C. (1999). Psychological safety and learning behavior in work teams. *Administrative Science Quarterly, 44*(4), 350–383.

Edmondson, A. C. (2002). The local and variegated nature of learning in organizations. *Organization Science, 13*(2), 128–146.

Edmondson, A. C. (2003a). Managing the risk of learning: Psychological safety in work teams. In M. West (Ed.), *International handbook of organizational teamwork and cooperative working* (pp. 255–275). London: Blackwell.

Edmondson, A. C. (2003b). Speaking up in the operating room: How team leaders promote learning in interdisciplinary action teams. *Journal of Management Studies, 40*(6), 1419–1452.

Edmondson, A. C. (2004). Psychological safety, trust and learning: A group-level lens. In R. Kramer & K. Cook (Eds.), *Trust and distrust across organizational contexts* (pp. 239–272). New York: Russell Sage.

Elliott, E. S., & Dweck, C. S. (1988). Goals: An approach to motivation and achievement. *Journal of Personality & Social Psychology, 54,* 5–12.

Ford, C., & Sullivan, D. M. (2004, March). A time for everything: How the timing of novel contributions influences project team outcomes. *Journal of Organizational Behavior, 25*(2), 279–292.

Frese, M., & Baer, M. (2003). Innovation is not enough: Climates for initiative, psychological safety, process innovations, and firm performance. *Journal of Organizational Behavior, 24*(1), 45–68.

Gersick, C. J. G. (1988). Time and transition in work teams: Toward a new model of group development. *Academy of Management Journal, 31,* 9–41.

Hackman, J. R. (1987). The design of work teams. In J. W. Lorsch (Ed.), *Handbook of organizational behavior* (pp. 315–342). Englewood Cliffs, NJ: Prentice-Hall.

Hansen, M. T. (1999). The search-transfer problem: The role of weak ties in sharing knowledge across organization subunits. *Administrative Science Quarterly, 44*(4), 82–111.

Janis, I. L. (1982). *Victims of groupthink* (2nd ed.). Boston: Houghton Mifflin.

Kramer, R. M. (1999). Trust and distrust in organizations: Emerging perspectives, enduring questions. *Annual Review of Psychology, 50,* 569–598.

Leary, M. R., & Atherton, S. C. (1986). Self-efficacy, social anxiety, and inhibition in interpersonal encounters. *Journal of Social and Clinical Psychology, 4*(3), 256–267.

Leary, M. R., Atherton, S. C., Hill, S., & Hur, C. (1986). Attributional mediators of social inhibition and avoidance. *Journal of Personality, 54*(4), 704–716.

Leary, M. R., Knight, P. D., & Johnson, K. A. (1987). Social anxiety and dyadic conversation: A verbal response analysis. *Journal of Social and Clinical Psychology, 5*(1), 34–50.

Leary, M. R., & Kowalski, R. M. (1995). *Social anxiety.* New York: Guilford.

Lee, F., Edmondson, A., Thomke, S., & Worline, M. (2004). The mixed effects of inconsistency on experimentation in organizations. Conditional acceptance. *Organization Science, 15*(3), 310–326.

Lewis, M. W., Welsh, M. A., Dehler, G. E., & Green, S. G. (2002). Product development tensions: Exploring contrasting styles of product management. *Academy of Management Journal, 45*(3), 546–564.

Nisbett, R., & Ross, L. (1980). *Human inference: Strategies and shortcomings of social judgment.* Englewood Cliffs, NJ: Prentice-Hall.

Peters, T. J., & Waterman, R. H. (1982). *In search of excellence.* New York: Warner.

Pichanick, J. S. (2003). *The regulation of well-being: Growth and action orientations.* Unpublished doctoral dissertation, Harvard University.

Ryan, K. D., & Oestrich, D. K. (1998). *Driving fear out of the workplace* (2nd ed.). San Francisco: Jossey-Bass.

Schein, E. H. (1985). *Organizational culture and leadership.* San Francisco: Jossey-Bass.

Schein, E. H., & Bennis, W. (1965). *Personal and organizational change via group methods.* New York: Wiley.

Schippers, M. C. (2003). *Reflexive learning in teams.* Unpublished doctoral dissertation, Vrije Universiteit, Amsterdam.

Schlenker, B. R., & Leary, M. R. (1982). Social anxiety and self-presentation: A conceptual model. *Psychological Bulletin, 92*(3), 641–669.

Stasser, G. (1999). The uncertain role of unshared information in collective choice. In L. Thompson, J. Levine, & D. Messick (Eds.), *Shared cognition in organizations* (pp. 49–69). Mahwah, NJ: Lawrence Erlbaum Associates.

Stasser, G., & Titus, W. (1985). Pooling of unshared information in group decision making: Biased information sampling during discussion. *Journal of Personality and Social Psychology, 48*, 1467–1478.

Tynan, R. (2005). The effect of threat sensitivity and face giving on dyadic psychological safety and upward communication. *Journal of Applied Social Psychology, 35*(2), 223–247.

Wanous, J. P., Reichers, A. E., & Hudy, M. J. (1997). Overall job satisfaction: How good are single-item measures? *Journal of Applied Psychology, 82*(2), 247–252.

West, M. A. (1990). The social psychology of innovation in groups. In M. A. West & J. L. Farr (Eds.), *Innovation and creativity at work: Psychological and organizational strategies* (pp. 309–333). Chichester: Wiley.

Wheelwright, S. C., & Clark, K. B. (1995). *Leading product development: The senior manager's guide to creating and shaping the enterprise.* New York: The Free Press.

Woolley, A. W. (2003). *The antecedents and consequences of procedural orientation in work teams.* Unpublished doctoral dissertation, Harvard University.

Chapter 7

Creativity and Innovation Implementation in Work Groups: The Paradoxical Role of Demands

Michael A. West
Claudia A. Sacramento
Doris Fay
Aston University, Birmingham

Three themes dominate the writings of researchers investigating creativity and innovation among work teams. The first is the importance of the group task and the demands and opportunities it creates for creativity and innovation. The second is the theme of diversity in knowledge and skills among team members, which researchers suggest is related to both team creativity and innovation. The third is the theme of team integration—when team members work in integrated ways to capitalize on their diverse knowledge and skills, researchers believe that both creativity and innovation implementation result. In this chapter, we propose an important fourth element—the extent of external demands or uncertainty. We propose that creativity and innovation implementation represent two stages in the innovation process and that external demands have quite opposite effects on each of these stages. We argue that external demands on the team *inhibit* creativity or idea generation, but *encourage* the implementation of creative ideas or innovation implementation. This proposition has important implications not only for theory in the area, but also for practice.

Creativity can be seen as the first stage in the innovation process. Creativity is the development of ideas, whereas innovation implementation is the application of ideas (e.g., for new and improved products, services, or ways of working) in practice (West, 1997). Aphoristically, creativity is thinking about new things, whereas innovation implementation is about doing new things (West & Rickards, 1999). Innovation, we argue, is therefore a two-component, but nonlinear, process encompassing both creativity and innovation implementation. At the outset of the process, creativity dominates, to be superseded later by innovation implementation processes. Innovation is restricted to intentional attempts to bring about benefits from new changes; these might include economic benefits, personal growth, increased satisfaction, improved group cohesiveness, better organizational communication, as well as productivity and economic gains. Various processes and products may be regarded as innovations. They include technological changes such as new products, but may also include new production processes, the introduction of advanced manufacturing technology, or the introduction of new computer support services within an organization. Administrative changes are also regarded as innovations. New human resource management (HRM) strategies, organizational policies on health and safety, and the introduction of teamwork are all examples of administrative innovations within organizations. Innovation implies novelty, but not necessarily absolute novelty (West & Farr, 1990).

It is generally assumed by researchers that innovation is not a linear process (see e.g., Van de Ven, Schroeder, Scudder, & Polley, 1986; Van de Ven, Polley, Garud, & Venkatraman, 1999). The innovation process may be conceived of as cyclical with periods of innovation initiation, implementation, adaptation, and stabilization (West, 1990). Creativity is likely to be most evident in the early stages of innovation processes or cycles, when those in teams are required to develop or offer ideas in response to a perceived need for innovation. Creative thinking is also likely when they initiate proposals for change and consider their initial implementation. Such considerations alert team members to possible impracticalities associated with their ideas and to potential negative reactions from stakeholders. The employee who discovered the practical value of Post-It notes in 3M was constrained not by technology (the adhesive properties required for the product were already available), but by the resistance and incredulity of others in the organization. His creative strategy was to provide Post-It notes to the secretaries of senior managers, and they in turn began to demand more of the product, so persuading the Marketing and Production departments of the value of the idea. Thus, creativity is primarily required at early stages of the innovation process. As the innovation is adapted to organizational circumstances and stabilized, there is less need for creativity. Of course it can be argued that creativity is important throughout the innovation process, but in general the requirements for creative ideas are greater at the earlier stages of the innovation process than the later.

This distinction might have limited theoretical import if the factors influencing both creativity and innovation implementation were identical. However, although task characteristics, integrated group functioning, and diversity of knowledge and skills are (we argue) requirements for both, the effects of external demands and threat on creativity and innovation implementation are, we propose, quite opposite (see Fig. 7.1).

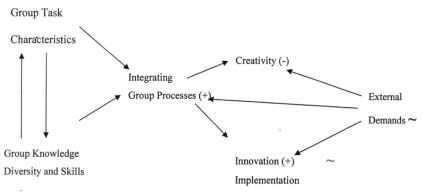

FIG. 7.1. A model of team innovation.

Four groups of factors principally determine the level of group innovation:

- Task characteristics
- Group knowledge diversity and skills
- External demands
- Integrating group processes

Figure 7.1 depicts the principal relationships among these elements. For the rest of the chapter, we analyze how they influence creativity and innovation, and we further explore the interaction effects between external demands and the other factors.

EXTERNAL DEMANDS

The external context of the group's work, be it organizational climate, support systems, market environment, or environmental uncertainty, is likely to have a highly significant influence both on its creativity and innovation implementation.

Throughout the annals of history, we find that some of the major advances and introduction of new technologies have been implemented for the first time during or in the aftermatch of severe wars. The development of technology goes hand in hand with the history of war. The invention of the wheel, around 4000 B.C., was further developed into a two-wheeled chariot 500 years afterward because the Sumerians thought it would be useful in battle. The hot air balloon was initially used as a surveillance engine in the American Civil War (Hoehling, 1958). It was during World War I that radio wireless communication became possible for the first time. World War II fostered the development of electronics and nuclear sciences (Devereux, 1990). Satellite technology was a consequence of the cold war, which drove Americans and Russians to compete for the space race (Evangelista, 1988). The severe constraints felt during war periods and the necessity of having some competitive advantage in relation to the enemy led to innovation.

We can conclude that people, groups, and organizations will innovate partly in response to external demands. Yet do such demands have a positive effect throughout the whole creative and innovation process? The ideas behind the innovations documented earlier did not take place during war time, but before. The hot air balloon was invented in 1783 by the brothers Montgolfier (Gillispie, 1983), long before the American Civil War. The radar, strongly used by the Allies' navy during World War II (Latham & Stobbs, 1996), was conceptualized in 1904 by a German engineer who patented a radio echo device meant to locate ships at sea. Nylon, which only became widely used during World War II, was in fact invented between 1930 and 1939 (Handley, 1999). The demands of war time drive forward the implementation of ideas developed before—during less constrained periods.

A wealth of research evidence suggests that, indeed, creative cognitions occur when individuals are free from pressure, feel safe, and experience relatively positive affect (Claxton, 1997, 1998). For example, using the Luchins Water jars problems (Rokeach, 1950), it is possible to demonstrate how time pressures inhibit creative problem solving. Moreover, psychological threats to face or identity are associated with rigid thinking (Cowen, 1952). Time pressure can also increase rigidity of thinking on work-related tasks such as selection decisions (Kruglansky & Freund, 1983). Wright (1954) asked people to respond to Rorschach inkblots tests; half were hospital patients awaiting an operation and half were controls. The former gave more stereotyped responses and were less fluent and creative in completing similes (e.g., as interesting as . . .), indicating the effects of stress or threat on their capacity to generate creative responses.

In contrast, among individual health workers, we have found in a number of studies that high work demands are significant predictors of individual innovation. West (1989) operationalized demands in terms of work load and measured it using a 9-item scale (adapted from Caplan, 1971). This scale included items concerning time constraints, lack of resources, and conflicting demands. He verified that work demands were the best role predictor of individual innovation. Bunce and West (1995) found innovative responses to occupational stress to be common among caring professionals. Bunce and West (1996) examined the level of stress arising directly out of the work using the Job-Induced Tension scale (House & Rizzo, 1972). This scale comprises items such as "I work under a great deal of pressure" or "Problems associated with my work have kept me awake at night." The authors verified that high levels of stress predicted individual innovation. Corroborating these findings, studies of work role transitions show that changing role objectives, strategies, or relationships is a common response to the demands of new work environments (West, 1987a, 1987b). More recently, in a study of over 10,000 health care workers, work overload emerged as a significant predictor of innovation (Hardy & West, 2000). Janssen (2000) verified that job demands had a positive relationship with innovative work behavior when individuals perceived effort rewards fairness.

Of course excessive work demands can also have detrimental effects on stress levels, absenteeism, and turnover. But the point here is that individuals innovate at least partly in response to high levels of demand, and groups are comprised of individuals.

At the organizational level, research in manufacturing organizations (West, Patterson, Pillinger, & Nickell, 1998) and hospitals (West & Anderson, 1992) suggests that external demands have a significant impact on organizational innovation (and therefore are likely to have an impact on group innovation). A longitudinal study of 81 manufacturing organizations showed that the lower the market share of the companies in relation to their primary products, the higher the level of companies' product and technological innovation. It seems that the threat of being a small player in a competitive situation spurs innovation. Moreover, the extent of environmental uncertainty reported by senior managers in these organizations (in relation to suppliers, customers, market demands, and government legislation) was a significant predictor of the degree of innovation in organizational systems (i.e., in work organization and people management practices; West et al., 1998). Taken together, these findings suggest that if the environment of teams and organizations is demanding and uncertain, it is likely that they will innovate to reduce the uncertainty and level of demand.

Why do demands enhance innovation? Why do diverse factors such as time pressure and high work load—as experienced by individuals or teams—and a loss in market share—which affects the entire organization—support innovation? The common theme among these factors is that they all indicate to the individual, the group, or the organization that there is a high necessity for action. These demands signal that there is an urge "to do something about it"—that "one shouldn't carry on like this." This signal could even be interpreted such that circumstances may get worse if one does not act. The idea of demands as a factor that motivates people to *act* is supported by research on initiative taking. People take initiative when they leave their prescribed work role to improve something about their work. A longitudinal study showed that stressors lead to higher levels of initiative taking (Fay & Sonnentag, 2002).

The seemingly contradictory effects of high demands reported earlier can be explained by the model presented before. It was suggested earlier that creative processes (idea generation) occur in the earlier stages of the innovation process, whereas innovation implementation processes occur predominantly at later stages. What is suggested, therefore, is that external demands will *inhibit* creativity, which occurs in the earlier stages of the innovation process, but they will *facilitate* innovation (via innovation implementation) at later stages. Creativity requires an undemanding environment, whereas implementation requires precisely the opposite. Because demands actually impair the creativity necessary to start the innovation process, where do people actually get their creative ideas? A preliminary answer to this may be generated from the anecdotal examples presented at the beginning of the chapter. In times of high demands, creative ideas may originate more frequently from outside the organization. For example, individuals can take up an idea or invention developed earlier or elsewhere that has not been used on a large scale and successfully adapt it to the new circumstances. In contrast, in times of low demands, creative ideas may originate from within the organization. The necessity to act triggered by high demands may help individuals to pragmatically and quickly adapt an old or existing idea and implement it.

Why is there this consistency of findings about the influence of external demands across levels of analysis? Innovation implementation involves changing the status quo, which implies resistance, conflict, and a requirement for sustained effort. Innovative workers with high job involvement experience conflict and reduced satisfaction with relations with resistant co-workers (Janssen, 2003). A team that attempts to implement innovation is likely to encounter resistance and conflict among others in the organization, and therefore sustained effort is required to overcome these disincentives to innovate. Yet effort is aversive—like most species, we strive to achieve our goals while expending the minimum effort necessary. So the effort required to innovate has to be motivated, at least partly, by external demands. The necessity to do something ("or else the situation may get worse") associated with external demands may counterbalance the risks and effort involved in innovation.

But what form do external demands take? External demands are likely to take the form of uncertainty (experienced as potentially threatening)—compare this proposition with Burns and Stalker's (1961) finding that a strong relationship existed between environmental uncertainty and organic structures in organizations, which facilitate innovation. The price of crude oil is a constant uncertainty in petroleum refining and retailing organizations, and this prompts continuous innovation in retail operations to win customer loyalty. Another form of external demand is time constraints imposed by the organization or environment. Where customers demand ever-shorter lead times (the time from placing an order to its delivery), manufacturers or suppliers of services must innovate their work processes to satisfy their customers' demands. Competition is clearly a form of demand that economists have long identified as a force for innovation. The *severity or challenge* of the environment is also an important influence (Borrill et al., 2000).

What is intuitively apparent is that the relationship between external demands and innovation implementation cannot be linear. Extreme demands or sustained high levels are likely to produce paralysis or learned helplessness. When individuals are confronted by sustained demands that they cannot meet, they are likely to respond with apathy or learned helplessness (Maier & Seligman, 1976). So either very low or very high levels of demands are associated with relatively low levels of innovation implementation—an inverted U relationship.

Yet how does this component of the model described in Fig. 7.1 relate to other factors influencing innovation (task characteristics, team member knowledge and skill diversity, and integrating processes)? Next, we discuss the other factors in the model, and we also explore possible interactions between them and external demands.

GROUP TASK CHARACTERISTICS

The task a group performs is a fundamental influence on the work group, defining its structural, process, and functional requirements—the people in the group, their roles, how they should work together, and the nature and processes of the tasks they individually and collectively perform. Indeed in one sense, a team is defined by the task it is required to perform. Therefore, the task influences the level of creativity and innovation in the team.

Dimensions for classifying task characteristics include task difficulty; solution multiplicity; intrinsic interest; cooperative requirements (Shaw, 1976); tasks that are unitary versus divisible, conjunctive, disjunctive, and additive (Steiner, 1972); conflict versus cooperation elements (Tjosvold, 1998); and conceptual versus behavioral components (McGrath, 1984). These classification systems, developed by social psychologists, have not been fruitful for researchers exploring group performance and innovation in organizational settings probably because such goals as producing TV programs, battleground training, health care, product development, and providing financial services cannot be neatly categorized into discrete tasks and subtasks (Tschan & von Cranach, 1996). Health care teams that maintain and promote the health of people in local communities have multiple stakeholders and a wide variety of tasks. A primary health care team (PHCT), for example, comprises general practitioners, community nurses, practice nurses, administrative staff, district, health visitors, and one or more practice managers (Borrill et al., 2000). These teams represent the first point of contact for people seeking medical advice or treatment through the UK National Health Service (NHS). They serve virtually the whole population of the United Kingdom, and all services are provided free of charge. PHCTs across the UK perform much the same task—delivering primary health care for routine ailments and chronic ill health (e.g., the treatment of diabetes and chronic high blood pressure) and acting as gatekeepers to secondary care services, referring patients when necessary to specialist medical services. PHCT doctors and nurses provide specialist clinics (e.g., diabetes, baby, and antenatal clinics) and also visit patients at their homes who cannot, through reasons of disability or illness, travel to the team premises. They are paid on the basis of numbers of patients registered and clinics provided (e.g., diabetes clinics), and this produces considerable homogeneity of activity across PHCTs throughout the country. Teams will typically include two or more doctors who are self-employed contractors paid by the NHS, administrative and clerical staff, team managers and practice nurses (all of whom are employed by the doctors), and other nurses including midwives, district nurses, and health visitors (all employed by the NHS). Teams may also include a physiotherapist, counselor, pharmacist, or a range of other professions allied to medicine, but the core membership is as described earlier. Some of their tasks can be divided into individually assignable subtasks, like paying home visits to patients, whereas others require the teams' synergy, such as performing a surgery. Quite often teams work in a cooperative way, but they also engage in conflict. For example, when divergent opinions exist, it is necessary to discuss them to identify the correct diagnosis. Health care teams' tasks are then simple and difficult; unitary and divisible; involve conflict and cooperation; and demand both behavioral and conceptual responses. Consequently, these tasks cannot be easily categorized into one of the dimensions presented previously.

Sociotechnical systems theory (STST) provides a powerful framework for examining the effects of task design on work group innovation. Sociotechnical systems theorists (Trist & Bamforth, 1951) argue that autonomous work groups provide a structure through which the demands of the social and technical subsystems of an organization can be jointly optimized. Thus, STST proposes that the technical subsystems of any work unit must be balanced and optimized concurrently with the social subsystem—technological and spatial working conditions must be designed to meet the human demands of the social system. The two subsystems are connected by team members' occupational roles and by cooperative and interdependent relationships. The key to effective performance is then whether the work group can control variation in quality and quantity of task performance at source (Cordery, 1996). Such variance control implies innovation because the work group will introduce new and improved methods of working or technologies to achieve control of variance in task performance appropriately. What characteristics of the work group and the group's task encourage innovation?

The joint optimization of the two subsystems is more likely when work groups have the following characteristics:

- The team is a relatively independent organizational unit that is responsible for a whole task.
- The tasks of members are related in content so that awareness of a common task is evoked and maintained, and members are required to work interdependently.
- There is a unity of product and organization (i.e., the group has a complete task to perform), and group members can identify with their own product (Ulich & Weber, 1996).

With reference to the task, it is possible to identify, according to STST, six characteristics that evoke task focus or intrinsic motivation (and therefore innovation). Tasks that involve completion of a whole and identifiable piece of work (completeness), which the team can look on afterward as the product of their efforts, are more meaningful for the group. Second, tasks comprising varied demands that consequently require the use of several skills are more motivating than repetitive tasks. A third influential characteristic is the amount of opportunities for social interaction. Tasks that involve team meetings or require exchange of information among colleagues or with people outside the organization are more intrinsically motivating than tasks in which individuals work alone. Autonomy is also extremely important. If the task allows the group substantial freedom and discretion to decide about their work, it fosters higher motivation. Another relevant factor for intrinsic motivation is the extent to which a task promotes development of knowledge. As a consequence of an intrinsic need for growth (Steers, Porter, & Bigley, 1996), tasks that offer the group opportunities for learning are more motivating than tasks that only require use of previously acquired knowledge. A last characteristic is the extent to which a task allows the development of new and challenging possibilities for the team. Hackman and Oldham (1980) also suggested the influence of task significance on intrinsic motivation (and consequently on innovation). Task significance is the degree to which a task has a substantial impact on the lives or work of other people.

EXTERNAL DEMANDS AND TASK CHARACTERISTICS

What of the relationship between external demands and task characteristics? So far it has been proposed that the task characteristics suggested by STST (a whole task, tasks of members are content interrelated, unity of team with its product or service, varied demands, opportunities for social interaction, autonomy, opportunities for learning, task development opportunities) will foster intrinsic motivation, and thereby innovation attempts. It has also been suggested that external demands will encourage innovation implementation. This leads to the following propositions:

- Where the level of group task characteristics that encourage intrinsic motivation and external demands are high, then innovation implementation will be at a high level.
- Where the levels of group task characteristics that encourage intrinsic motivation are high and external demands are low, then innovation implementation will be moderate.
- Where the level of group task characteristics that encourage intrinsic motivation are low and external demands are high, then innovation implementation will be moderate.
- Where the level of group task characteristics that encourage intrinsic motivation and external demands are low, then innovation implementation will be low.

These propositions suggest that either high levels of task characteristics encouraging intrinsic motivation or high levels of external demands are necessary for innovation implementation.

Karasek's (1979) job demand-control model provided an alternative framework to understand the interaction between external demands and task characteristics. Karasek posited that job control moderates the relationship between external demands and job outcomes. According to his model, increasing levels of job demands accompanied by decreasing levels of job control lead to psychological and physiological strain. However, the increase of both job demands and job control promotes active learning and fosters the adaptation of new and innovative patterns of behavior. Although this assumption has no empirical validation, it is reasonable to suggest that external demands interact with the autonomy a group has to perform a task to predict innovation (compare also Csikszentmihalyi's concept of *flow*—a state that is highly intrinsically motivating and characterized by high challenge accompanied by a belief that one has the necessary skills to meet the challenge; Csikszentmihalyi & Sawyer, 1995). Within a team with high task autonomy, external demands will foster innovation implementation. However, if the team has low task autonomy, it is not able to respond innovatively to external demands, and consequently these have a negative impact on the team's performance.

GROUP KNOWLEDGE DIVERSITY AND SKILLS

Diversity of knowledge and skills will contribute to team innovation dependent on the sophistication of group processes. Groups composed of people with differing professional backgrounds, knowledge, skills, and abilities will be more innovative than those whose members are similar because they bring usefully differing perspectives on issues to the group (Paulus, 2000). Their divergence of views offers multiple perspectives and the potential for constructive controversy. Diversity contributes to the magnitude of the team's total pool of task-related skills, information, and perspectives and to the potential for more comprehensive or creative decision making via informational conflict. If this informational conflict is processed in the interests of effective decision making and task performance, rather than on the basis of motivation to win or prevail or because of conflicts of interest, this in turn will generate improved performance and more innovative actions will be the result (De Dreu & De Vries, 1997; Paulus, 2000; Tjosvold, 1998). Moreover, task characteristics will dictate the requirements for diversity in group members' knowledge and skills.

In considering diversity, researchers tend to differentiate between attributes that are directly related to work roles (such as organizational position or specialized technical knowledge) and those that are more enduringly characteristic of the person (such as age, gender, ethnicity, social status, and personality; Maznevski, 1994). Existing research evidence suggests that diversity of professional background is associated with higher levels of innovation. For example, in a study of 100 primary health care teams, Borrill et al. (2000) found that the greater the number of professional groups represented in the team, the higher the levels of innovation in patient care.

If diversity is maximized at the expense of shared understanding about the group task, it will threaten the ability of the group to innovate effectively. The clarity of the task will therefore influence the level of requisite knowledge diversity in the team. Innovation requires agreement about the goals of any change and how these advance the overall objectives of the team. There must be sufficient overlap of group members' mental models for them to coordinate and communicate effectively. Thus, the common task (shared goals) will create shared understanding, but within this greater knowledge diversity will lead to more creativity and innovation.

What is proposed here is an inverted-U relationship between knowledge diversity and integrating group processes. Where diversity is very low, the group pressures will be toward conformity rather than integration. Where diversity is very high, there is unlikely to be adequate shared mental representation of the group and its task to enable integration, communication, and coordination of efforts for innovation. Thus, the research team composed of a statistician, Marxist sociologist, quantitative organizational psychologist, social constructionist, and political scientist may be so diverse that they are unable to develop a coherent and innovative program of research to discover under what circumstances nursing teams on hospital wards acknowledge and discuss medication errors.

EXTERNAL DEMANDS AND DIVERSITY

The relationship between external demands and task diversity is worthy of further discussion. We suggest that the effect of the interaction between external demands and diversity on innovation implementation depends on the type of diversity existent within the team. According to Maznevski (1994), diversity can be categorized into task- or relation-oriented diversity. Task diversity concerns attributes related to work roles, whereas relation-oriented diversity involves personal attributes. Task diversity is posited to have a positive effect on innovation, and we suggest that external demands emphasize that effect by necessitating the integration of diverse skills and knowledge (this relationship between external demands and group processes is discussed later). However, if a group has high relations diversity, external demands and the sense of emergence associated with them will amplify potential personal differences and interact to hinder innovation implementation.

GROUP PROCESSES

The key group processes that enable the team to translate the effects of task characteristics and the effects of diversity of knowledge into creativity and innovation are the following: clarifying and ensuring commitment to shared objectives, participation, minority influence processes, support for ideas to introduce new ways of doing things, and reflexivity (see also Paulus, Nakui, & Putman, chap. 4, this volume; Nijstad, Rietzschel, & Stroebe, chap. 8, this volume, for further discussion on aspects of group processes). We consider each of these processes in turn.

Clarifying and Ensuring Commitment to Shared Objectives

Ensuring clarity of and commitment to shared team objectives is a sine qua non for integrating knowledge diversity to meet task requirements for teamwork. In the context of group innovation, ensuring clarity of team objectives is likely to facilitate innovation by enabling focused development of new ideas, which can be filtered with greater precision than if team objectives are unclear. Theoretically, clear objectives will only facilitate innovation if team members are committed to the goals of the team because strong goal commitment is necessary to maintain group member persistence for innovation implementation in the face of resistance from organizational members.

Participation in Decision Making

Research on participation in decision making has a long history in both social and industrial/organizational psychology, and it suggests that participation fosters integration and commitment (Heller, Pusić, Strauss, & Wilpert, 1998). We should be wary of assuming a link with creativity at the early stages of the innovation process. Participation in teams can, under appropriate conditions, lead to high levels of creativity. Group members can be motivated to perform at higher levels of creativity by social comparison processes (providing group members and teams with a comparison standard) and providing feedback on individual performance (Paulus, Dzindolet, Poletes, & Camacho, 1993; Paulus, Larey, Putman, Leggett, & Roland, 1996). Yet it is clear that many of the benefits of group participation for the generation of creative ideas are manifested only if the group has appropriate teamworking skills (a point elaborated later).

Minority Influence

An important perspective on conflict and creativity is offered by minority influence theory. A number of researchers have shown that minority consistency of arguments over time is likely to lead to change in majority views in groups (Maass & Clark, 1984) or at least more comprehensive processing of information by majority members than would otherwise be the case. The experimental evidence suggests that, although majorities bring about attitude change through public compliance prior to attitude change (i.e., the individual first publicly conforms to the majority view prior to internalizing that view), minority influence works in the opposite direction. People exposed to a confident and consistent minority change their private views as a result of more thorough cognitive processing of information. Minority influence researchers have labeled this process *conversion*. Research on minority influence suggests that conversion is most likely to occur where the minority is consistent and confident in the presentation of arguments. Moreover, it is a behavioral style of persistence that is most likely to lead to attitude change and innovation (Nemeth & Owens, 1996). In a study of minority dissent, De Dreu and West (2001) integrated research on minority dissent and individual creativity, and team diversity and the quality of group decision making, with research on team participation in decision making. From these lines of research, it was proposed that minority dissent would predict innovation in teams, but only when teams have high levels of participation in decision making. This hypothesis was tested in two studies—one involving a homogenous sample of self-managed teams and one involving a heterogeneous sample of cross-functional teams. Study 1 suggested a newly developed scale to measure whether minority dissent has discriminant validity. Studies 1 and 2 both showed more innovations under high rather than low levels of minority dissent, but only when there was a high degree of participation in team decision making. They concluded that minority dissent stimulates creativity and divergent thought, which, through participation, manifests as innovation.

Supporting Innovation

Innovation is more likely to occur in groups where members have taken a decision to be innovative and where there is consequent support for innovation. In such teams, attempts to innovate are rewarded rather than punished (Amabile, 1983; Kanter, 1983). Support for innovation is the expectation, approval, and practical support of attempts to introduce new and improved ways of doing things in the work environment (West, 1990). Within groups, new ideas may be routinely rejected or ignored or attract verbal and practical support. Such group processes powerfully shape individual and group behavior (for reviews, see Hackman, 1992) and will encourage or discourage team members to introduce innovations. In a longitudinal study of 27 hospital top management teams, support for innovation emerged as a powerful group process predictor of team innovation (measured by independent evaluations of implemented innovations; West & Anderson, 1996). Further studies in TV production teams (Carter & West, 1998), primary health care and community mental health teams (Borrill et al., 2000), have strongly supported this finding (see also Agrell & Gustafson, 1996).

Reflexivity

Team reflexivity will also predict group innovation (as well as effectiveness; West, 1996, 2000). Team reflexivity is "the extent to which team members collectively reflect upon the team's objectives, strategies and processes as well as their wider organizations and environments, and adapt them accordingly" (West, 1996, p. 559). There are three central elements to the concept of reflexivity—*reflection, planning,* and *action* or *adaptation.* Reflection consists of attention, awareness, monitoring, and evaluation of the object of reflection. Planning is one of the potential consequences of the indeterminacy of reflection because, during this indeterminacy, courses of action can be contemplated, intentions formed, plans developed (in more or less detail), and the potential for carrying them out is built up. High reflexivity exists when team planning is characterized by greater detail, inclusiveness of potential problems, hierarchical ordering of plans, and long as well as short-range planning. The more detailed the implementation plans, the greater the likelihood that they will manifest in innovation (Frese & Zapf, 1994; Gollwitzer, 1996). Indeed the work of Gollwitzer and colleagues suggested that innovation will be implemented almost only when the team has articulated implementation intentions. This is because planning creates a conceptual readiness for and guides team members' attention toward relevant opportunities for action and means to implement the innovation. *Action* refers to goal-directed behaviors relevant to achieving the desired changes in team objectives, strategies, processes, organizations, or environments identified by the team. In a variety of studies, links between reflexivity and team innovation and effectiveness have been demonstrated (Carter & West, 1998; West, Patterson, & Dawson, 1999). Borrill et al. (2000) verified that reflexivity moderated the relationship between knowledge diversity and innovation. The relationship between knowledge diversity and innovation was stronger in teams with high levels of reflexivity than those with low levels.

EXTERNAL DEMANDS AND GROUP PROCESSES

We now discuss the relationship between external demands and integrating group processes. In a study comprising 98 health care teams, West, Dawson, Utsch, and Borrill (2003) operationalized external demands as the severity of health and social problems and level of deprivation in the community served by each health care team. External demands were assessed using a reliable national index—Jarman Index (Jarman, 1983)—which is a measure of pressure of work on general practitioners. This measure is calculated on the basis of 10 social factors (e.g., unemployment, poor housing, ethnic minorities, and proportion of elderly living alone), which are combined with census data to calculate composite workload scores for each borough. The researchers investigated the relationships between external demands, group processes, and levels of team innovation. Team objectives and task focus did not have a direct effect on team innovation: Well-functioning teams working in less demanding areas did not exhibit high levels of innovation in patient care. Also no direct relationship between external demands on teams and their level of innovation was found. However, group processes moderated the relationship between external demands and innovation, such that good group processes and high levels of external demands were associated with high levels of team innovation. It is feasible to argue then that external demands interact with existing good team processes to predict innovation. Building on this reasoning, we claim that external demands have a positive effect on innovation implementation, but only when the group has good integrative processes.

We argue that external demands always have a negative impact on group creativity. Creativity requires a nonconstrained, undemanding environment (West, 2002), and the existence (or perception) of threat reduces creative cognition (Claxton, 1997, 1998). Good group processes will obviously help the team thwart the negative effect of external demands. Nevertheless, the creative output will still be partially hindered. Building on this reasoning, we posit that, although group processes play an extremely important role in predicting innovation, they do not explain it per se. External demands influence creativity and innovation implementation differently, and it is therefore important to differentiate these stages in the innovation cycle.

We suggest that high levels of external demands increase group cohesion—and the corollary, high levels of internal group cohesion enable the group to cope more effectively with demands and uncertainty (Mullen & Copper, 1994). External demands can interact with existing good processes, such as task focus and team objectives, to predict innovation implementation, and they can also influence group performance by fostering other processes like group cohesion.

Is there any difference between innovations that arise from demanding environments and those that are products of teams performing under low levels of external demands? This question begs for data as a basis for an answer. However, we speculate that time will be an important factor. High-demand environments will constrain the time available for implementing innovations, and so we expect that teams operating under high levels of external demands will innovate more rapidly.

THEORETICAL AND PRACTICAL IMPLICATIONS

The model of group creativity and innovation implementation described here treats these phenomena as if they were simply dependent variables in a precise experiment in, say, the physical sciences. However, innovation implies reciprocal relationships between variables. For example, innovation may affect the group's level of external demands. The production team on the shop floor may decide to establish direct relationships with customers to speed information flow and reduce task uncertainty. As the primary health care team clarifies its commitment to encourage patients/clients to take responsibility for their own health care, they may change their own membership (taking on a counselor and health promotion adviser rather than another doctor). The team may also reduce clients' demands for their services as a consequence. Moreover, an innovative group will change managers' perceptions of the team, and team members may consequently find they have increasing influence in their organizations. This in turn will affect their subsequent innovation and group processes. Creativity and innovation implementation are also reciprocally interdependent. Of course innovation implementation is dependent on the quality of the ideas initially developed. Similarly, creativity will be demanded during the innovation implementation process because unanticipated problems are likely to demand yet more creative ideas to aid in their solution.

Innovation is dynamic, so we must aspire to construct dynamic models representing how groups both shape and are shaped by their environments and their innovations. Yet we are still at an early stage of understanding of group creativity and innovation, requiring that we establish basic principles before confronting such complex challenges. We need models in the future that reciprocally link the organization and wider environment of the group to characteristics of the group and its task, and to group creativity and innovation implementation. Such dynamic models will enable us to confront this research area more confidently.

In organizational settings, where the intent is to encourage teams to be innovative, there are clear practical recommendations that can be derived from the propositions outlined above.

Select People With Diverse Experience and Knowledge to Form the Team. To build a balanced team, you have to ensure that, between them, the team members have the skills to get the job done, but also to ensure they are sufficiently diverse in their backgrounds. Diversity in skills, life experience, culture, and work experience ensures a variety of perspectives in the team's work and decision making. This diversity will translate into effectiveness and sparkling fountains of innovation, but only if you can teach team members to manage their differences as a valuable asset, rather than as a threat to their individual identities. Teams of like-minded clones will experience a comfortable existence, but will be ineffective and, in relation to creativity, stagnant ponds. Teams should have the right balance of skills and experience. Take the case of a team putting together a staff attitude survey for an organization that has hundreds of outlets across the country (e.g., gas stations). The team needs people who have experience of questionnaire design and understand what the differences are between good and poor measures. They also need a statistician to help design the questionnaire and analyze the data. The team needs someone who has experience of running surveys across many sites—a skilled project manager. Other key skills are likely to be setting up a telephone help desk for staff to call when they

have questions or confusions in relation to the survey and a Web site de-
signer to provide relevant Web-based information. The manager may need
to involve union and HR representatives to offer their perspectives. The
task dictates the skills required, and from the list of skills you can then select those people who have the best of them for your team.

Diversity is valuable. By having culturally diverse membership in a team
that works in a culturally diverse community, the team can respond knowl-
edgeably to the needs of its customers because members have an understanding of the cultural communities. But diversity can threaten the team
too. When we bring together a wide range of ages, skills, cultural backgrounds, functional backgrounds, and life experiences, there is the possibility of friction. These differences should be the grit in the oyster that becomes a pearl. That means that managers have to create the right medium.
They must model the skills of teamwork, listen openly and actively, and constantly test their understanding of what team members have said. Team
members must thoroughly explore their different viewpoints over task issues and summarize their understanding of these explorations. Leaders
can emphasize the shared goal or mission of the team, show that dissent
and disagreement are valuable by emphasizing it, and encourage discussion
to conclusion and consensus rather than compromising or voting on issues.

A Team Task and One That Challenges the Team.   Painting a supertanker's
hull requires a group of painters, all working in parallel on their section of
the hull, but they do not need to work as a team to do the job. The lifeboat
crew in a rural coastal area with busy shipping lanes must work as a team to
do the job. Practically, we need to take a number of steps to decide whether
a team is appropriate for the task. First, analyze the task and decide whether
the goals are clear and the task is challenging. If so, it is a task that may require a team. If not, the task may need to be clarified or made more challenging. A group of secretaries may take responsibility not just for adminis-
tration, but also for the budget or office space redesign. Second, is the task
a complete piece of work (e.g., not simply putting the studs on the car
wheels, but assembling the whole transmission system plus wheels)? If it is,
it is likely to be appropriate for a team. If it is not, it needs to be broadened
to make it into a whole piece of work. Call center operators handle complaints from customers. Broadening the task might involve having them
meet regularly to discuss common themes in complaints, identifying areas
in the organization that cause the problems, and coming up with solutions.
Third, does the task require a range of skills spread across a number of different individuals? If that is the case, the task is probably best done by a
team. If not, the first two steps need to be revisited to make the task more
challenging, broader, and complete (the painters on the supertanker
would not fulfill this condition). Finally, if the task requires people to work

together in interdependent ways, communicating, sharing information, and debating decisions about the best way to do the job, then it is a team task. When team members have to dance as a team, rather than individually, to get the job done, then it is a task best done by a team. If not, the task should be redesigned.

The team's task must be a whole task (i.e., perceived by the team as significant to the organization or the wider society). That makes varied demands on team members and requires them to use their knowledge and skills interdependently. It also provides opportunities for social contact between them, and provides opportunities for learning, skill development, and task development. The group should be relatively autonomous in the conduct of its work.

Emphasize Team Creativity, Not Just Productivity . . . and Stop Work.   The group should be given time during the early stages of the innovation process, in a relaxed environment, to generate creative ideas for new and improved products or ways of working. This may mean taking time away from the usual workplace and working in (ideally) a pleasant environment. The services of a skilled facilitator, knowledgeable about research evidence on group creative processes (as opposed to popular belief and consultancy mythology), can help groups maximize their creative output. An intragroup psychosocial environment experienced by group members as unthreatening will best facilitate such processes.

To help teams deal with the paradoxical effect of external demands, we recommend the following actions.

Ensure That Team Members Face Challenging Tasks and Environments That Stretch Them.   It is important that teams are exposed to high, but not extreme, levels of external demands (West, Hirst, Richter, & Shipton, 2004). At later stages of the innovation process, if group members feel pressured or uncertain, they are more likely to implement innovations as long as the demands and uncertainties are created by extra- not intragroup agents (this is sometimes called the *burning platform* effect) and the level of demand is not crippling. Today competition, threat, pressure, and uncertainty are characteristic of most public and commercial sector environments, particularly as globalization increases apace—there is rarely reason to increase the level of demand. But there is much more reason to improve the level of safety and the integration skills of team members.

Regularly Check That the Team Is Functioning Well.   Group members must individually and collectively develop the skills to work well as a team, encouraging integrating group processes to ensure that they innovate effectively. This means continually clarifying and ensuring group member commitment to shared objectives; encouraging information sharing, regular group member interaction, and shared influence over decision making; and encouraging high levels of emphasis on quality and practical support (time, money, and cooperation) for innovation. It means encouraging group members to regularly reflect on and adapt their objectives, strategies, and processes—consciously and continually improving their functioning as a group.

Assign Creativity Generation and Implementation of Ideas to Different Individuals or Teams. Having some team members (or teams within an organization) work on the generation of ideas with other team members (or other teams) responsible for implementing those ideas offers a strategy for dealing with the paradoxical effect of external demands. If the organization's resources allow it and task division is possible, tasks that involve generation of creative ideas should be performed by individuals or teams working free of pressure, whereas the implementation of those ideas should be assigned to individuals or groups that experience the pressure to innovate rapidly.

Provide a More Relaxing Climate While Individuals or Groups Are Generating Ideas and Create a Sense of Urgency at the Time of Implementation. The team's leader is able to influence the perception of threat and pressure. Therefore, he or she can promote a more relaxed, pressure-free climate at the time the team has to be creative and afterward create a sense of urgency to foster the effective implementation of those ideas.

CONCLUSION

For creativity and innovation implementation to emerge from group functioning—for groups to be vibrant sources of ideas and changes—the context must be demanding, but there must be strong group integration processes. This requires that members have the integration abilities to work effectively in teams, and that they develop a safe psychosocial climate and appropriate group processes (clarifying objectives, encouraging participation, constructive controversy, reflexivity, and support for innovation). Such conditions are likely to produce high levels of group innovation, but crucially too the well-being, which is a consequence of effective human interaction in challenging and supportive environments.

ACKNOWLEDGMENTS

The authors would like to thank Leigh Thompson, Honk-Seok Choi, and the reviewers for their helpful comments and suggestions.

REFERENCES

Agrell, A., & Gustafson, R. (1996). Innovation and creativity in work groups. In M. A. West (Ed.), *Handbook of work group psychology* (pp. 317–344). Chichester: Wiley.

Amabile, T. M. (1983). The social psychology of creativity: A componential conceptualization. *Journal of Personality and Social Psychology, 45,* 357–376.

Borrill, C. S., Carletta, J., Carter, A. J., Dawson, J. F., Garrod, S., Rees, A., Richards, A., Shapiro, D., & West, M. A. (2000). *The effectiveness of health care teams in the National Health Service.* Birmingham: Aston Centre for Health Service Organization Research.

Bunce, D., & West, M. A. (1995). Changing work environments: Innovative coping responses to occupational stress. *Work and Stress, 8,* 319–331.

Bunce, D., & West, M. A. (1996). Stress management and innovation interventions at work. *Human Relations, 49,* 209–232.

Burns, T., & Stalker, G. M. (1961). *The management of innovation.* London: Tavistock.

Caplan, R. D. (1971). *Organizational stress and individual stain: A social psychological study of risk factors in coronary heart disease among administrators, engineers and scientists.* Institute of Social Research, University of Michigan, University Microfilms No. 72-14822, Ann Arbor, Michigan.

Carter, S. M., & West, M. A. (1998). Reflexivity, effectiveness and mental health in BBC-TV production teams. *Small Group Research, 29,* 583–601.

Claxton, G. L. (1997). *Hare brain, tortoise mind: Why intelligence increases when you think less.* London: Fourth Estate.

Claxton, G. L. (1998). Knowing without knowing why: Investigating human intuition. *The Psychologist, 11,* 217–220.

Cordery, J. L. (1996). Autonomous work groups and quality circles. In M. A. West (Ed.), *Handbook of work group psychology* (pp. 225–246). Chichester: Wiley.

Cowen, E. L. (1952). The influence of varying degrees of psychological stress on problem-solving rigidity. *Journal of Abnormal and Social Psychology, 47,* 420–424.

Csikszentmihalyi, M., & Sawyer, K. (1995). Creative insight: The social dimension of a solitary moment. In R. J. Sternberg & J. E. Davidson (Eds.), *The nature of insight* (pp. 329–364). London: MIT Press.

De Dreu, C. K. W., & De Vries, N. K. (1997). Minority dissent in organizations. In C. K. W. De Dreu & E. Van De Vliert (Eds.), *Using conflict in organizations* (pp. 72–86). London: Sage.

De Dreu, C. K. W., & West, M. A. (2001). Minority dissent and team innovation: The importance of participation in decision making. *Journal of Applied Psychology, 86*(6), 1191–1201.

Devereux, T. (1990). *Messenger Gods of battle: Radio–radar–sonar: The story of electronics in war.* London, UK: Brassey's.

Evangelista, M. (1988). *Innovation and the arms race: How the United States and Soviet Union develop new military technologies.* New York: Cornell University Press.

Fay, D., & Sonnentag, S. (2002). Rethinking the effects of stressors: A longitudinal study on personal initiative. *Journal of Occupational Health Psychology, 7,* 221–234.

Frese, M., & Zapf, D. (1994). Action as the core of work psychology: A German approach. In H. C. Triandis, M. D. Dunnette, & L. M. Hough (Eds.), *Handbook of industrial and organizational psychology* (Vol. 4, 2nd ed., pp. 271–340). Palo Alto, CA: Consulting Psychologists Press.

Gillispie, C. C. (1983). *The Montgolfier brothers and the invention of aviation, 1783–1784: With a word on the importance of ballooning for the science of heat and the art of building railroads.* Princeton, NJ: Princeton University Press.

Gollwitzer, P. M. (1996). The volitional benefits of planning. In P. M. Gollwitzer & J. A. Bargh (Eds.), *The psychology of action: Linking cognition and motivation to behavior* (pp. 287–312). New York: Guilford.

Hackman, J. R. (1992). Group influences on individuals and organizations. In M. D. Dunnette & L. M. Hough (Eds.), *Handbook of industrial and organizational psychology* (Vol. 3, pp. 199–267). Palo Alto, CA: Consulting Psychologists Press.

Hackman, J. R., & Oldham, G. (1980). *Work redesign.* Reading, MA: Addison-Wesley.

Handley, S. (1999). *Nylon, the manmade fashion revolution: A celebration of design from art silk to nylon and thinking fibres.* London: Bloomsbury.

Hardy, G. E., & West, M. A. (2000). *Interpersonal attachment and innovation at work.* Unpublished manuscript, Department of Psychology, University of Sheffield.

Heller, F., Pusić, E., Strauss, G., & Wilpert, B. (1998). *Organizational participation: Myth and reality.* Oxford: Oxford University Press.

Hoehling, M. D. (1958). *Thaddeus Lowe, America's one-man air corps.* New York: Messner.

House, R. J., & Rizzo, J. R. (1972). Towards the measurement of organizational practices: Scale development and validation. *Journal of Applied Psychology, 56*(5), 388–396.

Janssen, O. (2000). Job demands, perceptions of effort–reward fairness and innovative work behavior. *Journal of Occupational and Organizational Psychology, 73,* 287–302.

Janssen, O. (2003). Innovative behavior and job involvement at the price of conflict and less satisfactory relations with co-workers. *Journal of Occupational and Organizational Psychology, 76,* 347–364.

Jarman, B. (1983). Identification of underprivileged areas. *British Medical Journal, 286,* 1705–1709.

Kanter, R. M. (1983). *The change masters: Corporate entrepreneurs at work.* New York: Simon & Schuster.

Karasek, R. A. (1979). Job demands, job control and mental strain: Implications for job redesign. *Administrative Science Quarterly, 24,* 285–308.

Kruglansky, A. W., & Freund, T. (1983). The freezing and unfreezing of lay influences: Effects on impressional primacy, ethnic stereotyping and numerical anchoring. *Journal of Experimental Social Psychology, 19,* 448–468.

Latham, C., & Stobbs, A. (1996). *Radar: A wartime miracle.* Gloucestershire: Sutton.

Maass, A., & Clark, R. D. (1984). Hidden impacts of minorities: Fifty years of minority influence research. *Psychological Bulletin, 95*(3), 428–450.

Maier, S. F., & Seligman, M. (1976). Learned helplessness: Theory and evidence. *Journal of Experimental Psychology: General, 105,* 3–46.

Maznevski, M. L. (1994). Understanding our differences: Performance in decision-making groups with diverse members. *Human Relations, 47*(5), 531–552.

McGrath, J. E. (1984). *Groups, interaction and performance.* Englewood Cliffs, NJ: Prentice-Hall.

Mullen, B., & Copper, C. (1994). The relation between group cohesiveness and performance: An integration. *Psychological Bulletin, 115,* 210–227.

Nemeth, C., & Owens, P. (1996). Making work groups more effective: The value of minority dissent. In M. A. West (Ed.), *Handbook of work group psychology* (pp. 125–142). Chichester: Wiley.

Paulus, P. B. (2000). Groups, teams and creativity: The creative potential of idea-generating groups. *Applied Psychology: An International Review, 49,* 237–262.

Paulus, P. B., Dzindolet, M. T., Poletes, G., & Camacho, L. M. (1993). Perception of performance in group brainstorming: The illusion of group productivity. *Personality and Social Psychology Bulletin, 19,* 78–89.

Paulus, P. B., Larey, T. S., Putman, V. L., Leggett, K. L., & Roland, E. J. (1996). Social influence process in computer brainstorming. *Basic and Applied Social Psychology, 18,* 3–14.

Rokeach, M. (1950). The effect of perception of time upon the rigidity and concreteness of thinking. *Journal of Experimental Psychology, 40,* 206–216.

Shaw, M. E. (1976). *Group dynamics: The psychology of small group behavior.* New York: McGraw-Hill.

Steers, R. M., Porter, L. W., & Bigley, G. A. (Eds.). (1996). *Motivation and leadership at work.* Boston, MA: McGraw-Hill.

Steiner, I. D. (1972). *Group process and productivity.* New York: Academic Press.

Tjosvold, D. (1998). Co-operative and competitive goal approaches to conflict: Accomplishments and challenges. *Applied Psychology: An International Review, 47,* 285–342.

Trist, E. L., & Bamforth, K. W. (1951). Some social and psychological consequences of the longwall method of coal getting. *Human Relations, 4,* 3–38.

Tschan, F., & von Cranach, M. (1996). Group task structure, processes and outcome. In M. A. West (Ed.), *Handbook of work group psychology* (pp. 95–121). Chichester: Wiley.

Ulich, E., & Weber, W. G. (1996). Dimensions, criteria and evaluation of work group autonomy. In M. A. West (Ed.), *Handbook of work group psychology* (pp. 247–282). Chichester: Wiley.

Van de Ven, A. H., Polley, D. E., Garud, R., & Venkatraman, S. (1999). *The innovation journey.* New York: Oxford.

Van de Ven, A. H., Schroeder, R., Scudder, G., & Polley, D. (1986). Managing innovation and change processes: Findings from the Minnesota Innovation Research Programme. *Agribusiness Management Journal, 2,* 501–523.

West, M. A. (1987a). A measure of role innovation at work. *British Journal of Social Psychology, 26,* 83–85.

West, M. A. (1987b). Role innovation in the world of work. *British Journal of Social Psychology, 26,* 305–315.

West, M. A. (1989). Innovation among health care professionals. *Social Behavior, 4,* 173–184.

West, M. A. (1990). The social psychology of innovation in groups. In M. A. West & J. L. Farr (Eds.), *Innovation and creativity at work: Psychological and organizational strategies* (pp. 309–333). Chichester: Wiley.

West, M. A. (Ed.). (1996). *The handbook of work group psychology.* Chichester: Wiley.

West, M. A. (1997). *Developing creativity in organizations.* Leicester: British Psychological Society.

West, M. A. (2000). Reflexivity, revolution, and innovation in work teams. In M. M. Beyerlein, D. A. Johnson, & S. T. Beyerlein (Eds.), *Product development teams: Advances in interdisciplinary studies of work teams* (pp. 1–29). Stamford, CT: JAI.

West, M. A. (2002). Sparkling fountains or stagnant ponds: An integrative model of creativity and innovation implementation in work groups. *Applied Psychology—An International Review, 51*(3), 355–387.

West, M. A., & Anderson, N. (1992). Innovation, cultural values and the management of change in British hospitals. *Work and Stress, 6,* 293–310.

West, M. A., & Anderson, N. (1996). Innovation in top management teams. *Journal of Applied Psychology, 81*(6), 680–693.

West, M. A., Dawson, J. F., Utsch, A., & Borrill, C. S. (2003). *Necessity is the moderator of innovation.* Working paper. Birmingham, England: Aston Business School.

West, M. A., & Farr, J. L. (1990). Innovation at work. In M. A. West & J. L. Farr (Eds.), *Innovation and creativity at work: Psychological and organizational strategies* (pp. 3–13). Chichester: Wiley.

West, M. A., Hirst, G., Richter, A., & Shipton, H. (2004). Twelve steps to heaven: Successfully managing change through developing innovative teams. *European Journal of Work and Organizational Psychology, 13*(2), 269–299.

West, M. A., Patterson, M. G., & Dawson, J. F. (1999). A path to profit? Teamwork at the top. *Centrepiece, 4,* 6–11.

West, M. A., Patterson, M., Pillinger, T., & Nickell, S. (1998). *Innovation and change in manufacturing.* Institute of Work Psychology, University of Sheffield, Sheffield, S10 2TN.

West, M. A., & Rickards, T. (1999). Innovation. In M. A. Runco & S. R. Pritzker (Eds.), *Encyclopedia of creativity* (Vol. 2, pp. 45–55). London: Academic Press.

Wright, M. (1954). A study of anxiety in a general hospital setting. *Canadian Journal of Psychology, 8,* 195–203.

Chapter 8

Four Principles of Group Creativity

Bernard A. Nijstad
Eric F. Rietzschel
University of Amsterdam

Wolfgang Stroebe
Utrecht University

The scientific study of creativity dates back at least to 1869, when Francis Galton published his *Hereditary Genius* (Simonton, 2003). Galton argued that genius was born rather than made: He considered "natural ability" the most important factor for creative achievement. In the scientific literature and consistent with Galton's individual differences approach, *creativity* is often defined as an individual-level phenomenon. Mumford and Gustafson (1988), for example, defined *creativity* as

> . . . a syndrome involving a number of elements: (a) the processes underlying the *individual's* capacity to generate new ideas or understandings, (b) the characteristics of the *individual* facilitating process operation, (c) the characteristics of the *individual* facilitating the translation of these ideas into action, (d) the attributes of the situation conditioning the *individual's* willingness to engage in creative behavior, and (e) the attributes of the situation influencing evaluation of the *individual's* productive efforts. (p. 28; italics added)

Although the situation may exert an influence on creative behavior, creativity still is largely assumed to be an individual act.

On many occasions, however, creative ideas are born in situations where two or more creators cooperate. For example, it is not likely that the Manhattan project would have succeeded if Robert Oppenheimer had worked independently of his collaborators. The double helix structure of DNA might not have been discovered by either Crick or Watson had they

161

not worked on the project in collaboration. The Walt Disney studios might not have been so successful without the input of a number of creative artists (see e.g., Bennis & Biederman, 1997). Further, more and more organizations structure their work around teams, and teams are becoming the basic building blocks of many modern organizations (e.g., Lawler, Mohrman, & Ledford, 1995). It is thus important to consider the factors that lead to high levels of creativity when people work collaboratively in a group context, and complement the individual differences approach with an approach that considers the group context in which people work.

In our own work, we have focused on idea-generating groups (for overviews, see Nijstad, Diehl, & Stroebe, 2003; Stroebe & Diehl, 1994). In this chapter, we attempt to go beyond these studies and propose a framework to understand group creativity more generally. The framework is a combination of contributions framework, in which the level of creativity of the group is determined by the way the resources of individual group members are combined. We derive four principles of group creativity from this framework. Because we will illustrate these principles with studies of group idea generation, it will be helpful to first describe the basic findings in that field of research.

GROUP IDEA GENERATION

Group idea generation research has a relatively long history. In the 1950s, Osborn (1957), an advertising executive, proposed brainstorming as a method to improve the creativity of groups. He suggested that creativity is enhanced when groups adhere to a set of simple rules: generate as many ideas as possible, do not criticize ideas, combine and improve ideas, and generate wild and unusual ideas. Research has confirmed that groups using these rules are more creative than groups that do not (Parnes & Meadow, 1959). Further, Osborn (1957) expected that brainstorming would best be performed in a group because hearing the ideas of others would be stimulating and lead to ideas individuals alone would not have generated. Most people agree and think that they can generate more and better ideas in a group setting than when working alone (Paulus, Dzindolet, Poletes, & Camacho, 1993; Stroebe, Diehl, & Abakoumkin, 1992).

However, as early as 1958, Taylor, Berry, and Block found that groups are actually *less* creative than individuals. When they compared interactive groups of four with four individuals who worked alone and whose non-redundant ideas were pooled after the session (groups with no interaction or nominal groups), it appeared that the interactive groups produced fewer ideas and ideas of lower quality than did the equivalent number of individuals. This so-called *productivity loss* of real groups as compared with nominal groups has since been replicated many times (see Diehl & Stroebe, 1987), is relatively large, and increases with group size (Mullen, Johnson, & Salas, 1991).

A great deal of research has been devoted to the causes of this surprising productivity loss of groups. There is evidence that, despite the instruction not to be critical, group members are still somewhat reluctant to share all their ideas (Diehl & Stroebe, 1987). This is especially true for shy people, who perform much worse in a group session than in an individual session (Camacho & Paulus, 1995). Further, in groups some members are usually more productive than others. Paulus and Dzindolet (1993) found that the high-performing group members tend to match the rate of performance of low-performing group members, which evidently leads to lower levels of performance of the group as a whole. A third important factor is mutual production blocking (Diehl & Stroebe, 1987, 1991). Production blocking arises from the constraint that group members must take turns to express their ideas. This implies that group members sometimes (and more often in larger groups) must wait for their turn to express their ideas. While waiting for one's turn, ideas can be forgotten or suppressed, or waiting can interfere with one's thought process (Diehl & Stroebe, 1991; Nijstad, Stroebe, & Lodewijkx, 2003). Indeed if turn taking is introduced in nominal groups, productivity dramatically declines (Diehl & Stroebe, 1987).

If blocking is an important cause of the productivity loss of brainstorming groups, it can be expected that procedures which do not require turn taking will reduce or eliminate the productivity loss. This does appear to be the case: If ideas are not shared orally, but by means of computers (electronic brainstorming [EBS]) or written notes (brainwriting), and people can type or write simultaneously, no productivity loss is found (e.g., Gallupe, Bastianutti, & Cooper, 1991; Paulus & Yang, 2000). Further, when turn taking is introduced in electronic groups, a productivity loss is found that is similar to that in orally interactive groups (e.g., Gallupe, Cooper, Grisé, & Bastianutti, 1994). Even more interesting is the finding that idea sharing in these groups can sometimes lead to productivity gains; that is, groups that can read each other's ideas on their screens or on written notes outperform groups without idea sharing (e.g., Dennis & Valacich, 1993; Paulus & Yang, 2000). It appears that, in the absence of production blocking, reading the ideas of others can be stimulating and lead to ideas that otherwise would not have been generated, provided that participants are motivated to attend to those ideas (also see Dugosh, Paulus, Roland, & Yang, 2000).

To summarize these basic findings, there are both costs and benefits associated with idea generation in groups. Fear of negative evaluation and production blocking are among the costs, whereas access to others' ideas seems to be stimulating. We believe that these findings, as well as other find-

ings in the area of group creativity, can be integrated and better understood with a general framework of group performance—called *combination
of contributions.*

A COMBINATION OF CONTRIBUTIONS FRAMEWORK
FOR GROUP CREATIVITY

The combination of contribution framework identifies two important determinants of group performance: (a) the resources that group members
bring to the group, and (b) the processes involved in the way these resources are combined to produce group-level outcomes. Combination of
contributions is not a new framework for the study of group processes. For
example, in Davis' (1973) Social Decision Scheme theory, group decisions
are modeled using individual preferences (contributions) and rules (or Social Decision Schemes) of how these preferences are combined into a
group decision. In his seminal work on group process and performance,
Steiner (1972) distinguished between potential and actual productivity of a
group. The resources of the group members in combination with the group
task determine the group's potential productivity. However, potential productivity is often not realized because resources are not combined in an optimal way, and actual productivity might lie under the potential productivity
of the group.

We argue that combination of contributions also provides a natural
framework to understand group creativity. Figure 8.1 provides an illustration of our framework. At the left-hand side of that figure are the representations of several individual group members (four in this case). Each group
member brings knowledge, skills, and abilities to the group. Using these resources, the member can generate ideas or find problem solutions (Arrow
1 in the figure). These individual outputs can then be shared with the other
group members (Arrow 2): They are contributed to what we call the *group
processing space* (cf. Hinsz, Tindale, & Vollrath, 1997). Once contributed, an
item of information (e.g., an idea) is in principle available to the other
members (Arrow 3). Information contributed by others can have various effects on group members: A contributed idea may lead to the development
of additional ideas, and a suggestion by another may lead to the generation
of a problem solution. Eventually, the group must come to some kind of
collective response, such as a decision about which creative ideas to implement or a proposed solution to a problem that can next be tested for effectiveness (Arrow 4). To summarize: Individual group members contribute
information to the group, and the individual contributions must somehow
be combined to produce a group response that can vary in creativity (e.g.,
in originality and usefulness; Amabile, 1983).

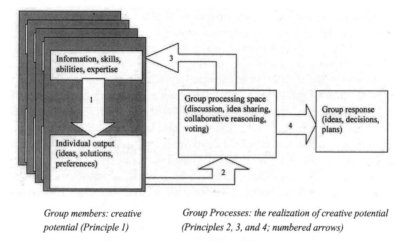

Group members: creative   Group Processes: the realization of creative potential
potential (Principle 1)   (Principles 2, 3, and 4; numbered arrows)

FIG. 8.1.   A combination of contribution model of group creativity.

In the remainder of this chapter, we propose four principles of group creativity, which correspond to the four numbered arrows in Fig. 8.1: the creative potential principle, the effective sharing principle, the accessibility principle, and the effective convergence principle. These principles are illustrated with recent work on group idea generation, as well as with research in other areas.

PRINCIPLES OF GROUP CREATIVITY

The Creative Potential Principle

The first principle, the creative potential principle, is derived from the work of Ivan Steiner (1972). As described earlier, Steiner distinguished between a group's potential and actual performance. He argued that the potential performance of the group is determined by two factors: the resources of the group members and the characteristics of the task. If the group members possess the resources that are necessary to perform the task, potential productivity will be high (e.g., in a problem-solving task, when at least one of the group members is capable of finding the correct solution, the group's potential is high). However, the group's potential is not always realized because process losses may occur: Group members may not be motivated to perform at their best level (motivation loss; e.g., the group member with the correct solution is unmotivated to share it with the others), or the contributions of individual members may not be combined in an optimal way (coordination loss; e.g., the other group members do not recognize the correct solution and decide on a wrong solution). Because of process loss, the group's actual performance may lie below potential performance.

The creative potential principle similarly states that the group's potential to be creative is a function of the resources of the group members (knowledge, skills, abilities) in combination with the demands of the group task. According to Amabile (1983), two types of resources are important for creative achievement: domain skills and creativity skills. Domain skills include factual knowledge, technical skills, and special talents in a particular domain (e.g., in mathematics). Creativity-relevant skills include cognitive style, knowledge of creative heuristics, and working style. Amabile argued that, to be creative, a person must have both domain skills (one cannot be creative in mathematics without knowledge of that domain) and creativity skills (one needs creativity skills to come up with something new in a particular domain). Once group members have the adequate level of these skills, the group has a high potential for creativity—at least in the domain for which they have the required domain skills. If group members lack these skills, the group as a whole will not be creative no matter how effective the group works.

Some groups have more potential than other groups. One factor that is important in this respect is group diversity. It has often been argued that more diverse groups have more creative potential (e.g., Milliken & Martins, 1996; Williams & O'Reilly, 1998). In principle, the resources of a group as a whole are larger than the resources of any individual within the group. However, when certain group members have information that others do not, or they have skills and abilities that complement the skills and abilities of other members, the potential of the group is higher. If group members have similar knowledge, skills, and abilities, one would not expect collaboration to add much value. From the creative potential principle, however, it is clear that diversity should be related to the task. Thus, diversity in ethnicity, gender, or age (or hair color for that matter) will only increase creative potential when it is associated with diversity in task-relevant knowledge, skills, or abilities.

In the idea-generation literature, there is evidence that task-related diversity enhances performance. Diehl (1991; also see Stroebe & Diehl, 1994) manipulated knowledge diversity in the laboratory. He had participants take an association test on the topic of preserving the environment (they had to write down their first associations). He then composed groups of four that were similar in associations (homogenous groups) or dissimilar in associations (heterogeneous groups). In addition, he assigned some participants randomly to groups. Some of these groups worked together in a normal brainstorming session (interacting groups), whereas other groups worked in separate rooms and could not communicate with each other (nominal groups). These groups were then asked to generate ideas about how to preserve the environment. Diehl (1991) found that group diversity did not make a difference for nominal groups. However, heterogeneous interacting groups produced more ideas than either homogenous or random interacting groups. As a result, the homogenous and random interacting groups showed the usual productivity loss; however, this loss was substantially reduced in the heterogeneous interacting groups.

Other studies have also found a positive link between group diversity and creativity. Valacich, Wheeler, Mennecke, and Wachter (1995) distributed task-related information to group members in such a way that all members either had the same information (all members were given all the information; homogenous groups) or different information (the information was divided among group members; diverse groups). In addition, they used groups of different sizes (5–10 members). The participants had to generate solutions to a policy problem on computers and could see each other's solutions on their screens. Valacich et al. (1995) found that the number of solutions and the number of high-quality solutions were constant across group size for the homogenous groups. However, for diverse groups, the number of solutions and the number of high-quality solutions increased with group size. As a consequence, larger diverse groups ($n > 7$) generated more solutions and more high-quality solutions than equivalent homogenous groups.

Although these studies suggest that diverse groups are more creative than homogenous groups, two caveats should be noted. First, there probably is an optimal level of diversity beyond which the potential for creativity may not rise or even go down, and this optimal level of diversity may be different for different tasks. For example, Dunbar (1995), in his research in real-life microbiology labs, has found that diverse teams were more effective problem solvers than homogenous teams. Diverse teams were more successful because they were able to map principles from one domain within microbiology to a problem in a related but different domain. However, these teams still consisted of microbiologists only, although they had slightly different areas of expertise. One can easily imagine that, when working on a specialist problem in chemistry, it will not be of great value to add a psychologist to the team—the psychologists probably will not even understand the problem. The tasks used by Diehl (1991) and Valacich et al. (1995), however, were relatively simple, in that no specialist domain knowledge was required. Problems that require less specialist knowledge probably have a different optimal level of diversity than problems that require much domain knowledge and skills.

A second caveat is that the creative potential principle does not imply that diverse groups, even if they are close to their optimal level of diversity, will always be more creative than homogenous groups. The reason is that potential creativity often is not realized, and the actual level of the group's creativity may fall below its potential. Group diversity has often been shown to also negatively affect group functioning and performance, and it may lead to high levels of conflict, low identification with the group, and negative affective reactions in general (e.g., Milliken, Bartel, & Kurtzberg, 2003). Whether (diverse) groups will reach their potential depends on various group processes. Thus, whereas the first principle deals with the resources of group members and their potential contributions, the next three principles deal with group process and the degree to which potential creativity materializes.

The Effective Sharing Principle

For groups to be creative and tap their members' potential, it is necessary that group members communicate their ideas, preferences, solutions, and knowledge. In our framework, this means that group members have to contribute information to the group processing space (Arrow 2 in Fig. 8.1). The group processing space can be a (face-to-face) group discussion, but could equally well be a virtual discussion on the Internet or an exchange of written comments. The effective sharing principle states that the creative potential of groups will not be realized without an adequate exchange of information and ideas (also see Hinsz et al., 1997). This requires group members to be both motivated and able to share their ideas.

In particular, the potential positive effects of group diversity depend on an effective sharing process. For high levels of group creativity to occur, the members of diverse groups need to share their unique ideas, information, and perspectives with the other members. Unfortunately, there is much evidence that groups, when left to their own devices, are not effective when it comes to the sharing of unique knowledge or ideas. There is abundant evidence that groups mainly discuss information that group members already have in common (i.e., information they all held before discussion), at the expense of unique information that is only held by one or two group members (e.g., Stasser & Titus, 1985). This tendency will constrain the creativity of groups because emergent ideas—ideas that can only be found when group members combine their unique insights—are unlikely to occur (Stasser & Birchmeier, 2003). Further, research has documented that minority dissent can have beneficial effects on group members' creativity. When one or a few group members express a minority opinion that goes against the majority of group members, this leads to higher levels of elaboration of the problem and more creative solutions (e.g., Nemeth, 1986). However, due to conformity pressures, the standpoint of the minority is often not expressed or is disregarded (see Nemeth & Nemeth-Brown, 2003), which severely limits the potential benefits of dissent.

Group members must thus be willing to share their ideas with the other members even when they hold a minority position. An unsafe group climate, where members face the risk of ridicule and rejection, will negatively affect the willingness to share ideas (e.g., Edmondson, 1999). Similarly, newcomers in a group can have beneficial effects on group creativity due to their fresh look on old problems, but these positive effects are constrained when newcomers are unwilling to share their ideas, for example, because they fear their ideas are not taken seriously (Levine, Choi, & Moreland, 2003).

Besides willingness to share ideas, group members must also be able to share their ideas. A study by De Dreu and West (2001) nicely illustrated this. They argued that minority dissent will lead to higher creativity, as was shown in previous research. However, if groups do not meet on a regular basis and group members do not participate in decision making, high tolerance for dissent will not lead to new ideas and innovations because group members do not have the opportunity to share their thoughts. Indeed De Dreu and West found that tolerance for dissent was positively associated with team innovation, but only for teams with high levels of participation in decision making.

The point is even more fundamental than this. We argue that groups have a limited capacity processing space: The opportunities to contribute to the group processing space are by definition limited. Because time is a scarce resource, one simply cannot share all of one's information with the group. However, the size of the group processing space is not constant, but depends on the way the group interacts. Earlier we discussed that one of the reasons that verbally interacting groups are less effective idea generators than nominal groups is mutual production blocking. Because usually only one member can share information at one time, the others have to wait for their turn. Verbal communication thus limits the opportunities to contribute ideas because of its serial nature. These limitations are less severe in electronic or writing groups because group members can type or write simultaneously (see e.g., Gallupe et al., 1991). Thus, the medium by which groups communicate affects the size of the group processing space. The fact that one has to wait for one's turn in verbal groups makes these groups unsuited for some activities: One would not want to write a report as a group, but rather leaves it to one of the group members.

Further, the limited processing space can be used in an efficient or inefficient way. Through an adequate division of labor, the group processing space can be used more effectively. Group members should perform those tasks that they can perform best. This is a tricky problem because it requires that group members know who is best at which task. However, there is substantial evidence that mutual recognition of expertise helps the sharing of unique information and group problem solving. The tendency of groups to mainly discuss information that everybody already holds (at the expense of their unique information) is weakened when group members have mutually recognized areas of expertise (Stewart & Stasser, 1995). Thus, when group members are aware of their specialized areas of expertise, they are more likely to share their unique knowledge. A similar finding has been obtained in group problem solving. When performing a problem-solving task, those groups in which members knew who were best in which part of the task performed better (Liang, Moreland, & Argote, 1995). This type of meta-knowledge, in which group members have mutually recognized areas of expertise, has been called a *transactive memory system* (Wegner, 1986). If group members know whom to turn to with problems, and if they know who holds the relevant information, the limited group processing space can be used more effectively.

To summarize, effective sharing of information and ideas entails willingness and opportunities to share ideas. The opportunities to share ideas are by definition limited, so an adequate sharing process as well as an adequate division of labor are necessary. We now turn to the question of what happens when information or ideas have been shared, and to the question of how information contributed by one group member affects the other members.

The Accessibility Principle

Even if group members share their information effectively, information needs to be processed by the other members before it will have any effects on group creativity (Arrow 3 in Fig. 8.1). If information is attended to, it can have various effects. For example, an idea suggested by one group member may trigger ideas in other members, and information suggested by different members may be combined to solve a problem. The accessibility principle states that information shared by others, provided that it is attended to, makes related information more accessible in memory. In turn, more accessible information is likely to be mentioned later in the discussion.

What is important for this principle is the distinction between available and accessible knowledge and ideas (e.g., Tulving & Pearlstone, 1966). Knowledge may in principle be available to a person, meaning that it is stored in long-term memory (LTM), but not all knowledge is equally accessible. The tip-of-the-tongue phenomenon—when we know that we know something, but cannot retrieve it from memory—is a well-known demonstration of this fact. Accessibility of knowledge depends on the context in which we try to remember it (e.g., a waitress may recognize a regular client when she walks into the restaurant, but not when she accidentally bumps into her in the supermarket). In a group, the utterances of others are part of the context: What others say makes related knowledge more accessible.

First of all, information needs to be attended to before it will have any effects. A brainstorming study by Dugosh et al. (2000) showed this. They had groups of four generate ideas at computer terminals. Some groups could not read each other's ideas on monitors, whereas other groups could. Of the latter groups, some groups were instructed to pay close attention to the ideas of the other members because they would be tested for recall of these ideas later on, whereas other groups did not receive this instruction. It appeared that idea sharing was stimulating: Groups that could read each other's ideas were more productive than groups that could not. However, this stimulating effect only occurred when group members expected that they would later be tested for recall. This shows that the ideas of others can be stimulating, but only if they are attended to properly.

In one of our own studies, we found more direct evidence for the accessibility principle (Nijstad et al., 2002). We had individual participants generate ideas on how to help protect the environment at computer terminals. There were three conditions. In two of these conditions, participants were shown ideas of others on their monitors, which were randomly drawn from previously prepared files. One of these files consisted of ideas that came from two different semantic categories (e.g., energy conservation and water conservation), and this file was used in Condition 1. In Condition 2, participants were shown ideas that came from a wide range of different categories (we used 34 categories). In a final control condition, participants were not shown ideas of others. According to the accessibility principle, ideas of others should make related knowledge more accessible in memory; as a consequence, participants should generate ideas that are semantically similar to those shown at their monitors. This was indeed what we found. Participants in both conditions were more productive than those in the control condition. However, this was due to two different processes. Participants who were shown ideas from just two categories generated many ideas in these two categories, and were therefore more productive. In contrast, those who were shown ideas from 34 categories used more categories, and this increased diversity of ideas was responsible for their productivity gains relative to the control condition.

The accessibility principle, however, does not imply that attending to information or ideas suggested by others is always stimulating. To the contrary, attending to others can even have detrimental effects on creativity. Smith, Ward, and Schumacher (1993) asked people to draw alien species and design new toys. Some of their participants were shown a few examples before they started drawing. These examples had various features in common; all the example toys, for instance, involved a ball, an electronic device, and a high level of physical activity. Those participants who had seen the examples were much more likely to copy these features in their own drawings than those who had not seen these examples. This was even true when participants were explicitly instructed to design toys that were different from the example toys. Apparently, the features of the example toys were accessible in memory and were difficult to reject or neglect when designing one's own toys.

Similar effects have been found in brainstorming studies. Ziegler, Diehl, and Zijlstra (2000) compared electronic brainstorming groups who could and could not read each other's ideas on their screens. They found that groups in which idea sharing was possible used fewer semantic categories of ideas than groups in which this was not possible. In other words, the ideas of the sharing groups were more similar to each other than the ideas of the other groups—a finding they labeled *cognitive uniformity*. Similar findings have been obtained in verbally interacting groups, where interacting groups tend to survey fewer categories than nominal groups (Larey & Paulus, 1999). However, the previously described study by Diehl (1991) on group diversity suggests that this uniformity effect may only occur in relatively homogenous groups: Heterogeneous groups used more categories than did the homogenous groups.

In summary, ideas suggested by others sometimes are stimulating and make certain ideas accessible that would otherwise not be generated. However, increased accessibility of certain ideas or other knowledge may also lead to conformity effects or cognitive uniformity, but this seems less true in diverse groups. We now turn to our final principle, which is concerned with combining insights and ideas into a collective group response.

The Effective Convergence Principle

Group creativity involves both divergent and convergent processes. Idea generation is a divergent process: It is advisable to generate many ideas and not stop before one has generated a number of high-quality solutions. However, eventually a time should come when one stops generating ideas and start selecting the most promising solutions. This is a convergent process, in which agreement has to be reached on which ideas to further pursue. The quality and creativity of the final group response depends on the quality of this selection process. The effective convergence principle states groups will only be creative when they eventually converge on their best ideas (Arrow 4 in Fig. 8.1). At least two questions are relevant. When do groups end the divergent stage and switch to convergent idea selection? What determines the effectiveness of the convergent stage of the process?

At some point in time, groups should stop generating ideas and move on to the next phase of problem solving. Ideally, one should not stop generating ideas before a number of high-quality solutions have been found. However, how does one know that one has generated a sufficient number of high-quality ideas? In one of our papers (Nijstad et al., 1999), we therefore considered this question: "How do people know when to stop?" We argued that people can stop for a number of reasons. They may stop when they feel they have generated a sufficient number of high-quality ideas and are satisfied with their performance (satisfaction stop rule). They may also stop when they are getting bored with idea generation (enjoyment stop rule), or when they are running out of ideas and do not expect to generate many additional ideas (expectancy stop rule). We further argued that the specific stop rule people apply has consequences for how long they persist in the activity of idea generation.

Suppose that people apply the enjoyment rule and stop when they are getting bored with idea generation. In that case, we would expect groups to continue longer than individuals because group members usually enjoy themselves more than individuals (e.g., Diehl & Stroebe, 1987). However, if people apply the satisfaction rule, groups may be less persistent than individuals. Usually, group members are more satisfied with their performance than individuals (Paulus et al., 1993; Stroebe et al., 1992), and presumably they will reach satisfactory levels of performance before individuals do and thus stop earlier (and perhaps even prematurely). Finally, if people apply the expectancy rule, we predict groups to be more persistent than individuals. Periods of silence, in which no ideas are being generated, will be less prevalent for groups than for a single individual because groups are more productive in absolute numbers of ideas (although not per person). Periods of silence are a salient indicator of expectancy; when periods of silence become more prevalent, this might lead to the desire to end the session. This happens sooner for individuals than for groups and sooner for smaller than for larger groups.

Therefore, in a study we manipulated group size and had individuals, dyads, and four- and six-person groups brainstorm without externally imposed time constraints (Nijstad et al., 1999). We found that persistence increased linearly with group size, and groups were able to compensate part of their usual productivity loss by being more persistent (although six-person groups still showed a significant productivity loss when compared with six individuals). This result is consistent with the expectancy stop rule, as were the results of a postexperimental questionnaire. Most people (some 80%)—both those who had worked individually and those who had worked in a group—indicated that they had stopped because they were running out of ideas. Apparently they did not stop because they thought they had generated a sufficient number of high-quality ideas, but rather because they were unable to come up with new ideas.

Higher levels of persistence imply that more ideas will be available for later selection and development. Because the number of ideas and the number of good ideas therein are usually strongly correlated (e.g., Diehl & Stroebe, 1987), one would also expect more good ideas to be available for selection. However, does the availability of more ideas also lead to a higher quality solution when group members must choose some of their ideas for further development? We considered this question in another study, in which nominal groups (consisting of three individuals who worked alone) and interactive groups of three were compared (Rietzschel et al., 2003). These participants first had to generate ideas, either alone or in a group, and then select the best four ideas for further development. People who had worked in groups selected four ideas as a group, and people who worked alone selected four ideas each. The number of ideas of each (nominal or interactive) group was counted, and all ideas were rated on two dimensions of idea quality, which were originality and feasibility. High-quality ideas were those that were rated as high on both dimensions (Amabile, 1983).

We found the usual productivity loss: Interacting groups produced only half as many ideas as our nominal groups. In line with previous results, we also found that nominal groups had produced more high-quality ideas than had interacting groups. Thus, after the brainstorming and before selection, nominal groups had more high-quality ideas available to them than did interacting groups. However, the nominal groups lost this advantage after the selection phase: Neither the average originality nor the average feasibility of the selected ideas differed between nominal and interactive groups. We further found, much to our surprise, that people were actually not very good in selecting their best ideas. The average originality and feasibility of the chosen ideas was not higher than the average originality and feasibility of the produced ideas, although higher quality ideas were available.

This study thus shows that availability of good ideas is not enough. Instead an effective selection process is necessary, as our effective convergence principle implies. Apparently, the choice process of groups has not been optimal, which prevented groups from reaching their potential creativity. It would be interesting to investigate what factors may improve the selection process and lead to a higher quality group response. We suspect that groups reached a premature consensus, instead of discussing all the ideas that were available. Furthermore, they had no explicit selection criteria, so they might have chosen ideas they thought would work best, and they paid no attention to originality or feasibility of ideas. It might therefore be helpful to have explicit selection criteria and encourage groups to really consider all their ideas before making a final choice. Alternatively, one can give the set of ideas generated by one group to another group and have other people make the choice. This might prevent a premature consensus on the most dominant (but not necessarily the best) ideas.

CONCLUSION: WHEN TO USE GROUPS?

In this chapter, we argued that groups have the potential to be creative (our first principle of group creativity) because groups have more resources at their disposal than individuals. Contrary to some of the literature on creative genius, where it is argued that isolation and individual reflection is key to creative achievement (Ochse, 1990), we believe that collaboration can at times stimulate creativity. Relatively recent research has shown that group members can mutually stimulate each other and groups can be more creative than individuals (e.g., Dugosh et al., 2000; Nijstad et al., 2002; Paulus & Yang, 2000). Further, open debates and authentic dissent within groups can have beneficial effects on creativity (Nemeth & Nemeth-Brown, 2003), and diverse groups in particular have creative potential (e.g., Dunbar, 1995; Milliken et al., 2003).

Principle 1 was concerned with creative potential, whereas Principles 2, 3, and 4 deal with the conditions under which creative potential is or is not realized. Unfortunately, much of the research evidence we cited suggests that groups often do not reach their creative potential. First, groups suffer from production blocking (Diehl & Stroebe, 1987), lack of trust (Edmondson, 1999), and inadequate sharing of unique information (Stasser & Titus, 1995). According to our effective sharing principle, this limits their creativity. Second, according to our accessibility principle, idea sharing can lead to cognitive stimulation, but also to cognitive uniformity (Ziegler et al., 2000) and conformity (e.g., Smith et al., 1993; for a more extensive discussion of this issue, see Smith, Gerkens, Shah, & Vargas-Hernandez, chap. 1, this volume). Third, the effective convergence principle suggests that groups sometimes perform suboptimally when it comes to selecting their best ideas for further development (Rietzschel et al., 2003). The important question, at least from a practical point of view, is thus: How can these negative effects be prevented while maintaining the creative potential of the group?

In the course of this chapter, we already suggested a number of solutions. Effective sharing of ideas can be achieved by using effective means of communication, such as brainwriting or electronic brainstorming, and by creating a group climate in which members feel psychologically safe and do not fear ridicule or rejection. Further, the group processing space can be used more effectively when group members have mutually recognized areas of expertise and an adequate division of labor (i.e., group members should perform the tasks they are good at). The right level of diversity seems to be essential to avoid cognitive uniformity and conformity: Group members who have different approaches to the same problem are less likely to get *stuck in a rut*. Finally, idea selection and implementation can probably be improved by carefully going through all the generated ideas and solutions and use explicitly defined criteria to judge each idea—although, due to lack of research on this topic, this advice is somewhat speculative. Other good advice on the issue of how to improve group creativity can be found in other chapters of this volume (see Paulus, Nakui, & Putman, chap. 4; Santanen, chap. 2; Smith et al., chap. 1; West et al., chap. 7).

Besides these remedies, we believe another important issue is that groups should be used in the right stages of the creative process. Thus, instead of focusing exclusively on the question of *whether* to use groups, we should focus more on the question of *when* to use groups (see Nijstad & De Dreu, 2002). We have argued that groups are fundamentally unsuited to perform certain activities. Groups have a limited processing space: Not all information and ideas can be shared, and because only one person usually contributes information and ideas at a time, it is often inefficient to perform certain activities in a group. Indeed the historian Alfred Whitney Griswold (1906–1963) hit the nail on the head when he rhetorically asked: "Could Hamlet have been written by a committee, or the Mona Lisa painted by a club? Could the New Testament have been composed as a conference report?" Sometimes work should not be performed by groups, but instead left to individuals (i.e., an adequate division of labor is necessary). However, at times, it may be effective to use groups in the creative process.

Unfortunately, the question of when groups can be used most effectively in the creative process is unanswered. However, two possibilities suggest themselves. First, one may turn to a group when stuck in a rut—that is, when one has worked on a problem for some length of time but does not see a solution. Dunbar's (1995) studies of teams of microbiologists suggest that this is exactly what these teams do. In their weekly lab meetings, these teams devoted most of their time to unexpected and unexplained results. Moreover, at several occasions, Dunbar observed that solutions to problems arose in these meetings: Team members came to the meeting with a problem they were unable to solve, and this problem was solved during discussion. At another level, one may also get stuck: People may simply give up when they have struggled for some time and were unable to solve a problem. Our studies of brainstorming persistence (Nijstad et al., 1999) indicate that one advantage of group work is that people can keep each other going. If one group member is running out of ideas, another may still have some, and this indicates to the first that more ideas are still possible.

Second, some evidence suggests that groups may not be better when it comes to idea generation, but perhaps are better when it comes to idea selection or implementation. Although groups in general do not perform at an optimal level when making decisions, they do perform better than the average individual (e.g., McGrath, 1984). Further, one might expect that the implementation of ideas, which arguably is part of the creative process, is facilitated when the people who are affected participated in decision making (cf. De Dreu & West, 2001).

To conclude, we argue that group creativity is possible and that collaboration can stimulate creativity. However, to optimally use the creative potential of groups, groups should be composed in the right way, use effective procedures, and be used in the right stages of the creative process. Only then may groups come close to their potential.

ACKNOWLEDGMENTS

Financial support for this research was provided by the Netherlands Organization for Scientific Research (NWO), grants 575-31.007 and 410-21-010, and is gratefully acknowledged.

REFERENCES

Amabile, T. M. (1983). *Social psychology of creativity.* New York: Springer-Verlag.

Bennis, W., & Biederman, W. P. (1997). *Organizing genius: The secrets of creative collaboration.* Reading, MA: Addison Wesley.

Camacho, L. M., & Paulus, P. B. (1995). The role of social anxiousness in group brainstorming. *Journal of Personality and Social Psychology, 68,* 1071–1080.

Davis, J. H. (1973). Group decisions and social interaction: A theory of social decision schemes. *Psychological Review, 80,* 97–125.

De Dreu, C. K. W., & West, M. A. (2001). Minority dissent and team innovation: The importance of participation in decision making. *Journal of Applied Psychology, 86,* 1191–1201.

Dennis, A. R., & Valacich, J. S. (1993). Computer brainstorms: More heads are better than one. *Journal of Applied Psychology, 78,* 531–537.

Diehl, M. (1991). *Kollektive Kreativität: Zur Quantität und Qualität der Ideenproduktion in Kleingruppen* [Collective creativity: On the quantity and quality of idea production in small groups]. Habilitation, University of Tübingen.

Diehl, M., & Stroebe, W. (1987). Productivity loss in brainstorming groups: Toward the solution of a riddle. *Journal of Personality and Social Psychology, 53,* 497–509.

Diehl, M., & Stroebe, W. (1991). Productivity loss in idea-generating groups: Tracking down the blocking effect. *Journal of Personality and Social Psychology, 61,* 392–403.

Dugosh, K. L., Paulus, P. B., Roland, E. J., & Yang, H. C. (2000). Cognitive stimulation in brainstorming. *Journal of Personality and Social Psychology, 79,* 722–735.

Dunbar, K. (1995). How scientists really reason: Scientific reasoning in real-world laboratories. In R. J. Sternberg & J. E. Davidson (Eds.), *The nature of insight* (pp. 365–395). Cambridge, MA: MIT Press.

Edmondson, A. (1999). Psychological safety and learning behavior in work teams. *Administrative Science Quarterly, 44,* 350–383.

Gallupe, R. B., Bastianutti, L. M., & Cooper, W. H. (1991). Unblocking brainstorms. *Journal of Applied Psychology, 76,* 137–142.

Gallupe, R. B., Cooper, W. H., Grisé, M. L., & Bastianutti, L. M. (1994). Blocking electronic brainstorms. *Journal of Applied Psychology, 79,* 77–86.

Galton, F. (1869). *Hereditary genius: An inquiry into its laws and consequences.* London: Macmillan.

Hinsz, V. B., Tindale, R. S., & Vollrath, D. A. (1997). The emerging conceptualization of groups as information processors. *Psychological Bulletin, 121,* 43–64.

Larey, T. S., & Paulus, P. B. (1999). Group preference and convergent tendencies in small groups: A content analysis of group brainstorming performance. *Creativity Research Journal,* *12,* 175–184.

Lawler, E. E., Mohrman, S. A., & Ledford, G. E. (1995). *Creating high performance organizations: Practices and results of employee involvement and total quality management in Fortune 1000 companies.* San Francisco: Jossey-Bass.

Levine, J. M., Choi, H. S., & Moreland, R. L. (2003). Newcomer innovation in work teams. In P. B. Paulus & B. A. Nijstad (Eds.), *Group creativity: Innovation through collaboration* (pp. 202–224). New York: Oxford University Press.

Liang, D. W., Moreland, R., & Argote, L. (1995). Group versus individual training and group performance: The mediating role of transactive memory. *Personality and Social Psychology Bulletin,* *21,* 384–393.

McGrath, J. E. (1984). *Groups: Interaction and performance.* Englewood Cliffs: Prentice-Hall.

Milliken, F. J., Bartel, C. A., & Kurtzberg, T. R. (2003). Diversity and creativity in work groups: A dynamic perspective on the affective and cognitive processes that link diversity and performance. In P. B. Paulus & B. A. Nijstad (Eds.), *Group creativity: Innovation through collaboration* (pp. 32–62). New York: Oxford University Press.

Milliken, F. J., & Martins, L. (1996). Searching for common threads: Understanding the multiple effects of diversity in organizational groups. *Academy of Management Review,* *21,* 402–433.

Mullen, B., Johnson, C., & Salas, E. (1991). Productivity loss in brainstorming groups: A meta-analytic integration. *Basic and Applied Social Psychology,* *12,* 3–24.

Mumford, M. D., & Gustafson, S. G. (1988). Creativity syndrome: Integration, application, and innovation. *Psychological Bulletin,* *103,* 27–43.

Nemeth, C. J. (1986). Differential contributions of majority and minority influence. *Psychological Review,* *93,* 23–32.

Nemeth, C. J., & Nemeth-Brown, B. (2003). Better than individuals? The potential benefits of dissent and diversity for group creativity. In P. B. Paulus & B. A. Nijstad (Eds.), *Group creativity: Innovation through collaboration* (pp. 63–84). New York: Oxford University Press.

Nijstad, B. A., & De Dreu, C. K. W. (2002). Creativity and group innovation. *Applied Psychology: An International Review,* *51,* 400–406.

Nijstad, B. A., Diehl, M., & Stroebe, W. (2003). Cognitive stimulation and interference in idea generating groups. In P. B. Paulus & B. A. Nijstad (Eds.), *Group creativity: Innovation through collaboration* (pp. 137–159). New York: Oxford University Press.

Nijstad, B. A., Stroebe, W., & Lodewijkx, H. F. M. (1999). Persistence of brainstorming groups: How do people know when to stop? *Journal of Experimental Social Psychology,* *35,* 165–185.

Nijstad, B. A., Stroebe, W., & Lodewijkx, H. F. M. (2002). Cognitive stimulation and interference in groups: Exposure effects in an idea generation task. *Journal of Experimental Social Psychology,* *38,* 535–544.

Nijstad, B. A., Stroebe, W., & Lodewijkx, H. F. M. (2003). Production blocking and idea generation: Does blocking interfere with cognitive processes? *Journal of Experimental Social Psychology,* *39,* 531–548.

Ochse, R. (1990). *Before the gates of excellence: The determinants of creative genius.* New York: Cambridge.

Osborn, A. F. (1957). *Applied imagination* (2nd ed.). New York: Scribner.

Parnes, S. J., & Meadow, A. (1959). Effects of "brainstorming" instructions on creative problem solving by trained and untrained subjects. *Journal of Educational Psychology,* *50,* 171–176.

Paulus, P. B., & Dzindolet, M. T. (1993). Social influence processes in group brainstorming. *Journal of Personality and Social Psychology,* *64,* 575–586.

Paulus, P. B., Dzindolet, M. T., Poletes, G., & Camacho, L. M. (1993). Perceptions of performance in group brainstorming: The illusion of group productivity. *Personality and Social Psychology Bulletin,* *19,* 78–89.

Paulus, P. B., & Yang, H. C. (2000). Idea generation in groups: A basis for creativity in organizations. *Organizational Behavior and Human Decision Processes, 82,* 76–87.

Rietzschel, E. F., Nijstad, B. A., & Stroebe, W. (2003). Productiviteit is niet genoeg: Een vergelijking van groepen en individuen bij de productie en selectie van ideeën [Productivity is not enough: A comparison of individuals and groups at the production and selection of ideas]. In E. van Dijk, E. Kluwer, & D. Wigboldus (Eds.), *Jaarboek sociale psychologie* (pp. 255–263). Delft: Eburon.

Simonton, D. K. (2003). Creative cultures, nations, and civilizations: Strategies and results. In P. B. Paulus & B. A. Nijstad (Eds.), *Group creativity: Innovation through collaboration* (pp. 304–325). New York: Oxford University Press.

Smith, S. M., Ward, T. B., & Schumacher, J. S. (1993). Constraining effects of examples in a creative generation task. *Memory & Cognition, 21,* 837–845.

Stasser, G., & Birchmeier, Z. (2003). Group creativity and collective choice. In P. B. Paulus & B. A. Nijstad (Eds.), *Group creativity: Innovation through collaboration* (pp. 85–109). New York: Oxford University Press.

Stasser, G., & Titus, W. (1985). Pooling of unshared information in group decision making: Biased information sampling during discussion. *Journal of Personality and Social Psychology, 48,* 1467–1478.

Steiner, I. D. (1972). *Group process and productivity.* New York: Academic Press.

Stewart, D. D., & Stasser, G. (1995). Expert role assignment and information sampling during collective recall and decision making. *Journal of Personality and Social Psychology, 69,* 619–628.

Stroebe, W., & Diehl, M. (1994). Why groups are less effective than their members: On productivity losses in idea-generating groups. In W. Stroebe & M. Hewstone (Eds.), *European review of social psychology* (Vol. 5, pp. 271–303). London: Wiley.

Stroebe, W., Diehl, M., & Abakoumkin, G. (1992). The illusion of group effectivity. *Personality and Social Psychology Bulletin, 18,* 643–650.

Taylor, D. W., Berry, P. C., & Block, C. H. (1958). Does group participation when brainstorming facilitate or inhibit creative thinking? *Administrative Science Quarterly, 3,* 23–47.

Tulving, E., & Pearlstone, Z. (1966). Availability versus accessibility of information in memory for words. *Journal of Verbal Learning and Verbal Behavior, 5,* 381–391.

Valacich, J. S., Wheeler, B. C., Mennecke, B. E., & Wachter, R. (1995). The effects of numerical and logical group size on computer-mediated idea generation. *Organizational Behavior and Human Decision Processes, 62,* 318–329.

Wegner, D. M. (1986). Transactive memory: A contemporary analysis of the group mind. In B. Mullen & G. R. Goethals (Eds.), *Theories of group behavior* (pp. 185–205). New York: Springer-Verlag.

Williams, K. Y., & O'Reilly, C. A. III (1998). Demography and diversity in organizations: A review of 40 years of research. *Research in Organizational Behavior, 20,* 77–140.

Ziegler, R., Diehl, M., & Zijlstra, G. (2000). Idea production in nominal and virtual groups: Does computer-mediated communication improve group brainstorming? *Group Processes and Intergroup Relations, 3,* 141–158.

Part III

ORGANIZATIONAL INFLUENCES OF CREATIVITY AND INNOVATION

Chapter 9

Begging, Borrowing, and Building on Ideas From the Outside to Create Pulsed Innovation Inside Teams

Deborah Ancona
Henrik Bresman
Massachusetts Institute of Technology

The "kiddie corps" team at Microsoft worked long and hard (*Newsweek*, February 24, 2003) to come up with a new software product called *three degrees*. Tammy Savage and her team realized that Microsoft was not meeting the needs of the 13 to 24 set and came up with some ideas. Selling these to the top brass was not easy. Bill Gates was not that interested, but finally another top manager gave them his support. The team brought a set of college students together and asked them to work on a business plan—not because they were interested in the plan, but because they were interested in how they used technology as they worked together. After a week they understood a lot more. Thus began the development and production of three degrees. The team got a new space and many new members. They looked around to find out how products had been developed before, borrowed lots of ideas from others, and built on what they learned. They worked through many technical glitches and internal disagreements. Yet in the end, they brought the product to market.

Will it be successful? It will take some time to tell. What is clear is that this was an innovative team. *Innovation* here means not only coming up with a new idea for a new market, but also the ability to win support for the idea, refine the idea through interaction with others, and actually implement the idea in an organizational context. Innovation here is about creating new products, services, or processes and getting them accepted and implemented within the organization (cf. Burns & Stalker, 1961). An innovative team within an organization is like a small entrepreneurial venture, build-

183

ing something new within the corporation. Although the promise of innovation is often present, in our own work we have seen many teams fail. We believe that this failure is due to a reliance on outdated models of team innovation and performance.

We argue that a team like kiddie corps is able to be innovative not just because of creative internal brainstorming, but also because of its ability to influence top management, use external ties, maintain a flexible structure, borrow and build on the ideas of others, and operate in synchrony with the organization and customer. In this chapter, we build on three streams of research that have been part of our own quest to learn how to create and maintain innovative teams.

In the first stage, small-group theory had two different approaches as to how to help teams be more innovative. One stream of research focused inside the team's boundaries at different processes and techniques aimed at improving the creativity of the team. Here teams were designed to bring different orientations together—functional backgrounds, industry experience, academic disciplines—and to structure their interaction so as to generate many new ideas and divergent thinking (Nemeth, 1994; Sutton & Hargadon, 1996). A second stream focused on team member outreach beyond the team to bring in technical information or coordinate with interdependent groups (Hansen, 1999; Katz, 1982; Tushman, 1977, 1979). This external perspective also moved beyond technical information and task coordination to include scouting for market and organizational information, and lobbying upper management for legitimacy and resources (Ancona & Caldwell, 1992).

A second stage of research in articulating the design of an innovative team has come in the form of the X-team. This entrepreneurial, adaptive team (Ancona, Bresman, & Kaufer, 2002) combines the internal and external perspectives, and considers issues of implementation and the need to change the form of teams across stages of the task.

Beyond the X-team, we introduce a third emerging stage of research on innovation in teams. Although the X-team is a rather novel concept, we argue that our understanding of team innovation can be further enhanced by focusing on the roles of vicarious learning (Bandura, 1977; Bresman, 2004) and temporal design that facilitates pulsed entrepreneurship and temporal coordination across teams (Ancona & Waller, 2003). A major hypothesis here, which has inspired the title of this chapter, is that innovative teams need to go beyond their boundaries to beg, borrow, and build on ideas, key routines, knowledge about networks, and stories of failure from other teams and individuals that have the experience of completing similar tasks in the past. They then have to apply these lessons in ingenious ways to be successful.

Furthermore, firms need to manage this begging, borrowing, and building among teams by making it rhythmic. By *rhythmic* we mean that teams need to manage the timing of their activities so as to entrain or move in sync with key cycles of the firm, such as the fiscal year or product development cycle. When multiple teams follow the same temporal rhythm, the firm can take advantage of increased coordination across teams and pulsed innovation. Here all teams stop work at the same time. Management then evaluates existing work and considers all new ideas. Decisions are made about which projects to stop and which new ideas to implement. Resources and personnel are reallocated, and then teams all go back to work taking into account changes that need to be implemented. This work continues until the next pause signaling another pulse of innovation. When that temporal rhythm is also in sync with external customer and technology cycles, performance can be enhanced even more. We now move on to discuss the three stages of research on innovation in teams in more detail.

STAGE 1: TWO STREAMS OF RESEARCH FOR INNOVATIVE TEAMS

Two streams of research have dominated the literature. The first examines how team composition and internal team processes can improve the creativity of the team (e.g., West, 1994). On the team composition end, research suggests that increasing the diversity of team membership can improve the number and type of innovative ideas coming into the team (Jackson, 1992). Similarly, changes in team composition can spur creativity (Choi & Thompson, chap. 5, this volume).

It has been shown that diversity of functional and disciplinary backgrounds brings different *thought worlds* together in the team, offering different ways to view the situation and problem at hand (Dougherty, 1992). Creating teams with members from varying disciplines and industry backgrounds also enables the team to borrow ideas from one context and apply them to another (Hargadon & Sutton, 1997). For example, the Specialized Water Bottle, designed by the IDEO product development consulting company, used a technology from medical devices to create the valve that allows people to easily open and close the bottle. Structural diversity (Cummings, 2004), whereby members represent different organizational affiliations, roles, or positions, can also expose the team to unique sources of knowledge. In general, the more heterogeneous the team, the more likely the team is to engage in divergent thinking—taking the problem in many possible directions and not blindly following the majority—rather than convergent thinking—moving in one direction as chosen by the majority (Guilford, 1967; Nemeth & Kwan, 1987).

Yet heterogeneous composition is not enough to guarantee innovation. Indeed research has shown that greater heterogeneity can actually make it more difficult for a team to consolidate information and avoid negative conflict (Jehn, 1997). Thus, another part of the internal emphasis of teams is a focus on team process. Here researchers have looked at ways that team members can work together to improve innovation. Several techniques have been developed to help teams generate many ideas and move from idea generation to choice. This would include brainstorming (Osborn, 1957; Paulus & Dzindolet, 1993; Paulus et al., 2002), the nominal group technique, and the Delphi technique. Many of these techniques get members to write down their ideas individually, share and build on other people's ideas, and then choose (through a variety of techniques) among the ideas.

Other process interventions call for (a) creating an open climate to encourage minority opinion and thus increase the amount of divergent thinking in a team (Nemeth, 1994), (b) getting a team to use analogical reasoning as they learn to use knowledge from one experience to gain insights on a new problem, and (c) applying dimension extension, a structured way to design new products by breaking the product down into its basic dimension and thinking of new alternatives for each one and then recombining the possibilities to create new product ideas. Many different process interventions exist and all help the team to think in new and different ways and generate many new ideas.

The second stream of research looks not at how the team is organized internally, but at how members manage across the team boundaries. In particular, those studying innovation have focused on the transfer of technical information across the team boundaries (Aldrich & Herker, 1977; Allen, 1984; Katz & Tushman, 1979). These researchers have found that when tasks are highly uncertain and complex, more boundary activity is necessary to have innovative and effective teams.

More recently, the emphasis has moved to examine how teams can effectively coordinate and link to other groups. In particular, Hansen (1999) showed that both strong and weak ties to outside groups can help a team bring in different types of knowledge. Still another direction for this external approach came from Ancona and Caldwell (1992), who demonstrated that teams needed to move beyond the transfer of technical information and use external boundary activity to link to the information, task, and power structures within the firm to be innovative. Thus, teams need to bring in technical information; coordinate with other groups; get information from disparate areas to learn more about the market, technology, and the customer; and get the support of top management. In general, this work has supported the external perspective, which argues that teams are more innovative to the extent that they have extensive interactions with other parts of the organization and task environment.

Thus, this first stage of research illustrates the need for innovative teams to have diverse membership and be able to engage in team processes that focus that membership on divergent thinking and idea generation. It also focuses on the need for teams to engage in extensive external boundary spanning to coordinate with other teams, being in technical information, and bring in the support from top management. Yet the past decade has seen changes in the demands on innovative teams that have simultaneously put demands on group theory to go beyond Stage 1.

STAGE 2: THE X-TEAM

The challenges on innovative teams in organizations have broadened in the past decade (Brown & Eisenhardt, 1995). Five trends seem to be in evidence. First, team tasks are more interdependent with other teams' tasks (Ancona, Kochan, Scully, Van Maanen, & Westney, 1999). The new product is now part of a family of products, and all new products must fit into top management's new strategic direction. Second, teams are not necessarily given a task to perform; they are required to be more entrepreneurial and come up with ideas about what to do themselves (Edmondson, 1999). Part of the entrepreneurial process is to *sell* your ideas to top management and get funding and support. Third, team size is also increasing as more expertise is needed to solve complex problems (Staudenmayer, Tripsas, & Tucci, 2000). With increased size comes the need for greater coordination within the team.

Fourth, there is a need for teams to work faster and take on multiple tasks across the value chain (Brown & Eisenhardt, 1997). Thus, not only are teams designing new products, they are also taking them through the manufacturing stage. Not only are teams coming up with new ideas, they need to implement those ideas. The challenge for teams under this scenario is that they need to shift composition, task, structure, and process more often and to a greater degree than before. Finally, much of the expertise and information that the team needs exists outside of the team boundaries and often outside of the organization (Chesbrough, 2003). For some teams, even their core technologies come from outside the firm (Bresman, 2004).

These changes mean that even more is required of innovative teams, both in terms of internal process and external outreach. In addition, the team needs a more flexible structure that will enable it to shift its composition and process as it moves across various tasks and levels of interdependence with other groups. To capture these changes, the two streams of Stage 1 need to be integrated and pushed forward. Enter the X-team.

In our research on teams, we found that a particular kind of team (characterized by external orientation, adaptability, and entrepreneurship) is seeing positive results across a wide variety of innovation-driven functions and industries. So named because of the alliteration across key characteris-

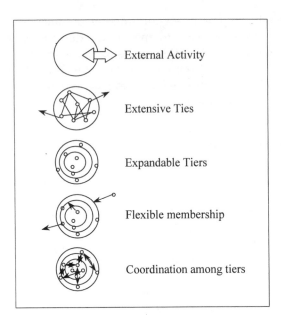

FIG. 9.1.   X-team components.

tics, X-teams share these five hallmarks: external activity, extensive ties, expandable tiers, flexible membership, and mechanisms for execution (see Fig. 9.1).

External Activity

The first component of the X-team is members' external activity. Because teams are more interdependent with other teams than ever before, more entrepreneurial, and hence need to get buy-in and resources from top management and need to search broadly for ideas and expertise to be creative, X-teams maintain high levels of external activity throughout their lives. This external activity is broad in its type and reach. As noted in prior research (Ancona & Caldwell, 1992), ambassadorial, scouting, and task coordinator activity are key. Again the difference from prior research is that external activity now seems to be needed across all phases of the team task and to a higher degree than before (Ancona, Bresman, & Kaufer, 2002).

Ambassadorial activity is aimed at managing upward—that is, marketing the project and team to the company power structure, maintaining the team's reputation, lobbying for resources, and keeping track of allies and competitors. Ambassadorial activity helps the team link its work to key strategic initiatives, and to alert team members to shifting organizational strategies and organizational upheaval.

Scouting activity helps a team gather information located throughout the company and the industry. It involves lateral and downward searches through the organization to understand who has knowledge and expertise. It also means investigating markets, new technologies, and competitor activities. Scouting activity brings in new perspectives that are critical to the creative process.

Task-coordinator activity is much more focused than scouting. It is for managing the lateral connections across functions and the interdependencies with other units. Team members negotiate with other groups, trade their services, and get feedback on how well their work meets expectations.

Extensive Ties

To engage in such high levels of external activity, team members need to have extensive ties with outsiders. In fact it has been argued that team composition may be best served by finding members who have the most appropriate set of ties needed for the task at hand (Ancona & Caldwell, 1998). Because these ties need to be more far reaching than ever before and need to cover all kinds of information transfer, multiple kinds of ties are needed in X-teams. Using Granovetter's (1973) terminology, *weak ties* (i.e., infrequent and distant relationships) are good for certain purposes—for instance, when teams need to round up handy knowledge and expertise within the company or the industry. In contrast, *strong ties* are good for purposes of transferring knowledge, particularly when this knowledge is complex in nature. As Hansen (1999) argued, "the two-way interaction afforded by strong ties is important for assimilating [complex] knowledge, because the recipient most likely does not acquire the knowledge completely during the first interaction but needs multiple opportunities to assimilate it" (p. 88).

Expandable Tiers

How then is a team structured to deal with dense ties and external interactions? Furthermore, how is a team structured as it gets larger and needs to adapt to different tasks (e.g., product design vs. building the product)? Our research shows that X-teams manage by operating through a flexible structure made up of three distinct tiers that create differentiated types of membership—the core tier, operational tier, and outernet tier—and that members may perform duties within more than one tier. In contrast to most small-group theory, which stresses one team boundary between the team and its external environment (Alderfer, 1976), the X-team illustrates a new structure with multiple boundaries and multiple forms of team membership (Ancona, Bresman, & Kaufer, 2002).

The core of the X-team is often, but not always, present at the start of the team. Core members carry the team's history and identity. While coordinating the multiple parts of the team, they create the team strategy and make key decisions. The core is not to be confused with a management level, however. In fact core members frequently work beside other members of equal or higher rank and serve on other teams as operational or outernet members.

The team's operational members do the ongoing work; they get the work done. Often they make key decisions, but are focused on one part of the task while leaving oversight to the core.

Outernet members often join the team to handle some task that is separable from ongoing work. They may be part-time or part-cycle members, tied barely at all to one another, but strongly to the operational or core members. They bring specialized expertise, and different individuals may participate in the outer net as the team task changes. For example, when a team of authors (the core) and the case writers who worked with them (operational members) ran out of material, the core members sought out authors who had other forms of expertise (net members) to write specific modules for the new book. These outernet members are often the source of new ways of thinking that spurs innovation in the team.

Flexible Membership

How do teams get lots of heterogeneous members to brainstorm ideas at the start of a project and then shift into implementation mode where a more homogenous team with different skills is needed? X-team membership is fluid. People may move in and out of the team during its life or move across layers. Some layers are more flexible than others, however, and outernet membership tends to be the most fluid. In contrast to most group theory that assumes a constant team membership and the ability of all members to recognize one another (Alderfer, 1976), X-teams have fluid membership, variable group size, and members of the team who may not know each other.

Mechanisms for Execution

An increasing focus on the external context makes it a challenge to achieve effective internal coordination. We have found three different coordination mechanisms particularly useful in this context: integrative meetings, transparent decision making, and scheduling tools such as shared timelines. First, through integrative meetings, team members share the external information each has obtained. That helps keep everyone informed, but it also helps team members representing different disciplines adapt their own work according to the expertise of others and pull off an often difficult integration. For example, we know of a pharmaceutical drug development team that worked on a new and innovative drug involving a kind of biology that few of the team members had ever encountered before. By integrating the specialized pieces of knowledge and external networks that each of the members possessed in the forum of regular meetings, this team was able to produce a coherent knowledge base and orchestrate a process resulting in an approval for human testing.

Second, transparent decision making, which keeps people informed about the reasons behind choices, is good for nudging everyone in the same direction and maintaining motivation. The drug development team just mentioned provides an instructive example yet again. Because of the exceptionally differentiated bases of expertise in this team, opinions often differed, and some members had to be overruled. The team leader of this team made a point of being very clear about the basis for every controversial decision that he made while taking ample time to answer team members' questions. Not everyone was happy with the final decisions, but this openness prevented resentment from festering.

Finally, measures such as clearly communicated but flexible deadlines allow members to pace themselves and coordinate work with others. The just-in-time flexibility allows for deadline shifts and adjustments. If external circumstances change, then work changes and new deadlines are established. For example, in one product development team, different subgroups worked independently on various parts of a new computer. The subgroups were coordinated by a shared deadline by which everyone had to be finished. As it turned out, the customer decided he wanted fewer features for a lower price, and so the product was redesigned, new subgroups were formed, and new deadlines were put in place.

An important function of the coordination mechanisms described here is that they foster and leverage the team's "transactive memory system"—in short, this is the set of individual memory systems in the team in combination with the communication that takes place between individuals. First introduced by Wegner (1987), the notion of a team's transactive memory system has increasingly gained empirical support (Austin, 2003; Lewis, 2003). For example, Moreland (1999) found that team members who are trained together perform better than those who are trained apart. He attributed the performance differences to the fact that members trained together learned what other team members knew and, furthermore, that they learned how to communicate and draw on each others' skill sets. A well-functioning transactive memory system is particularly important in innovative teams because they heavily depend on their ability to draw on and integrate the diverse and nonredundant knowledge held by members. To build and make use of such a system, we have found that integrative team meetings in particular are important. Beyond the obvious benefits in terms of brainstorming, these meetings facilitate implementation in that they help team members from different disciplines to take each other's functional demands into consideration and integrate them into a coherent whole.

More important, the X-team components form a self-reinforcing system. To engage in high levels of external activity, team members bring to the table outside ties forged in past professional experience. To be responsive to new information and new coordination needs, X-teams have flexible membership and a structure featuring multiple tiers and roles. To handle information and multiple activities, they have coordination mechanisms and a strong core. The five components cannot work in isolation. They complement one another. Although small or new teams may not display all five hallmarks described here, fully developed X-teams usually do.

The X-team concept provides an overall structure for innovation in teams. It shows how teams can be organized to manage high levels of interdependence, be entrepreneurial, shift structures to move across phases of a task, and focus on implementation. It enables the team to find, integrate, and use divergent perspectives and information. Yet two empirical studies of teams have shown us that the X-team concept can be taken even further. One is an in-depth ethnographic study of six drug development teams in a large multinational pharmaceutical firm (Bresman, 2004). Another is a study of five teams studied over a 2-year period in the software industry (Ancona & Waller, 2003). Stage 3 introduces the concept of vicarious learning and temporal rhythms as processes that enable innovative teams to work faster and better by learning from others, and to better coordinate with other parts of the organization.

STAGE 3: VICARIOUS TEAM LEARNING AND TEMPORAL DESIGN

Vicarious Team Learning

Vicarious team learning is the process by which a team learns from the experiences of others outside the team, either by observing them or talking to them about their experiences (cf. individual level work by Bandura, 1977). This may sound similar to the scouting activity described earlier; vicarious team learning is a specialized form of scouting. Rather than focusing on scanning the environment for all kinds of technical and market knowledge needed to help complete a task, vicarious team learning typically concerns learning how to complete the task at hand in the absence of critical experience inside the team. Vicarious learning is scouting aimed at teams and team members already engaged in some aspect of the task at hand, and finding some way to profit from the knowledge that those experienced members have accrued.

Consider the case of the team in charge of the development of an aircraft at an aerospace company that we know. Facing intense competition and pressure to cut costs, the team was told by management to cut the assembly time for the aircraft by 30%. It was immediately clear to the team members that they had to radically rethink the entire assembly process. But where would they start? They had already taken the level of efficiency as far as their own experiences allowed. An internal process by trial and error was therefore not a realistic option. The notion of traditional scouting was not helpful either—after all, finding information about a particular technology is not useful unless one knows if and how the technology should be used. The only conceivable way for the team to meet its challenge was to learn vicariously from others who had gone through a similar process in the past. Hence, the team tracked down and learned from experienced people both inside and outside the firm. Specifically, the team in charge of a different aircraft program at the company and consortium members of the Lean Aerospace Initiative at MIT proved particularly helpful. Although the process involved considerable stress and frustration, in the end the team was able to meet its challenge. In this particular example, most of the vicarious learning pertained to knowledge about process—the process involved in streamlining aircraft assembly—but it may also involve content knowledge, and most often it involves a bit of both. Yet another important kind of knowledge in this context is knowledge about from whom a team may learn vicariously.

What does vicarious team learning look like? Although we have only started our investigation of this process, an inductive study that we recently completed provides some insights (Bresman, 2004). Specifically, the study involved a study of six teams in a large pharmaceutical firm charged with the task of identifying, evaluating, and acquiring a molecule from an outside source with the view to develop it into a marketable drug. More important, because the molecule was developed outside the team's own organization, the knowledge base on which it rested was external as well. In the absence of task-particular experiences of their own, we found that all these teams—albeit with varying degrees of success—engaged in vicarious team learning. The sources of this learning included independent consultants and even academics, but the most important source by far was members of teams that had completed similar tasks in the past.

We identified a number of different modalities by which these past experiences of others were applied to the task at hand. One such modality was what we refer to as *bypass application*, through which the team in essence was able to bypass learning a particular practice. For example, one team was able to use toxicology data from an experiment that another team had run in the past so it did not have to learn how to run the experiment. Another frequent occurrence was that of avoiding the repetition of past mistakes. This way teams could avoid learning that something was not worth learning, and thereby save time, but potentially also avoid more disruptive mistakes. An important prerequisite for bypass application is that the knowledge involved is modular. In other words, knowledge interdependency must be low enough for the team not to have to manage repercussions on other subtasks. Another modality we identified was what we refer to as *imitative application*, which involves copying a practice from the outside, but also some amount of adaptation to the context at hand. For example, after some adjustment and having spent some time learning how to operate it, one team was able to use a piece of equipment developed by a previous team. This saved them significant amounts of both money and time. In other examples, teams were able to extract lessons in everything from how to structure animal models to how to manage negotiations that could then be adapted and applied creatively and productively to their own tasks.

In summary, vicarious team learning allowed many of the teams in our study to avoid repeating mistakes, to figure out what does and does not work, to figure out where to go to find things out, to shortcut the process, and to start at a higher level of competence altogether. The knowledge involved in these vicarious learning processes may be know-how, but also knowing who knows what. Furthermore, it may be knowledge related to technology, but also process, and typically some component of both.

The notion of vicarious team learning adds to Stage 2. In particular, our research suggests that the concept of scouting as used in the X-team terminology needs to be broadened to encompass vicarious team learning. Referring back to the trends facing innovative teams that we outlined earlier, vicarious team learning is particularly well suited to address how teams manage the needs to work faster and to integrate critical expertise that exists only outside the team and still come up with new innovative solutions.

Temporal Design

Up to this point, we have emphasized how teams can become more innovative—learning to deal with new challenges through new modes of internal coordination and external outreach. Yet innovative teams still often suffer from several problems. One problem is that teams often get stuck in the early phase of idea generation and are unable to shift to implementation. March (1991) showed us that the same structures and processes that promote idea generation (exploration) are detrimental to implementation (exploitation). Indeed a study of new product development teams (Ancona & Caldwell, 1992) showed teams continuing to scan for new information and ideas beyond the point at which it was productive.

A second problem for innovative X-teams is how to coordinate with other parts of the organization. An X-team member might want to start working with another team, but the team is working on a top priority project and has no time. Similarly, an X-team core might want to add several engineers to a project only to find that they are working on another project and will not be available for several months.

A recent study of software development teams (Ancona & Waller, 2003) demonstrated how these problems could be dealt with through temporal design. Temporal design is the use of time and timing to organize work. In other words, managers could orchestrate when, how fast, and in conjunction with which other cycles work was done. In this study, all new product development teams in a particular business unit had to report their progress at a budgeting and review meeting that took place with top unit management every 4 months. The 4-month cycle acted as a deadline for teams to finish particular phases of work so that they could show progress and get continued support.

This cycle served several important functions for the teams and the organization in which they resided. First, this external nudge moved teams that otherwise would have been stuck in one phase of product development. The temporal trigger seemed to push teams into accelerated activity so they would be prepared for the review. After the review teams would receive feedback that would help them stop work or move on to the next phase of the project. Second, all teams had the same deadlines. Thus, all teams paused simultaneously in their work. This simultaneous temporal pause created a "temporal crossing point," during which different teams could share information and personnel could be moved around. Having all teams stopping simultaneously made them all open to change at the same time. Finally, this temporal trigger allowed the firm to engage in *pulsed innovation*. All new ideas could be considered simultaneously, facilitating comparisons (cf. Carter & West, 1998). Also ideas that were rejected could be killed, rather than lingering. Furthermore, when ideas were killed, resources in those teams could be redeployed immediately.

Thus, temporal design, in the form of a coordinated temporal (4-month) rhythm for all teams, facilitated innovation. In particular, it enables teams to be better able to handle their multiple interdependencies, encourages entrepreneurial activity (all new ideas would be considered on an ongoing basis), and helped teams shift from one phase of activity to another. From the perspective of the firm, there was improved coordination across teams, a mechanism to handle the flow of personnel to where they were most needed, and the ability to create ongoing innovation.

In this chapter, we outlined three stages of scientific inquiry that have enabled us to gain some insights into how to create and maintain innovative teams. This journey has led us from the first stage of two separate streams of research—one concentrating on internal processes and one focusing on external boundary spanning—to the second stage that integrates the two separate streams and pushes it further into a new form of team. This new team, the X-team, combines internal creativity with high levels of external activity. It shifts our definitions of *team* to include multiple boundaries and fluid membership. It takes an adaptive form that changes as the task shifts over time. As we have learned more about such teams, we have begun to enter a third stage—seeing new forms of external outreach, including vicarious learning, which can help teams learn more quickly and deeply. Furthermore, we have seen the importance of managing the team context through temporal design. Here the benefits of innovative teams are enhanced through pulsed entrepreneurship and simultaneous coordination.

We have only just begun the journey of understanding how teams really foster and maintain innovation. The objective of this chapter has been to provide a foundation of past research and a promising direction for future research in this exciting and important field of inquiry. Hopefully, by articulating three stages of research we fulfilled that objective. Now the question is what will be coming in Stage 4.

REFERENCES

Alderfer, C. P. (1976). Boundary relations and organizational diagnosis. In M. Meltzer & F. Wickert (Eds.), *Humanizing organizational behavior* (pp. 142–175). Springfield, IL: Charles C. Thomas.

Aldrich, H., & Herker, D. (1977, April). Boundary spanning roles and organization structure. *Academy of Management Review*, pp. 217–230.

Allen, T. J. (1984). *Managing the flow of technology: Technology transfer and the dissemination of technological information within the R&D organization.* Cambridge, MA: MIT Press.

Ancona, D. G., Bresman, H. M., & Kaufer, K. (2002). The comparative advantage of X-teams. *Sloan Management Review, 43*, 33–39.

Ancona, D. G., & Caldwell, D. F. (1992). Bridging the boundary: External activity and performance in organizational teams. *Administrative Science Quarterly, 37*, 634–665.

Ancona, D. G., & Caldwell, D. F. (1998). Rethinking team composition from the outside in. In D. H. Gruenfeld (Ed.), *Research on managing groups and teams* (pp. 21–37). Stamford, CT: JAI.

Ancona, D., Kochan, T., Scully, M., Van Maanen, J., & Westney, E. (1999). *Managing for the future: Organizational behavior and processes* (2nd ed.). South-Western College Publishing.

Ancona, D., & Waller, M. J. (2003). *The dance of entrainment: Temporally navigating through threat and opportunity.* Working paper.

Austin, J. R. (2003). Transactive memory in organizational groups: The effects of content, consensus, specialization, and accuracy on group performance. *Journal of Applied Psychology, 88*, 866–878.

Bandura, A. (1977). *Social learning theory.* Englewood Cliffs, NJ: Prentice-Hall.

Bresman, H. M. (2004). *Vicarious learning behavior and performance in organizational teams.* Paper presented at the Academy of Management Annual Meetings, New Orleans, LA.

Brown, S. L., & Eisenhardt, K. M. (1995). Product development: Past research, present findings and future directions. *Academy of Management Review, 20,* 343–378.

Brown, S. L., & Eisenhardt, K. M. (1997). The art of continuous change: Linking complexity theory and time-paced evolution in relentlessly shifting organizations. *Administrative Science Quarterly, 42,* 1–34.

Burns, T., & Stalker, G. M. (1961). *The management of innovation.* London: Tavistock.

Carter, S. M., & West, M. A. (1998). Reflexivity, effectiveness and mental health in BBC-TV production teams. *Small Group Research, 29,* 583–601.

Chesbrough, H. W. (2003). Thriving in the era of open innovation. *Sloan Management Review, 44,* 35–41.

Cummings, J. N. (2004). Work groups, structural diversity, and knowledge sharing in a global organization. *Management Science, 50,* 352–364.

Dougherty, D. (1992). Interpretive barriers to successful product innovation in large firms. *Organization Science, 3,* 179–202.

Dougherty, D., & Hardy, C. (1996). Sustained product innovation in large, mature organizations: Overcoming innovation-to-organization problems. *Academy of Management Journal, 39,* 1120–1153.

Edmondson, A. C. (1999). Psychological safety and learning behavior in work teams. *Administrative Science Quarterly, 44,* 350–383.

Granovetter, M. S. (1973). The strength of weak ties. *American Journal of Sociology, 6,* 1360–1380.

Guilford, J. P. (1967). The nature of human intelligence. *Intelligence, 1,* 274–280.

Hansen, M. T. (1999). The search-transfer problem: The role of weak ties in sharing knowledge across organization subunits. *Administrative Science Quarterly, 44,* 82–111.

Hargadon, A. B., & Sutton, R. (1997). Technology brokering and innovation in a product development firm. *Administrative Science Quarterly, 42,* 716–749.

Jackson, S. E. (1992). Team composition in organizational settings: Issues in managing an increasingly diverse work force. In S. Worchel, W. Wood, & J. A. Simpson (Eds.), *Group process and productivity* (pp. 138–173). Newbury Park, CA: Sage.

Jehn, K. A. (1997). A qualitative analysis of conflict types and dimensions in organizational groups. *Administrative Science Quarterly, 42,* 530–557.

Katz, R. (1982). The effects of group longevity on project communication and performance. *Administrative Science Quarterly, 27,* 81–104.

Katz, R., & Tushman, M. L. (1979). Communication patterns, project performance, and task characteristics: An empirical evaluation and integration in an R&D setting. *Organizational Behavior and Human Performance, 23,* 139–162.

Lewis, K. (2003). Measuring transactive memory systems in the field: Scale development and validation. *Journal of Applied Psychology, 88,* 587–604.

March, J. G. (1991). Exploration and exploitation in organizational learning. *Organization Science, 2,* 71–87.

Moreland, R. L. (1999). Transactive memory: Learning who knows what in work groups and organizations. In L. L. Thompson, J. M. Levine, & D. M. Messick (Eds.), *Shared cognition in organizations: The management of knowledge* (pp. 3–31). Mahwah, NJ: Lawrence Erlbaum Associates.

Nemeth, C. J. (1994). The value of minority dissent. In A. Mucchi-Faina, A. Maass, & S. Moscovici (Eds.), *Minority influence* (pp. 3–15). Chicago: Nelson Hall.

Nemeth, C. J., & Kwan, J. (1987). Minority influence, divergent thinking and the detection of correct solutions. *Journal of Applied Social Psychology, 17,* 786–797.

Osborn, A. F. (1957). *Applied imagination.* New York: Scribner.

Paulus, P. B., Dugosh, K. L., Dzindolet, M. T., Coskun, H., & Putnam, V. L. (2002). Social and cognitive influences in group brainstorming: Predicting production gains and losses. *European Review of Social Psychology, 12,* 299–325.

Paulus, P. B., & Dzindolet, M. T. (1993). Social influence processes in group brainstorming. *Journal of Personality and Social Psychology, 64,* 575–586.

Paulus, P. B., & Yang, H.-C. (2000). Idea generation in groups: A basis for creativity in organizations. *Organizational Behavior and Human Decision Processes, 82,* 76–87.

Staudenmayer, N., Tripsas, M., & Tucci, C. (2000). Development webs: A new paradigm in product development. In M. Hitt, R. Bresser, D. Heuskel, & R. Nixon (Eds.), *Winning strategies in a deconstructing world* (pp. 135–161). New York: Wiley.

Sutton, R., & Hargadon, A. B. (1996). Brainstorming groups in context: Effectiveness in a product design firm. *Administrative Science Quarterly, 41,* 685–718.

Tushman, M. (1977). Special boundary roles in the innovation process. *Administrative Science Quarterly, 22,* 587–605.

Tushman, M. (1979). Work characteristics and subunit communication structure: A contingency analysis. *Administrative Science Quarterly, 24,* 82–98.

Wegner, D. W. (1987). Transactive memory: A contemporary analysis of the group mind. In B. Mullen & G. R. Goethals (Eds.), *Theories of group behavior* (pp. 185–208). New York: Springer-Verlag.

West, M. A. (1994). *Effective team work.* Leicester: BPS Books.

Chapter 10

Bridging Old Worlds and Building New Ones: Toward a Microsociology of Creativity

Andrew B. Hargadon
University of California, Davis

Why, after almost 50 years of focused study, does creativity remain so elusive yet fascinating a topic? There is no denying the valued role creativity plays in spurring individual, organizational, and social change. Yet after half a century's effort, we are little closer to prescribing the process. In Greek mythology, the Chimera is a fire-breathing monster with a lion's head and a goat's body. One reason for creativity's continued allure, this chapter suggests, is that it is a chimera. Not in the first sense, as a figment of the imagination or wildly unrealistic idea, but in the second, as an organism made of two completely different genetic materials. Its vainglorious lion's head reflects creativity as an intensely personal process of deviating from the conformity of shared custom and culture, of rebelling against a tradition-bound social system. Its humble goat's body reflects a backstage process that is intensely social, rooted in established social systems and ultimately seeking acceptance within those systems for its own set of ideas. To explore this tension between the personal and the social, between front-stage defiance and backstage dependence, this chapter introduces the perspective of microsociology, which is concerned with understanding how individuals are shaped by and in turn shape their social surrounds.

Creativity involves the generation of novel, valuable, and nonobvious solutions (Amabile, 1983, 1988). It is a process that Jevons (1877; cited in Albert & Runco, 1999; see also Becker, 1995) eloquently called the "divergence from the ordinary grooves of thought and action" (p. 25), and it reflects our appreciation for the difficulty of breaking free from the bounds (cognitive, emotional, and behavioral) of socially shared conceptions of what is appropriate or even possible. Albert Szent-Gyorgi (n.d.) described the process as "seeing what everyone else has seen and thinking what no one else has thought."

At the same time, however, creativity is a social process that initially constructs solutions from pieces of the known world and ultimately depends on the approval of audiences in that world. In the original conception, paraphrasing E. H. Gombrich (1961), there is no such thing as the immaculate perception. All perceptions and the actions they inspire are built on existing understandings, and the construction of creative solutions, as Weick (1979) argued, involves "putting new things in old combinations and old things in new combinations" (p. 252). Once an idea has emerged, it still awaits the judgment of a particular audience before it becomes creative: "Creativity is not the product of single individuals, but of social systems making judgments about individuals' products" (Csikszentmihalyi, 1999, p. 314). These judgments are far from detached—they are reflections of the extent to which others within the social system converge around the new ideas.

We measure the creative value of works by Albert Einstein, Pablo Picasso, or Martha Graham, for instance, by some intuitive combination reflecting their deviation from what came before and the convergence that followed. The former process involves a sort of social deconstruction, a taking down of established thought and action, whereas the latter involves social construction, the building up of new thoughts and actions first by an individual or small group and later by the larger social system. These processes firmly place creativity in the relationship between the individual and society— first, for how the individual diverges from ordinary thought and action and, second, for how such divergence shapes and is shaped by the social context. A useful way to examine the interplay of these two processes is from the theoretical perspective of microsociology, and this chapter applies such a perspective to the creative process across a range of different contexts—from science to business to the performing arts.

A MICROSOCIOLOGY OF CREATIVITY

A microsociological approach has much to offer the study of creativity. Sociology's enduring question asks how individual behavior can be both consequence and cause of the larger social order. Microsociology is essentially concerned with a social theory of the mind. As a tradition, this focus originated with the work of the American pragmatists Charles Peirce and William James in the 19th century and continued through Charles Horton

Cooley, John Dewey, George Herbert Mead, Harold Garfinkel, and Erving Goffman (for a historical review, see Collins, 1994).[1] Microsociology focuses on how the social manifests itself not in external institutions, but in constructing the individualized representations of those exterior institutions and on how those representations shape comprehension and action.

Like modern psychology, a microsociological approach is concerned with how individuals comprehend their situations and craft responses. Unlike cognitive psychology, microsociology gives primacy to social structure and context; unlike social psychology, microsociology addresses a social structure and context that extends far beyond the immediate and local. Charles Peirce's original formulation was that man is "simply the sum total of his thoughts, and this sum is always a historical bundle of his society's experience" (Collins, 1994, p. 252).

From a microsocial perspective, an individual's social surrounds shape his or her thought and action by constituting (and simultaneously constraining) individuals to a range of definitions for a given situation and the appropriate responses available (Barley & Tolbert, 1997; DiMaggio, 1997; Friedland & Alford, 1991; Goffman, 1959). As Goffman (1974) stated,

> A "definition of the situation" is almost always to be found, but those who are in the situation ordinarily do not create this definition, even though their society often can be said to do so; ordinarily all they do is to assess correctly what the situation ought to be for them and then act accordingly. (p. 2)

To describe this constitutive nature, sociologists have variously used the language of frames, logics of action, cultural tools, and schemas and scripts (Barley & Tolbert, 1997; DiMaggio, 1997; Friedland & Alford, 1991; Goffman, 1974); acknowledging similar work within the field of psychology, this chapter adopts the use of schemas and scripts (Schank & Abelson, 1977). DiMaggio (1997) defined *schemas* as "knowledge structures that represent objects or events and provide default assumptions about their characteristics, relationships, and entailments under conditions of incomplete information" (p. 269). Scripts, as more localized forms of schemas, direct individual action and understanding within highly particularized situations (Barley, 1986; DiMaggio, 1997). The presence of schemas helps us to see, the presence of scripts to act. Most important for our purposes, schemas and scripts represent the means through which understanding and action are embedded within established social worlds—individual cognition serves as the nexus between institutions and action.

---

[1]Although this tradition has spawned the fields of ethnomethodology and symbolic interactionism, this chapter takes an approach more akin to Goffman's attendance to the interaction between social structure and cognition (e.g., Goffman, 1974).

Applying a microsocial perspective to the study of creativity shifts the focus away from the novelty of a creative solution—the extent to which an idea diverges from ordinary thought and action—and toward the ways in which that divergence is constructed from pieces of existing thought and action. People create novel insights by importing and recombining schemas and scripts learned in other contextual domains—in other words, people do not think out of the box, they think in other boxes (Hargadon & Fanelli, 2002). Psychologists, sociologists, economists, and historians have long recognized creativity as a recombinant process. Bethune (1837) considered it the ability to "originat[e] new combinations of thought," and William James (1880) called it "the most unheard-of combinations of elements" (cited in Albert & Runco, 1999; see also Becker, 1995). Similarly, the technological historian Usher (1929) described innovation as the "constructive assimilation of pre-existing elements into new syntheses," and sociologist Ogburn (1922; cited in Basalla, 1988) defined it as a result of "combining existing and known elements of culture in order to form a new element" (p. 21). Consider the following examples:

• Henry Ford did not invent mass production, but rather gathered together elements of technologies that had developed, some for almost a century, in other industries. In armory production, he found the technologies of interchangeable parts. In canneries, granaries, and breweries, he found the technologies of continuous flow production; in the meatpacking plants of Chicago, the assembly line; and in the emerging electric industry, the electric motor (Hargadon, 2003; Hounshell, 1984). Ford (Gordon, 2001) once even testified:

I invented nothing new. I simply assembled into a car the discoveries of other men behind whom were centuries of work . . . Had I worked fifty or ten or even five years before, I would have failed. So it is with every new thing. (p. 103)

• Polymerase chain reaction (PCR) is the biochemical process that enables the replication of single strands of DNA in great quantities. As such, PCR underlies the recent biotechnology revolution (Rabinow, 1996). Kary Mullis once described his achievement:

I put together elements that were already there, but that's what inventors always do. You can't make up new elements, usually. The new element, if any, it was the combination, the way they were used. (Rabinow, 1996, pp. 6–7)

• In 1972, Ray Tomlinson wrote the first electronic mail application by combining the code of an existing *intra*-computer messaging application with an *inter*-computer file transfer protocol (Segaller, 1998). As Tomlinson described:

> It seemed like an interesting hack to tie these two together to use the file-transfer protocol to send the email to the other machine. So that's what I did. I spent not a whole lot of time, maybe two or three weeks, putting that together and it worked. (Segaller, 1998, p. 104)

• In 1953, Elvis Presley's first record and hits came by combining the lyrics and melodies of country music with the beat and energy of Rhythm and Blues. "Blue Moon of Kentucky" was a bluegrass standard, written by Bill Munroe, which through a series of recorded rehearsals can be heard transforming itself, combining with R&B rhythms to become a hybrid tune with a rocking beat. A decade later, the Beatles similarly made their start by combining American folk, R&B, and rockabilly. David Crosby, of the Byrds and later Crosby, Stills, Nash, and Young, described what the Beatles brought to Rock and Roll as a recombination of what had come before:

> I heard folk sort of changes with rock and roll sort of beat [in the Beatles music]. Now, most new musical forms are created that way, the synthesis takes place by two disparate streams of stuff hitherto unrelated being mushed together. ("History of Rock and Roll," 1995)

• Einstein developed a theoretical framework that combined existing understandings of what were previously unconnected ideas and phenomena. Einstein built on the ideas of Boltzmann, Hertz, Poincare, Mach, Planck, and others, but combined them in a way that enabled him to take what was best and leave behind the vestiges of their origins in older scientific practices and communities. As Gardner (1993) wrote,

> Einstein's breakthrough was classic in that it sought to unify the elements of a physical analysis, and it placed the older examples and principles within a broader framework. But it was revolutionary in that, ever afterward, we have thought differently about space and time, matter and energy. (p. 114)

From a microsocial perspective, the origins of these creative acts lie in the same social structures, the same "ordinary thoughts and actions," that prevent most of us from being creative. Recombining existing ideas is possible because the ideas are drawn from a range of otherwise disconnected contexts—different worlds—and so appear new (and are new) to new audiences. Over time these roots become obscured by the continued evolution of new combinations in new settings. The preexisting elements of Ford's mass production—the machines, people, and ideas—quickly adapted to the new surroundings. The Beatles quickly moved past the original combinations they created, placing their own original imprint on the evolution of Rock and Roll. Yet this does not diminish the critical role played by the continuity of their creative process. As the artist Nathan Oliveira argues, originality is an end rather than a point of departure (Keats, 2002).

The question remains: How is it that these existing elements constrain so many of us to the grooves of ordinary thought and action and yet enable others to construct from them radically new and different ideas and actions? Following earlier work that embeds creativity within a context of social networks (Hargadon, 2003; Hargadon & Fanelli, 2002), one explanation rests in how individuals relate to their social surrounds. Creativity remains elusive because it requires individuals to relate to the established social system in two different ways. In a language of social networks, creativity entails (a) bridging existing contexts to acquire and recombine existing thoughts and actions, and (b) building new communities around those new combinations to gain their acceptance. These are different processes. Bridging describes a network position (and path) that exposes individuals to a range of relatively different social situations because it involves building wide-ranging, but weak, relationships with others who are not connected to one another. Building new communities around creative opportunities describes a network position (and path) that embeds individuals within a single community because it involves building strong relationships with and between others. Bridging different contexts enables individuals to acquire many new and different ideas, to break from existing frames, and to pursue independent thinking. Building new followings around novel ideas requires committing to a single or few ideas, to seeking the acceptance of others, and in other ways pursuing the benefits of shared thoughts and actions. Taken together, the creative process requires the ability to rebel against existing ideas and yet wholly commit to a new one—the ability to scoff at existing customs, yet ceaselessly promote your own.

Creativity's chimerical quality can be seen in the paradoxical constraints and opportunities posed by these different ways individuals relate to the surrounding social structure. Social structures reflect dense networks—not the simple social networks defined by network theory, but rather the webs of thought and action that tie individuals to the ideas and objects they experience in everyday life. These are the networks that Weber meant when he said, "Man is suspended in webs of significance he himself has spun" (cited in Geertz, 1973, p. 5). In the larger landscape that encompasses many different communities, these dense networks show up as many small worlds only loosely connected to each other. We should view them as small worlds for two reasons. First, because this is the way they are experienced. To someone on the inside, the world easily shrinks to encompass only those whom they interact with on a daily and weekly basis, who occupy the same places and share the same ideas. The second reason these are small worlds is related though academic. To network theorists, the label *small world* comes from the surprisingly short distances that connect so many relatively isolated pockets of dense interactions. We are, on average, somewhere between three and five degrees, or links, away from anyone else in the world (Watts, 1999). That means everyone, on average, knows someone (one link) who knows someone (two links) who knows someone (three links) who knows anybody else (four links) in the world. This small-world phenomenon is so surprising because we are continually surprised when these latent connections are made apparent and the artificiality of our distance and distinctiveness is made clear.

Small worlds both enable and constrain action. The dense connections give any single world its structure and stability; as a result, they enable a complex set of people, ideas, and objects to work smoothly together as a single, coherent system. But these same dense ties also make it extremely difficult to change any one part of that system without affecting the rest. Consider what happened to the world that Ford built. The development of mass production at the Ford Motor Company shows the creative potential of finding new ways to use old ideas. It shows how Ford managed to create an organization capable of pulling the best people, ideas, and objects from a range of otherwise distant and disconnected worlds. Yet in the decade after Ford established mass production of the Model T, General Motors began a systematic strategy of dividing and conquering Ford's mass market by introducing a range of mid- to low-cost models.

Compared with the bold and experimental approach Ford took in manufacturing the Model T, his response to this new threat was stunning for its defense of the status quo. Rather than adopt the new marketing practices, Ford focused on what he knew best—lowering the cost of the Model T yet further. He had few options. With the River Rouge factory, he had constructed such a tightly linked manufacturing operation that any changes in the design of a part or process rippled painfully through the entire organization. The tight-knit relations among people, ideas, and objects that Henry Ford constructed around mass production and the Model T made it almost impossible to respond to General Motor's introduction of multiple models and annual design changes. Ultimately, the River Rouge plant, the pinnacle of Ford's system, had to shut down completely for 9 months to abandon the Model T and convert over to a new model. In short, Ford's success in piecing together a system of mass production sowed the very seeds of its failure—the inability to easily accommodate changes in particular elements.

From 1908 to 1914, Ford revolutionized mass production by recognizing the latent potential in bringing together the people, ideas, and objects of

distant worlds. He successfully built a new world around this new combination. The world he built, however, quickly became small—its inhabitants
unable to change their thoughts and actions in response to the new and
valuable possibilities that arose just outside its boundaries.

In a similar story, 4 years after Edison threw the switch at the Pearl Street
Station in downtown New York, George Westinghouse opened an electric
generating plant in Buffalo and began one of the most famous standards
wars in technological history. Edison's system produced a low-voltage, direct current (DC) for transmission and use. In contrast, the new Westinghouse plant produced high-voltage, alternating current (AC). The arguments for and against each system are many and muddled—but simply put,
the advantage of AC electricity lay in more efficient transmission over distances, whereas the disadvantage lay in the complexities and danger of an
undeveloped system. The Battle of the Systems, as it became known, was
played out mainly in the press roughly from 1887 to 1892. In the end, Edison lost more than just the technical standard—he also lost his reputation
as inventive genius. Passer once wrote, "In 1879, Edison was a brave and
courageous inventor, in 1889, he was a cautious and conservative defender
of the status quo" (cited in Millard, 1990, p 101).

What happened in between? If we believe that creativity is a persistent individual quality, we are at a loss for explanation. But if we consider how Edison, like Ford, first relied on and then explicitly abandoned a strategy of
bridging the many small worlds, we can better understand such outcomes.
In 1882, Edison announced: "The electric lighting system is now perfected.
I will now bend all my time and energies to its introduction to the public."
Despite Edison's usual hyperbole, in this he was telling the truth. He moved
from Menlo Park to Manhattan to be close to the business headquarters of
Edison Electric Light Company, saying, "I'm going to be a business man,
I'm a regular contractor for electric lighting plants and I'm going to take a
long vacation in the matter of invention" (Millard, 1990, p. 3). Edison
turned his attention to building the necessary community around his
emerging innovation, but in doing so burned his bridges to other worlds.

It is easy to single out a few individuals and groups that cannot let go of
their old knowledge, refusing to see and adapt to breakthrough technologies that pushed them aside. But often it is the same people who led the
previous revolution. The transformation of both Edison and Ford from
courageous inventors to defenders of the status quo reveals the paradox inherent in creativity. The skills required to bridge distant worlds and generate novel combinations are ill suited to the focused process of building new
worlds around such innovations, and those skills required to build new
worlds are ill suited to ranging widely in search of alternatives. The novelist
Robertson Davies (1990) once wrote that knowledge "makes you wise in
some ways, but it can make you a blindfolded fool in others" (p. 534). The

difference, I suggest, lies in the relations between individuals and their so-cial systems.

The dense connections that make up small worlds do more than just make change costly—they actually make it difficult to recognize the possi-bilities for such change in the first place. The many strong and frequent in-teractions within any single world ensures that inhabitants are surrounded by other people who are doing the same things, sharing the same ideas, and using the same objects. As Beach (1997) wrote in *The Psychology of Decision Making*, "people who share cultures often arrive at similar frames for situa-tions, frames that might be very different from those arrived at by outsiders" (p. 25), or as Cohen and Prusak (2001) put it, the ties that bind are the ties that blind. Whether we draw the boundary of a small world around a group, and organization, or an industry, we must recognize that small worlds shape perceptions in ways that prevent inhabitants from seeing the value of peo-ple, ideas, and objects that reside outside of their traditional boundaries (Chatman, 1991; Chatman & Jehn, 1994).

Weick's (1993) study of the team of smoke jumpers who died when a fire turned against them shows the sometimes tragic inability to value ideas and actions outside one's perceived context—and to recognize when one's con-text is no longer a valid interpretation (see Maclean, 1992). One cause con-tributing to their deaths was their inability to drop their tools during their retreat up a steep hillside despite that those tools were now worse than use-less. To these firefighters, both Maclean and Weick argued, those tools were more than simple objects, they represented who they were, why they were there, and what they were trained to do. Dropping their tools meant abandoning their existing knowledge and relationships. This may not seem such a hard choice to make, but because they had not been trained for such a moment they had no alternative models of behavior. In moments of un-certainty and danger, clinging to the old ways may seem a better alternative than no ways at all. Even in more tranquil settings, people often fail to come up with new understandings of what's happening, new ways of dealing with problems, because they lack the wide-ranging set of ideas from which to piece together alternatives.

BRIDGING OLD WORLDS

Bridging activities bring people into contact with the wide variety of well-developed technologies that already exist in other worlds. Yet bridging ac-tivities provide another critical advantage that can easily be overlooked. The act of bridging distant worlds actually changes the way people see and think about the people, ideas, and objects they come in contact with. In this way, bridging activities overcome the parochialism that hinders individuals, groups, organizations, and even industries from seeing the value of people, ideas, and objects that reside outside their traditional boundaries.

Bridging old worlds offers a means to overcome the perceptual blocks that typically hinder the creative process. These activities work for two related reasons. First, by moving through other worlds, bridging puts people in the flow of the many different thoughts and actions that reside within any one world. Second, bridging changes the way people look at those different ideas they find in other worlds, and it also changes the way they look at the thoughts and actions that dominate their own.

At its heart, bridging activities provide the conditions for creativity—for the Eureka moment when new possibilities suddenly become apparent. But remember recombinant innovation. Creative insight, from this perspective, means seeing new ways to combine old ideas—not ignoring the past, but exploiting it. Nowhere is the learning process of individuals and organizations more critical or misunderstood than in this creative process. The notion that we can come up with new ideas has come under increasing attack by cognitive psychologists interested in understanding how people solve novel problems. A number of psychologists who have studied creativity, like Dean Simonton and Howard Gardner, for example, have argued that recombination is the fundamental mechanism behind creative insight. Einstein once said, such "combinatory play seems to be the essential feature in productive thought" (cited in Simonton, 1996, p. 468). We can see Einstein's theory of relativity through the lens of recombination.

Einstein developed a theoretical framework that combined current understandings of what were previously unconnected ideas and phenomena, building on the ideas of Boltzmann, Hertz, Poincare, Mach, Planck, and others, but combining them in a way that enabled him to take what was best and leave behind the vestiges of their origins in older scientific practices and communities. Those closest to Einstein's discovery, the very individuals whose work Einstein recombined (Mach, Max Planck, Lorentz, Poincare), never wholly embraced his work. Chance did not favor these very prepared minds. Quite the opposite; each was *too* familiar with and committed to what had come before to see how Einstein's new combination could be something greater than the sum of its parts. Max Planck referred to Einstein's theories as merely a generalization of Lorentz' work. Einstein once said of Mach, whose work he admitted to closely building on, "It is not improbable that Mach would have discovered the theory of relativity, if, at the time when his mind was still young and susceptible, the problem of constancy of the speed of light had been discussed among physicists" (cited in Simonton, 1996, p. 468).

Simonton (1996) argued that these recombinant thought processes shape how people approach their environment. Those who are more engaged in exploring new combinations are often more attuned to the world around them:

> Those people who make their minds accessible to chaotic combinatory play will also make their sense more open to the influx of fortuitous events in the outside world. Both the retrieval of material from memory and the orientation of attention to environmental stimuli are unrestricted. (p. 470)

Rather than believing they have seen it all or at least seen all that is worth seeing, those in the habit of finding unexpected connections begin to recognize in each new person they meet, each new idea they hear, and each new object they find, the potential for new combinations with others. The more worlds you bridge, the more you have a foot in each of these different flows, and the more you are able to see and exploit the existing technologies as they emerge and evolve in their own settings. At the same time, having one foot in another world also means have one foot outside any one world. Having one foot outside your world means you can be less beholden to the ties that would otherwise bind and blind you in that world because you have somewhere else to go.

The trick seems to be developing in-depth knowledge within a given field while retaining the willingness to take that knowledge apart and combine it in new ways. This is difficult because, as the fire at Mann Gulch shows us, people are reluctant to abandon their old knowledge. Bridging distant worlds provides a way to acquire knowledge without acquiring the ties that typically bind such knowledge to particular worlds.

Einstein admits that his ability to revolutionize physics came not from his intellect, but rather his position relative to others more deeply embedded in the field. He did his most innovative work while on the periphery of the scientific community he overturned. As he once said of this position:

> Such isolation is sometimes bitter but I do not regret being cut off from the understanding and sympathy of other men . . . I am compensated for it by being rendered independent of the customs, opinions and prejudices of others and am not tempted to rest my piece of mind upon such shifting foundations. (Gardner, 1993, p. 131)

In the same way, Elvis, who may have been no Einstein, also cut himself off from the "understandings and sympathies of other men" while growing up in Nashville, where he was accepted by neither the African-American community nor the White for his peripheral participation in each. We can give Einstein, Elvis, Edison, and Ford credit for seeing farther than others. Yet if we are truly interested in understanding the creative process, we need

210   HARGADON

to think about how they bridged different worlds to get where they did and
see what they saw.

BUILDING NEW WORLDS

Ralph Waldo Emerson's famous advice, "Build a better mousetrap, and the
world will beat a path to your door," is misleading. The world tends not to
beat a path to your door. As Hope (1996) described, since the patent office
opened in 1828, it has issued some 4,400 patents for mousetraps, and yet
only 20 or so have made any money (the most successful, the spring trap,
was patented in 1899). A better mousetrap, like anything else, succeeds
only when those who envision the idea convince others to join in their new
venture—as investors, suppliers, employees, retailers, customers, and even
competitors—each of whom, in turn, contributes his or her own contributions and connections. The revolutionary impacts we see from creative
efforts are often the result of the community that adopted the initial, well-
intentioned, but underdeveloped ideas. Case in point, Emerson's now famous quote. In actuality, he never said that. The quote originated some 7
years after Emerson's death. Emerson ( ) said, "If a man has good corn, or
wood, or boards, or pigs, to sell . . . you will find a broad, hard-beaten road
to his house" (p.). Emerson was not talking about creativity, but rather
about selling a good product. It became so much more only when others
joined in the process.

By a number of accounts, Edison was well aware of the need to sell his innovations to the public, to investors, to his employees, and to policy-
makers—and he used his image as a creative genius to do so (e.g., Hughes,
1989; Nye, 1983). Once, the story goes, Edison met with a cub reporter who
had come to interview the Wizard of Menlo Park:

> While the reporter was being ushered in, the Old Man disguised himself to re-
> semble the heroic image of "The Great Inventor, Thomas A. Edison." . . . Sud-
> denly gone were his natural boyishness of manner, his happy hooliganism.
> His features were frozen into immobility, he became statuesque in the arm-
> chair, and his unblinking eyes assumed a faraway look. . . . (Hughes, 1989, p.
> 91)

Francis Jehl, Edison's long-time assistant who joined him in Menlo Park
and remained with him through most of his career, remembers when they
first realized the power of Edison's name. At that point, he explained, they
began the process of turning Edison the man into Edison the myth. To the
public, Edison was an inventive genius. To Francis Jehl and many of the

other engineers in that lab, "Edison is in reality a collective noun and [means] the work of many men."

The role of the collective in the creative process can also be seen in the early days of the impressionist movement in the 1860s. Although history gives prominence to individuals artists—Renoir, Monet, and Cezanne—art historians have noted how these individuals began as a single, small group. Farrell (1982, 2001) recognized that these collectives enabled the individual artists to commit to and create a movement that directly challenged the established art world. In splitting from the dominant styles of the art world, the artists' circle of early impressionists worked closely to develop their emerging style and jointly construct an environment of support and motivation for their creative efforts. They worked so closely together that their paintings were often indistinguishable: When two paintings were on display in a gallery much later, Monet could not say which was his and which was Renoir's without looking to the signature. Only when the impressionist movement was established did each artist make efforts to distinguish themselves as individuals. Many such works of art, Farrell argued, and particularly those of the early stages of new movements, should be viewed as the product of these collectives and not of any individual artist.

Collectives like Edison's Menlo Park team and the impressionists provide two critical resources in the creative process: a broader pool of ideas and a stronger network of support. The first, a broader pool of ideas, comes about because the collective brings individuals together in ways that allow them to build on each others' ideas—to turn a wacky comment or hesitant suggestion into a brilliant insight. The collective works when it becomes difficult, if not impossible, to identify whose idea it was in the first place. For example, in describing the early days of the impressionists, Farrell (1982) explained how "A chance idea that might have been discarded if the painter had been alone was supported by the group. Risky decisions were validated and the group began to develop its own subculture . . ." (p. 459). The project team that developed the Reebok Pump at Design Continuum was another such collective. When someone suggested putting an inflatable splint into a shoe, the others could have laughed it off as one more wacky idea in a brainstorm filled with many wacky ideas. Instead someone else built on their idea. The idea (and object) of an IV bag to act as the inflatable bladder made the idea of an inflatable splint not only realistic, but good (see Hargadon, 2002). Fundamentally, the difference between a good idea and a bad one, in a collective, depends entirely on what the others decide to do with it.

These early collectives also provide a common belief in their cause and its chances for success just when these are needed most, when the ideas (and people) are attempting to go against the established ways of doing things. The Asch (1951) experiments revealed the ineffectiveness of individual judgment in the face of social pressures to conform. However, Asch also found that the easiest way to enable somebody to resist the larger group was by giving them a small group of their own. Adding one more independent subject to the group—from one to two—makes the effect of the group pressures disappear. When subjects had one other person who agreed with them, they were able to stand against the larger group. Asch also found that this collective deviance was a fragile thing. Take one of the partners away in the middle of experiments and the other often began conforming again.

In this way, collectives encourage individuals to think differently together. When you work with others who are visibly engaged in and passionate about their work, you feel better about it yourself. Emile Zola captured this power of collective deviance in his novel, *The Masterpiece*, which fictionalized his time spent working alongside the impressionists. When the central character, based on Monet, was in despair, he went walking with his friends:

> They . . . sauntered along, with an air of taking over the entire width of the Boulevard des Invalides. When they spread out like this, they were like a free-and-easy band of soldiers off to the wars. . . . In this company and under this influence, Claude began to cheer up; in the warmth of shared hopes, his belief in himself revived. (cited in Farrell, 1982, p. 459)

In this group, each artist's motivation (and identity) was shaped by his connections with the collective.

We tend to think that organizations play the role of collectives, providing all the necessary support for those within. Beyond the small firm or new venture, however, this is rarely the case. The role of the collective is often more critical *inside* large organizations, where standard operating procedures and "the way we do things around here" make just about any change seem deviant, and where hierarchies can turn even casual comments by superiors into powerful pressures to conform. The role of the collective, joining forces to fight the status quo, often spells the difference between good ideas stopping at the first conservative layer of management or pushing their way, painfully if necessary, all the way to the top.

The collective helps by pulling together previously disparate people, ideas, and objects and providing them with the necessary support to overcome their initial illegitimacy. Once a new venture crystallizes and acquires legitimacy, an established community can emerge. Whether pulling individuals together from across previously different social groups or within a single one, these communities take shape around emerging ideas such as the electric light or impressionist styles. As more and more people join, the community becomes more easily recognized from the outside. In organizations, it soon becomes officially sanctioned maybe as a new development project, as a research center, or even as a new division. Outside of organizations, it begins to look like an emerging market (one of the most defining characteristics of the evolving community being a readily identifiable set of customers), an industry, or a cluster of firms located in a particular region. This transition from collective to community is the focus of research on the social construction of industries (Garud & Karnoe, 2001; Garud & Rappa, 1994; Van de Ven & Garud, 1993) and social movements (for a review, see Swaminathan & Wade, 2001).

Most of the actual improvements in productivity and performance of a new technology, like the steam engine, the electric light, the transistor, or the computer, take place *in use*—and long after "individual inventors" have lost control of their ideas to those communities that form around them (Gilfillan, 1935; Rosenberg, 1963, 1982). As communities grow around new technologies, they create the necessary feedback loops that sustain them. As one group gets better at manufacturing integrated circuits, another exploits those gains to design more advanced chips, and another uses those to develop better computers, which spurs the demand for more and better manufacturing.

DISCUSSION AND CONCLUSION

The two complementary creative processes detailed here—bridging old worlds and building new ones—reflect the recognition that creativity is an intensely personal and cognitive process that derives both its content and meaning from the surrounding social system. First, because the combinatory process that underlies creative insight draws its raw materials from the established schemas and scripts—thoughts and actions—provided by the institutional environment of the creative individual. Second, because no matter how original the insight that results, the label of creativity still depends on how many others are convinced to adopt and extend these original ideas. The ability to think differently and then convince others to think the same requires different and sometimes conflicting attitudes and behaviors.

Individuals can sometimes take on both roles. For instance, Edison developed a working light bulb, but then publicly announced his retirement from invention to pursue the acceptance of his new innovation. However, many creative efforts seem to overcome this paradox through dyads and small groups: Henry Ford relied heavily on Max Wollering and Walter Flanders; Steve Wozniak designed the circuits that Steve Jobs turned into a Computer company; Bill Gates worked closely with Paul Allen (and Steve Ballmer) from the beginning; John Lennon and Paul McCartney (and Sir George) formed the creative nucleus of the Beatles; Watson and Crick;

Hewlett and Packard; Captain and Tenille. Even Edison established a partnership with Charles Batchelor, one of his engineers, which evenly split all patent royalties resulting from the work of the Menlo Park lab. Accounts describe how, when Edison was traveling, experiments at the lab continued, yet while Batchelor was away the experimentation ceased (Conot, 1979; Millard, 1990).

There is good reason to believe that we can all improve our creative abilities by attending to the different activities. First, we can seek a comfortable balance (unique for each of us) between the wide-ranging weak ties that enable us to bridge old worlds and the local, strong ties that embed us within a single world. More simply, we can seek out new people and new experiences or we can enjoy the comfortable rhythms of familiar context. Second, we can attend to shifting circumstances in the pursuit of our goals—at times it is better to bridge old worlds and at times to build new ones. Yet the process remains challenging. These opposing activities are difficult to balance, and most people, as Baker (2000) reported, end up favoring the local strong ties that provide community and continuity. Balancing between wide-ranging weak ties and local strong ties may be difficult within groups, where the attitudes and interests of individuals reflect the different paths by which they arrived at this collaboration. The locals distrust the shallow experiences and noncommittal nature of brokers, and the brokers distrust the parochial and intransigent nature of the locals. Perhaps this is why creativity remains so fascinating, reflecting as it does a momentary détente in the tension between the local and global, familiar and novel.

On the surface, the creative process takes awe-inspiring form as the source of revolutions in science, technology, and the arts. Yet this lion's head appearance belies a more humble body of practice in which novel and valuable ideas are pieced together from existing ones and in which the selling of new ideas must follow (or perhaps even precede) the anointing of those ideas as creative. This chimerical quality can distract from the intricacies of the creative process. This chapter has attempted to surface two of these intricacies—the influence of bridging or moving between different worlds and of building new worlds. The challenge remains to capture and study these influences more directly.

REFERENCES

Albert, R. S., & Runco, M. A. (1999). A history of research on creativity. In R. J. Sternberg (Ed.), *Handbook of creativity* (pp. 16–34). New York: Cambridge University Press.

Amabile, T. M. (1983). *The social psychology of creativity*. New York: Springer-Verlag.

Amabile, T. M. (1988). A model of creativity and innovation in organizations. In B. M. Staw & L. L. Cummings (Eds.), *Research in organizational behavior* (Vol. 10, pp. 123–167). Greenwich, CT: JAI.

Asch, S. E. (1951). Effects of group pressure upon the modification and distortion of judgments. In H. Guetzkow (Ed.), *Groups, leadership, and men* (pp. 177–190). Pittsburgh: Carnegie Press.

Baker, W. E. (2000). *Achieving success through social capital.* San Francisco: Jossey-Bass.

Barley, S. R. (1986). Technology as an occasion for structuring: Evidence from observations of CT scanners and the social order of radiology departments. *Administrative Sciences Quarterly, 31*, 78–108.

Barley, S. R., & Tolbert, P. S. (1997). Institutionalization and structuration: Studying the links between action and institution. *Organization Studies, 18*(1), 93–117.

Beach, L. R. (1997). *The psychology of decision making: People in organizations.* Thousand Oaks, CA: Sage.

Becker, M. (1995). Nineteenth century foundations of creativity research. *Creativity Research Journal, 8*, 219–229.

Chatman, J. A. (1991). Matching people and organizations: Selection and socialization in public accounting firms. *Administrative Science Quarterly, 36*, 459–484.

Chatman, J. A., & Jehn, K. A. (1994). Assessing the relationship between industry characteristics and organizational culture: How different can you be? *Academy of Management Journal, 37*, 522–533.

Cohen, D., & Prusak, L. (2001). *In good company: How social capital makes organizations work.* Boston: Harvard Business School Press.

Collins, R. (1994). *Four sociological traditions.* Oxford: Oxford University Press.

Conot, R. E. (1979). *A streak of luck* (1st ed.). New York: Seaview.

Csikszentmihalyi, M. (1988). Society, culture, and person: A systems view of creativity. In R. J. Sternberg (Ed.), *The nature of creativity: Contemporary psychological perspectives* (pp. 76–98). New York: Cambridge University Press.

Csikszentmihalyi, M. (1999). Implications of a systems perspective for the study of creativity. In R. J. Sternberg (Ed.), *Handbook of creativity* (pp. 313–335). New York: Cambridge University Press.

Davies, R. (1990). *World of wonder.* New York: Penguin.

DiMaggio, P. (1997). Culture and cognition. *Annual Review of Sociology, 23*, 263–287.

Farrell, M. P. (1982). Artists' circles and the development of artists. *Journal of Small Group Behavior, 13*(4), 451–474.

Farrell, M. P. (2001). *Collaborative circles: Friendship dynamics & creative work.* Chicago: University of Chicago Press.

Friedland, R., & Alford, R. (1991). Bringing society back in: Symbols, practices, and institutional contradictions. In W. W. Powell & P. DiMaggio (Eds.), *The new institutionalism in organizational analysis* (pp. 232–263). Chicago: University of Chicago Press.

Garud, R., & Karnoe, P. (Eds.). (2001). *Path dependence and creation.* Mahwah, NJ: Lawrence Erlbaum Associates.

Garud, R., & Rappa, M. A. (1994). A socio-cognitive model of technology evolution: The case of cochlear implants. *Organization Science, 3*(3), 344–362.

Geertz, C. (1973). *Interpretation of cultures.* New York: Basic Books.

Gilfillan, S. C. (1935). *Inventing the ship.* Chicago: Follet.

Goffman, E. (1959). *The presentation of self in everyday life.* Garden City, NY: Doubleday.

Goffman, E. (1974). *Frame analysis: An essay on the organization of experience.* New York: Harper & Row.

Gombrich, E. H. (1961). *Art and illusion; a study in the psychology of pictorial representation.* New York: Bollingen Foundation.

Hargadon, A. B. (2002). Brokering knowledge: Linking learning and innovation. *Research in Organizational Behavior, 24*, 41–85.

Hargadon, A. B. (2003). *How breakthroughs happen: The surprising truth about how companies innovate.* Cambridge: Harvard Business School Press.

Hargadon, A. B., & Fanelli, A. (2002). Action and possibility: Reconciling dual perspectives of knowledge in organizations. *Organization Science, 13*(3), 290–302.

History of Rock and Roll. (1995). Video. WGBH/PBS documentary.

Hope, J. A. (1996). A better mousetrap. *American Heritage*, pp. 90–97.

Hounshell, D. A. (1984). *From the American system to mass production.* Baltimore: Johns Hopkins University.

Hughes, T. P. (1989). *American genesis: A century of invention and technological enthusiasm, 1870–1890.* New York: Viking.

Keats, J. (2002). Oliveira stands alone: The heroic originality of our great figurative artist. *San Francisco.*

Maclean, N. (1992). *Young men and fire: A true story of the Mann Gulch fire.* Chicago: University of Chicago Press.

Millard, A. (1990). *Edison and the business of innovation.* Baltimore: Johns Hopkins University Press.

Nye, D. E. (1983). *The invented self: An anti-biography, from documents of Thomas A. Edison.* Odense, Denmark: Odense University Press.

Rosenberg, N. (1963). Technological change in the machine tool industry, 1840–1910. *Journal of Economic History*, pp. 414–443.

Rosenberg, N. (1982). *Inside the black box.* New York: Cambridge University Press.

Schank, R., & Abelson, R. P. (1977). *Scripts, plans, goals, and understanding: An inquiry into human knowledge structures.* Hillsdale, NJ: Lawrence Erlbaum Associates.

Segaller, S. (1998). *Nerds 2.0.1: A brief history of the Internet* (1st ed.). New York: TV Books.

Simonton, D. K. (1996). Foresight in insight: A Darwinian answer. In R. J. Sternberg & J. Davidson (Eds.), *The nature of insight* (pp. 465–494). Cambridge: MIT Press.

Swaminathan, A., & Wade, J. B. (2001). Social movement theory and the evolution of new organizational forms. In C. B. Schoonhoven & E. Romanelli (Eds.), *The entrepreneurship dynamic in industry evolution* (pp. 286–313). Stanford, CA: Stanford University Press.

Szent-Gyorgi, A. (n.d.). http://www.famous-quotations.com/asp/cquotes.asp?category= creativity+%2F+Ideas. Accessed January 19, 2005.

Van de Ven, A. H., & Garud, R. (1993). The co-evolution of technical and institutional events in the development of an innovation. In J. Singh & J. Baum (Eds.), *The evolutionary dynamics of organizations* (pp. 425–443). New York: Oxford University Press.

Watts, D. J. (1999). *Small worlds: The dynamics of networks between order and randomness.* Princeton, NJ: Princeton University Press.

Weick, K. E. (1979). *The social psychology of organizing.* Reading, MA: Addison-Wesley.

Weick, K. E. (1993). The collapse of sensemaking in organizations: The Mann Gulch disaster. *Administrative Sciences Quarterly, 38*, 628–652.

Chapter 11

Creative Associations and Entrepreneurial Opportunities

Cameron M. Ford
University of Central Florida

> *I refuse to recognize that there are impossibilities.*
> —Henry Ford, founder of Ford Motor Company

> *Ignore the conventional wisdom.*
> —Sam Moore Walton, founder of Walmart

> *Think unconventionally and do exactly what the competition tends to believe cannot be done.*
> —Michael Dell, founder of Dell computers

Heroic entrepreneurs like Henry Ford, Sam Walton, and Michael Dell are often described as creative for their transformational business ideas, visionary for their ability to attract supporters and consumers, and vanguards of change for their ventures' transformational impact on modern business practices. Although few entrepreneurs have had the impact of Ford, Walton, and Dell, all successful new ventures can be attributed to a combination of creative associations by an entrepreneur (Eckhardt & Shane, 2003), social networking processes that spur creativity and organizing efforts (Perry-Smith & Shalley, 2003), and markets that respond positively to a new venture's initial actions (Christensen, 1997). Consider Walter Robb's more typical circuitous journey during the invention of practical liquid membranes for gas separation that resulted in a new business venture at GE. His case demonstrates how a creative association between a technology (ultra-thin membranes) and a market (the Navy) instigated an iterative, evolutionary process where ideas attracted supporters who provided additional creative associations that improved the ideas, thus attracting further support, and so on until a new venture resulted.

Although Robb, a chemical engineer, was initially trying to make pure boron, he was diverted from that goal by talking to a physicist who posed a different application that might make his work more useful to a prominent constituent, the Navy (by using Robb's processes to separate oxygen from carbon dioxide to recycle oxygen in submarines). Robb had his doubts; the problem was offbeat and interesting all right, but seemed to have a low probability of success. Nonetheless, Robb was intrigued by the potential benefits of his creative idea. He saw these benefits as a substantial improvement on the performance of current technologies, so he convinced his superiors that this idea was worthy of initial investigation.

Robb was motivated to search for additional information and insights from technical reports and journals, but the most useful information came from suggestions and contributions offered by others only tangentially familiar with his work. The essential problem was to develop a thin membrane that would allow carbon dioxide, but not oxygen, to pass through. After much search and repeated failures, he solved that problem with a remarkably creative association leading him to bond two thin polymer films together. This success allowed Robb to win over enough admirers that he was able to form a team whose work led to the creation of a prototype showing that a hamster could breathe underwater when placed in a cage made of the new material. Their membrane was not yet good enough to purify air for people, however. Still they had reduced the uncertainty and risk associated with the initiative enough to attract continued sponsorship while they sought additional insights and further organized their business venture.

They benefited from new contributions from a stream of colleagues and acquaintances with nonobvious suggestions, many of whom were not involved in the work. These contributions led to additional creative ideas that advanced the quality of the membranes and attracted a widening circle of interested parties. The broader support and building success enabled the internal evaluators of the work to offer renewed funding that eventually resulted in a profitable new business venture.

Despite its initial appearance as yet another tale of triumph for a creative and relentless individual over vexing technical problems and skeptical naysayers, Walter Robb's story is even more interesting as an illustration of the dynamic interplay between creative associations and social support leading to opportunity recognition and new venture creation. As I describe in this chapter, *entrepreneurial opportunities*—defined as situations in which new products or services can be introduced through the formation of new means, ends, or means–ends relationships (Eckhardt & Shane, 2003)—are triggered by creative associations. *Creative associations* are defined here as combinations of knowledge or information that are both novel within a particular domain or setting and potentially valuable in some way (Ford, 1996). In entrepreneurship, creative associations often come in the form of fruitful product/technology—market combinations. For example, Walter

Robb associated characteristics of membranes with a potential market for recirculated oxygen. One entrepreneur I met associated the capabilities of a pressure-sensitive mat that serves as an electrical switch with the need for pets to let their owners know they would like to go indoors. The result was a pet doorbell—pets step on the doormat switch and ring the doorbell, thus alerting pet owners to their desire to enter the home. Creative associations may also link different technologies to create new functionality (e.g., associating a clock with a coffee pot provides the function of coffee brewed at a preset time), different organizing methods to create new business models (e.g., Dell's build to ship computer retailing model), among other possibilities. The point is that creative associations of existing knowledge form the basis for most innovations and new ventures (Hargadon & Sutton, 1997; see also Hargadon, chap. 10, this volume).

Here is a summary of the arguments I develop in this chapter. I follow Eckhardt and Shane (2003) in portraying creative associations as cognitive events (Mednick, 1962) that, therefore, must be viewed as an individual act. This does not deny the well-established impact of team members' (see Paulus, Nakui, & Putnam, chap. 4, this volume; Ancona & Bresman, chap. 9, this volume) or network ties' (Hargadon & Sutton, 1997) contributions to creative associations, of course. Rather, it views these factors as facilitating conditions that enhance individuals' capacity to associate knowledge in novel and valuable ways. Visions of a better future provoked by creative associations may raise an entrepreneur's aspirations (cf. March & Simon, 1958) and create heightened dissatisfaction with current performance and the status quo. Dissatisfaction resulting from the perceived gap between current performance and newly heightened aspirations motivates entrepreneurs to take risks (Shapira, 1995) and search for additional information necessary to refine and validate their creative insights (Greve, 2003). Problemistic search initially guides individuals to simple, easily accessed sources of information such as personal knowledge, the Internet, and close associates (Cyert & March, 1963). However, the complexities associated with articulating a new business venture are likely to necessitate search among new and weak network ties capable of spurring new creative associations and raising support for an entrepreneur's plans (Perry-Smith & Shalley, 2003). The additional knowledge acquired as a result of these interactions may incite new insights that affect the direction in which the new venture evolves, perhaps in unexpected ways. As the spiraling processes linking the refinement of the creative business concept to the development of a social network supporting the entrepreneur evolve (cf. Perry-Smith & Shalley, 2003), it is likely that important contributors with especially strong ties to the entrepreneur may join an entrepreneur's management team. This processes serves to incorporate diverse expertise necessary to fully articulate an entrepreneur's initial musings, and helps establish a creative coalition capable of providing the technical, marketing, financial, and administrative expertise necessary to keep the new venture concept moving forward.

Eventually, the iterative process between developing and refining creative associations and garnering social support for those ideas reaches a point of diminishing returns. At this point, a new venture concept may falter from lack of support or go forward as a new ends, means, or end–means combination capable of creating economic value. If a venture effectively addresses existing changes in consumer demand (e.g., growing demand for low-carbohydrate food products) or supplies products or services that are superior in design, quality, or price to consumers' current choices (e.g., Netflix home delivery of DVD rentals), it is likely to succeed as a consequence of addressing an existing market opportunity (Shane & Venkataraman, 2000). Highly creative venture proposals may instigate demand or supply changes, thus creating opportunities that would not have occurred absent an entrepreneur's initiative (e.g., there was no market or articulated need for sticky-back notes until consumers became aware of their existence). Although I believe all entrepreneurial opportunities emerge as a result of iterative creative and social dynamics just described, I focus a bit more attention on the special case of created opportunities that could be described as self-fulfilling prophecies resulting from entrepreneurial enactment (Weick, 1979). Unlike prototypical stories like Robb's, where an existing need may be readily apparent to those who happen to possess the right combination of knowledge, opportunity creation is a process that is based on a "build it and they will come" faith that poses the most extreme forms of uncertainty and risk on an entrepreneur. The quotes presented from Ford, Walton, and Dell all suggest that their visions were not based on widely available knowledge or beliefs, but instead were justified by their unshakable faith in the efficacy of their own creative visions. These men enacted their visions, implanting their ideas in markets and industries (cf. Weick, 1979) and, in doing so, created and exploited changes in demand and supply characteristics that transformed countless businesses. The remainder of this chapter elaborates the premises just presented in the form of research propositions that may help direct and motivate future entrepreneurship research on opportunity recognition, creation, and exploitation processes.

AN EVOLUTIONARY VIEW OF CREATIVITY AND ENTREPRENEURSHIP

One well-developed theoretical approach to modeling dynamic, iterative change processes is evolution theory. Consequently, it serves as a useful organizing heuristic for the arguments I have presented. Campbell (1960) is generally credited with applying evolution theory to individual creativity research in his influential description of blind variation and selective retention processes. Other creativity researchers have further developed and empirically explored the premises of this approach (e.g., Csiksentmihalyi, 1990; Gardner, 1993; Simonton, 1999), leading Simonton (1999) to argue that an evolutionary view may serve as a useful heuristic for understanding all creativity and change processes. Given this endorsement, perhaps it is not surprising to note that other prominent theories of organizing (e.g., Weick, 1979) and entrepreneurship (e.g., Aldrich & Kenworthy, 1998) have been based on Campbell's proposals. I recently proposed an evolutionary theory of individual creativity in organizational settings that describes how intentional actions influence and are influenced by evolutionary change processes in social contexts (see Ford, 1996). In short, this theory describes how interactions among actors (the source of variations), fields (stakeholders who affect the structure of a domain), and domains (customary practices, etc. that characterize a recognized area of action) produce and select creative actions. I believe this view is useful because it describes how ideas, actors, and context co-evolve as a consequence of creative action (Lewin, Long, & Carroll, 1999). Perry-Smith and Shalley (2003) presented a model based on evolutionary reasoning to describe spiraling processes that lead creative ideas and social networks to co-evolve. Drazen, Glynn, and Kazanjian (1999) also emphasized the dynamic, iterative nature of creative ventures by noting the shifting focus between administrative and technical challenges requiring creativity during the evolution of projects.

Depicting variation and selective retention processes at work among actors, fields, and domains is useful in the context of entrepreneurship research for several reasons. First, it is essential to distinguish between variation and selective retention processes. As Campbell (1960) and Weick (1979) both emphasized, variation and selective retention processes are inherently antagonistic. Creative ventures are disruptive to current practices, standards, and preferences, and the status quo often prevents creative ventures from gaining support. Thus, it is not surprising that variation and selective retention processes may be loosely coupled in the context of entrepreneurship. For instance, creative products or services often fare poorly relative to familiar offerings that conform to technological standards and consumer expectations (Aldrich & Fiol, 1994). In many markets, follow-the-leader strategies that conform to previously retained practices and norms are more successful, on average, than strategies that defy the conventional wisdom in an industry (Winter & Szulanski, 2001). Creative initiatives also run into problems of legitimacy in large firms (Dougherty & Heller, 1994). The loose coupling of variation and selective retention processes noted in prior organizational creativity research (e.g., Ford & Gioia, 2000) can be better understood using an evolutionary perspective.

Second, an evolutionary view emphasizes how processes relate to each other over time. It was this property of evolutionary reasoning that led Weick (1979) to advocate verbs as preferable to nouns in organizational theorizing. Entrepreneurship research has been criticized for its emphasis on static theorizing and cross-sectional research designs that fail to clarify processes related to developing variations, organizing new ventures, and exploiting markets (Eckhardt & Shane, 2003). Adopting an evolutionary view may help remedy this difficulty. Third, evolutionary concepts facilitate multilevel theorizing, wherein variations created at one level are intro-duced to selective retention processes at the next level, and so on (cf. Ford, 1996). I believe this is an important property with respect to entrepreneur-ship because of the need to describe how creative processes within entre-preneurs lead to team and venture formation, and ultimately to economic consequences in markets and industries. An evolutionary view allows one to build theories about how individual dispositions and interpretations are ex-pressed in social networks, and how patterns of social interaction at various levels of analysis impact creative outcomes (Perry-Smith & Shalley, 2003; Weick, 1979). Because entrepreneurship theory and research is broadly ori-ented toward explaining the creation of new business initiatives (Shane & Venkataraman, 2000), I believe the domain can benefit from developing dynamic, multi-level theories that explicitly recognize the inherent tensions between variation and selective retention processes (Aldrich & Kenworthy, 1998).

As I already foreshadowed, I seek to describe how creative associations (variations) motivate search processes that engage social networks and team members, ultimately leading to creative actions capable of instigating changes in demand-and-supply characteristics in the marketplace. The propositions offered herein are derived from an evolutionary view, and they provide a description of opportunity creation processes that reflects the dynamic, iterative, social processes necessary to enact creative new ven-tures. These propositions are represented graphically in Fig. 11.1.

A MODEL OF CREATIVE ASSOCIATIONS
AND ENTREPRENEURIAL OPPORTUNITIES

Creative Associations Lead to Performance—
Aspiration Level Gaps

Creative associations of existing knowledge, often embodied in tangible ob-jects and technology, provide unique insights to individuals and trigger the evolutionary processes described previously, leading to creative action and opportunity creation. Cognitive perspectives on creativity have long noted

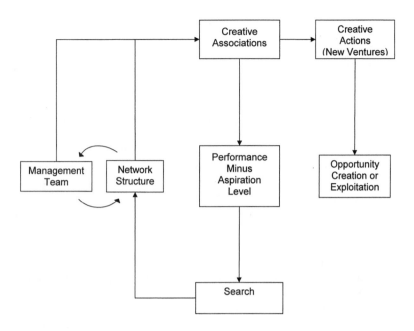

FIG. 11.1.   A model of creative associations and entrepreneurial opportunities.

the central role of associationistic processes and analogical thinking to the production of creative outcomes (Mednick, 1962; Ward, 1995). Evolutionary theory is similarly based on existing forms blending to form variations that alter both species and environments. Recent innovation and entrepreneurship research has also depicted creative business outcomes, or innovations, as the result of associations between previously retained forms of knowledge and technology (Hargadon & Sutton, 1997; Shane, 2000). This notion was captured by Thomas Edison (cited in Hargadon & Sutton, 2000), who noted that, "To invent, you need a good imagination and a pile of junk" (p. 160).

Creative associations result from generative cognitive processes that include retrieving information from memory and forming combinations, transformations, or analogies from those recollections (Ward, Smith, & Finke, 1999). Original and promising associations motivate extensive exploration of those ideas (Ward, Smith, & Finke, 1999). In the context of entrepreneurship, the initial generation of creative associations can motivate entrepreneurial exploration by producing information asymmetries—knowledge known to some but not others—capable of creating economic value. Information asymmetries such as these are the foundation of the Austrian perspective on entrepreneurship (Hayek, 1945; described by

Shane, 2000). This perspective argues that opportunities exist when all people do not possess the same information at the same time (a disequilibrium condition). The Austrian perspective states that entrepreneurs may obtain resources below their equilibrium market price because others do not recognize the value of recombining them in a creative way. Because each potential entrepreneur's experiences, resources, and social networks are unique, creative associations made by one entrepreneur are unlikely to be discovered by others possessing different knowledge, resources, and associations. When potential entrepreneurs believe they possess a creative idea not known to others, they may envision ways in which their proprietary, creative knowledge could lead to a successful business enterprise. Aspirations (the level or quality of desired consequences that organize individual motivation and decision making) are especially likely to increase when a potential entrepreneur imagines a venture's profits to be both large and sustainable (Shane, 2000).

The Austrian perspective is important because it recognizes entrepreneurs as creative actors capable of creating unique, potentially valuable knowledge unavailable to others. Entrepreneurs' beliefs regarding the efficacy and economic value of their creative associations can affect their aspirations relative to their current circumstances. Thus, I expect *creative associations*, defined previously as characterized by both novelty and perceived value within a particular setting, to lead to heightened aspirations relative to perceptions of current circumstances or performance. This expectation leads to the following research proposition:

Proposition 1: Creative insights that suggest enhanced future states will increase entrepreneurs' aspiration levels.

Performance—Aspiration Level Gaps Motivate Search

Cyert and March (1963) noted that decision makers are motivated to search for innovative solutions when current performance is no longer adequate. Decision makers imagine potential gains and losses related to various courses of action and assess the gap between their current performance and their aspirations. Gaps between performance and aspiration levels motivate search (Greve, 2003) and risk-taking behavior aimed at assessing and enacting the "domain of opportunities" (Shapira, 1995). Greve (2003) examined the proposed influence of "performance minus aspiration level" gaps on search, R&D, and innovation in the shipbuilding industry. He found that performance minus aspiration level gaps had a substantial impact on search and innovation (performance below aspirations had a mild positive relationship to innovation; performance above aspirations had a strong negative relationship to innovation). Greve's findings led him to conclude that performance minus aspiration level gaps is an important trigger for search and creative action. Consequently, he strongly advocates examining decision-making processes (i.e., aspiration levels, search, risk tolerance, etc.) related to innovation launch decisions as a means to better understand differences between firms' propensity to innovate.

The decision-making approach advocated by Greve provides valuable insights that can enrich our understanding of processes that affect the interplay between variation and selective retention processes in entrepreneurship. The variable performance minus aspiration level represents a dynamic relationship between an individual or firm's current situation and envisioned options. As a result, it may provide a better explanation for entrepreneurial search and new venture creation than static representations of individual differences examined in prior entrepreneurship research (Shane, 2000). In summary, I propose that creative associations lead to increased aspiration levels that motivate subsequent search. This leads me to propose the following research proposition:

Proposition 2: Increased aspiration levels, controlling for current performance, will increase entrepreneurs' search activities.

Search Creates and Strengthens Network Structure

Even those entrepreneurs fortunate enough to develop a genuinely valuable, creative association still have a lot of work to do. Analogous to joining two strands of DNA, an entrepreneur's initial creative association is likely to require sustained nourishment and development if it is to result in the birth of a healthy new venture. Consequently, search processes, especially those that involve the creation and development of social networks and a new venture management team, are critical to the new venture creation process (Bhave, 1994; Singh, Hills, Hybels, & Lumpkin, 1999). Search processes tend to be local and biased (Cyert & March, 1963), thus favoring currently possessed knowledge and existing network ties. Creative associations may thwart these tendencies, however, because it may be quickly apparent that easily accessible knowledge is less relevant to creative proposals. Networking efforts are likely to be highly instrumental—network contacts will be sought strategically to allay sources of uncertainty that are particularly troublesome. Thus, it is not surprising that solo entrepreneurs who rely primarily on their own knowledge for novel associations are limited in their ability to recognize or create opportunities (Shane, 2000). Alternatively, network entrepreneurs tend to create more opportunities because of their access to nonredundant knowledge and their exposure to serendipitous associations that characterize many business initiatives (Aldrich & Kenworthy, 1998).

Drazen et al. (1999) suggested that it may take a major discontinuity or crisis to provoke decision makers to go beyond prevailing sources of knowledge in a task domain. Perhaps entrepreneurs' creative associations, and the heightened aspirations they inspire, can create such a crisis—one of imagining a future that is more desirable than the present—sufficient to motivate search among weak and new network ties. Less familiar ties such as these are thought to have a strong contributing effect on subsequent creativity (Perry-Smith & Shalley, 2003). However, a creative association capable of engaging the interests of others may be a prerequisite to productive networking of this nature. In other words, a creative idea may attract network ties, and network ties may contribute to further creativity. Thus, as discussed previously, creative proposals and social networks co-evolve over time in a spiraling manner that leads proposals and networks to become more highly organized over time (Perry-Smith & Shalley, 2003).

Based on this reasoning, the journey between an initial creative association and the launch of a new venture can be described as an evolving negotiation process among an entrepreneur/founder, a management team, and critical stakeholders whose support is necessary to the venture's survival (see Fig. 11.1). Schrage (2000) described negotiation processes like these as characterized by "the tyranny of tradeoffs." The currency of these types of negotiation processes is an exchange between solution attributes and stakeholder support. In the beginning of the negotiation process, the creative idea is typically broad and relatively abstract; over time creative contributions become more highly developed as stakeholder inputs and interests are considered and incorporated. At the end of the journey stands a creative proposition endorsed by those who shepherded the idea along. This process can cause great ideas to be corrupted or diluted by stakeholders weighed down by convention, but the journey can also lead to new creative associations that magnify the creativity of the instigating proposal. I have sought to represent the evolutionary nature of these processes in Fig. 11.1 by depicting the relationships among creative associations, performance—aspiration level gaps, search, and network development as a cycle interrupted only when a decision is made to launch a new venture. This description leads to the following proposition:

Proposition 3: Increased search will be associated with increased numbers of network ties.

Strong Network Ties Promote Management Team Formation

Networking processes tend to evolve in a manner where ties become stronger over time (Perry-Smith & Shalley, 2003). New ventures typically include not only the original entrepreneur or founder, but a team of specialized contributors who form the top management team. Those individuals who join a founder's top management team must have great faith in the founder's vision and great trust in the founder's character to justify enlisting in a risky endeavor. Consequently, one would expect the top management team to be drawn from strong ties that predate an entrepreneur's initial creative association or developed during the networking process that refined the new venture concept.

The diversity of knowledge represented in the team is an important issue, as is the case in many creative efforts. In the context of entrepreneurship, there are four areas of domain-specific knowledge (Amabile, 1988) that seem especially critical to creative business venture performance and innovation. In business domains, knowledge tends to be segmented into four broad, interdependent, institutionally reinforced process domains (cf. resource-based view; Verona, 1999): product/production, marketing/sales, management/administration, and finance. As a practical matter, it is especially important that a new venture's top management team provide comprehensive representation of these key knowledge domains. Descriptions of these four generic functional areas are required in all formal business plans.

Assessments of creative venture proposals typically include reference to product/technology (does it work?), market (does it help?), organizational (can we do it? better than others?), and financial (can we profit?) dimensions. These four knowledge domains interact as sources of uncertainty affecting the valuation of novel proposals (Leifer, McDermott, O'Connor, Peters, Rice, & Veryzer, 2000). Unfortunately, due to a variety of institutional and organizational processes related to education, training, departmentalization, professional identification, and the like, knowledge of these four domains tends to be held by different people working in different places using different processes to enact different preferences (cf. Drazen, Glynn, & Kazanjian, 1999). Consequently, limitations in the functional comprehensiveness (extent to which relevant knowledge from all four functions are represented) of founder and management team knowledge restrict the range of creative associations that might manifest themselves in a new venture. When these knowledge domains are joined, however, creativity and opportunity recognition processes may be "ignited" to get others excited about implementing the new venture. The preceding arguments suggest that the structure *and* content of an entrepreneur's social/knowledge networks will influence the people and ideas that comprise a new venture. These expectations lead to the following related propositions:

Proposition 4: The number and strength of an entrepreneur's network ties will be positively associated with the formation of a management team.

Proposition 5: The function comprehensiveness of a management teams will positively affect creative associations developed by the team.

Creative Associations Promote Creative Action
(New Venture Formation)

The creative associations used to organize a new venture need to remain differentiated (creative) enough to create economic value, but conform enough to be viewed as legitimate by those whose support is required (Levitt & Nass, 1989). Well-developed and clearly differentiated entrepreneurial ventures backed by a credible management team and supportive stakeholders reduce uncertainty associated with the venture. Reduced uncertainty implies lower risk for those whose fates are likely to be affected by a decision to launch a venture. Thus, to the extent that iterations of search, networking, team building, and creative problem solving lead to a more compelling, comprehensive business proposal, new venture launch decisions will become increasingly more likely over time. Furthermore, new ventures initiated by creative associations that engage weak ties and functionally diverse team members are especially likely to evolve into highly creative proposals. Alternatively, new ventures initiated by widely diffused knowledge and developed primarily by a lone entrepreneur are likely to be less creative relative to other firms in an industry or market. Thus, following the rather straightforward logic that decision-making outcomes (new ventures) are a function of decision-making inputs (creative associations) leads me to offer the following proposition:

Proposition 6: Creative associations offered during the new venture formation process will be positively associated with the creativity of a new venture.

Creative Venture Launches Promote Opportunity Creation
(Supply or Demand Changes)

It is interesting to consider the locus of opportunities. Prior research on opportunities examines processes through which entrepreneurs gain knowledge regarding existing trends in supply and demand characteristics that affect particular markets (cf. the Austrian perspective; Shane, 2000). However, I believe it is useful to distinguish between processes best labeled as *opportunity recognition* and *opportunity creation* by considering the degree of knowledge diffusion related to each. In the case of opportunity recognition, knowledge regarding existing trends and changes is likely to be widespread. Therefore, one should expect simultaneous discovery of creative associations involving widely available knowledge to be widespread. This suggests that many competitors may race to implement their (similar) new venture proposals in hopes of beating the competition to the marketplace.

At the other extreme, knowledge may be held or created idiosyncratically by a single entrepreneur. Creative associations can provide a nascent entrepreneur with unique knowledge unknown to others. Entrepreneurial processes characterized by high degrees of creativity must proceed on the basis of an entrepreneur's vision of the future because characteristics of future demand in markets that do not yet exist are inherently unknowable (Eckhardt & Shane, 2003). Of course selective retention processes in business environments are often unkind to creative new ventures (Aldrich & Fiol, 1994). Perhaps it is not surprising, then, that highly creative knowledge often emerges from universities and other public agencies isolated from the selective retention processes of the marketplace. Given the lack of credible information available to articulate and justify highly creative new venture propositions, entrepreneurs are likely to have a more pronounced impact on new venture formation processes as the creativity of the proposal increases. Thus, entrepreneurs can either capitalize on well-established and understood market supply and demand characteristics, or they can enact a new venture that would be difficult to justify with existing information in hopes that the venture could instigate favorable changes in supply or demand characteristics.

To some degree, all businesses need to offer creative or unique characteristics to consumers (even if the characteristic is simply a unique location—i.e., a dry cleaner). Michael Porter (1996) articulated this perspective concisely when he argued that, "Competitive strategy is about being different. It means deliberately choosing a different set of activities to deliver a unique mix of value" (p. 64). Entrepreneurs play a unique role in creating changes in markets because they are more likely than existing firms to initiate radical, important, and sustainable new ventures (Shane, 2000). Highly creative or radical new ventures are difficult for established firms to pursue because they often lack legitimacy (Dougherty & Heller, 1994) and violate commitments to the established network of resource providers the firm has established through its prior efforts (cf. Christensen, 1997). Thus, in cases where knowledge is not widely diffused (i.e., the venture proposal is especially creative relative to current norms, practices, and preferences), entrepreneurs often enact ventures that instigate changes to markets and industries. The processes that distinguish opportunity recognition from opportunity creation lead to my final proposition:

Proposition 7: Highly creative business ventures are more likely to *instigate* supply and demand changes (opportunities) favoring venture success than ventures based on widely held knowledge.

The preceding theoretical arguments, also portrayed in Fig. 11.1, can be summarized as follows. Entrepreneurial opportunities are situations in which new products or services can be introduced through the formation of new means, ends, or means–ends relationships. Consequently, unlike optimizing or satisficing decisions, entrepreneurial decisions require creativity (Ekhardt & Shane, 2003). Unfortunately, relatively little theoretical or empirical work has examined how creativity influences the recognition, creation, or exploitation of opportunities (Shook, Priem, & McGee, 2003). I employed a Cambellian evolutionary view of creativity and entrepreneurship (Aldrich & Kenworthy, 1998; Campbell, 1960; Ford, 1996; Simonton, 1999; Weick, 1979) as a heuristic to describe how an individual entrepreneur's creative associations can reveal attractive potential future states that motivate search, networking, and team formation processes. I proposed that a promising creative association helps an entrepreneur attract network ties and management team members, and that these relationships may result in new associations and refinements that add value to the entrepreneur's original proposal. In this manner, creativity instigates organizing and organizing instigates subsequent creativity in a spiraling (cf. Perry-Smith & Shalley, 2003), cyclical, evolutionary manner (Ford, 1996). When these processes are sustained and coalesce into a new venture capable of enacting a specific domain or market niche, an entrepreneur's initiative may become a successful self-fulfilling prophesy (Weick, 1979) that "creates" an opportunity by instigating changes in market demand or supply characteristics that would not have existed absent an entrepreneur's actions.

Implications of a Dynamic View of Opportunity Creation

Although prior research suggests that entrepreneurs who present highly creative variations face significant obstacles, the quotes I used to introduce this chapter offer some encouragement. Highly creative ventures that instigate changes to markets and industries offer unique opportunities for those who lead the way, and they may serve as a catalyst for change and growth (Greve & Taylor, 2000) that pave the way for a broad range of positive consequences. For example, at the firm level, Levinthal and March (1993) contended that creative strategic actions are necessary for a business to rise above the competition and achieve preeminence. Others have cited creative actions as primary contributors to the continual evolution and well-being of an industry (Huff, Huff, & Thomas, 1992). In general, strategic variety promotes industry performance, and individual firms benefit from participating in industries characterized by diverse, creative competitive strategies (Barnett & Hansen, 1996; Lewin, Long, & Carroll, 1999; Miles, Snow & Sharfman, 1993). Findings such as these underscore the potential importance of creativity to entrepreneurship and strategy research, and they support Chakravarthy and Doz's (1992) conclusion that describing the process through which organizations renew themselves is the principle challenge facing strategy researchers.

Recent efforts to define the domain of entrepreneurship research argue that it can be distinguished from other domains of behavioral and business strategy research by emphasizing the nexus between enterprising individuals and valuable opportunities (Venkataraman, 1997). Consequently, opportunities should play a central role in any framework of entrepreneurship (Eckhardt & Shane, 2003). Until recently, dominant theories of entrepreneurship largely overlooked the role of opportunities. These theories tended to describe individual differences characterizing those who are more likely to recognize opportunities or launch new ventures, or market/industry characteristics associated with emerging or unmet market demands. Unfortunately, neither of these approaches adequately captures the dynamic processes associated with the creation, recognition, or exploitation of entrepreneurial opportunities (Eckhardt & Shane, 2003).

The primary contribution offered by integrating insights from creativity, social network, and entrepreneurship research is present opportunities as both responses to changing supply and demand characteristics *and* as creative initiatives capable of instigating changes (i.e., create opportunities). This contribution suggests an important avenue for integrating insights from prior organizational creativity research into the domain of entrepreneurship and new venture creation. The processes through which opportunities emerge and evolve are not well understood (Shane & Venkatraman, 2000). Relatively mature proposals from the creativity literature may serve to advance our understanding of this critical and pervasive process. Thinking of opportunities as something one creates rather than recognizes or discovers subtly reframes their causal locus. Opportunities are presented here as something that a particular person is uniquely able to cultivate, perhaps slowly and unevenly, over time, rather than as something that one stumbles over that is equally available for others to discover. This depiction may enable researchers to better articulate how individual-level characteristics and processes interact with instrumental social activities to create knowledge advantages capable of justifying new business ventures.

I also wanted to contribute to the opportunity recognition literature by speculating about the importance of functionally diverse knowledge to the new venture creation process. To comprehensively articulate the economic value associated with a novel business proposal, one needs to fully articulate the technological, market, organizational, and financial aspects of the proposition. These are the fundamental components of any business plan. As these four primary sources of uncertainty interact, new associations, conundrums, paradoxes, and predicaments are likely to arise (Leifer et al.,

2000). This sharply interactive and unpredictable process favors those who are alert to opportunities and open to exploring the implications of serendipitous associations and events. The need for comprehensive knowledge representation may be one reason that the quality of a management team is often more important than the quality of venture proposal in terms of attracting funding. Funding agents seem to think that a strong, comprehensive foundation of knowledge will create a profitable opportunity eventually. Alternatively, incomplete intellectual capital portends of greater uncertainties that magnify risks associated with a creative venture.

In summary, the model presented here offers initial proposals regarding opportunity creation and exploitation that result from creative associations. New knowledge reflected in a creative association is information that may be known only by an entrepreneur at first. Economic approaches to entrepreneurship research describe conditions wherein one party knows something that others do not as representing information asymmetry. When information asymmetries exist, those who possess unique knowledge may create or claim economic value necessary to justify a new business venture. The value-generating potential of a creative association is likely to be underspecified and uncertain at first. However, if an initial generated insight is deemed worthy of further exploration and development, then problemistic search will ensue. Search will be strategically directed to address knowledge gaps pertaining to four loosely coupled business knowledge domains—product/production, marketing, managing, and financing. Search is likely to be local and biased (cf. Cyert & March, 1963), engaging networks in which the creator(s) already participate. However, novel associations and comprehensive value articulation is facilitated by nonredundant knowledge held by weak ties (Perry-Smith & Shalley, 2003). Creative associations emerging from these social exchanges serve to improve and differentiate new venture proposals, and they strengthen ties among those most interested in the venture. When this interest coalesces into the formation of a management team, the founder and team can consider launching the new venture within a specific market domain.

I have argued that venture proposals based on widely diffused knowledge may capitalize on existing trends. Ventures based on recognizing opportunities are likely to present lower potential due to the presence of competition, but they also portend lower risks because market characteristics and trends are well understood. Highly creative new ventures have the potential to command dominant positions in newly created, emerging markets, but they also face daunting levels of uncertainty and risk. Entrepreneurs play a unique role to inciting markets and industries with new insights. I hope others will take the opportunity to contribute their efforts to the emerging field of entrepreneurial opportunity research.

REFERENCES

Aldrich, H. E., & Fiol, C. M. (1994). Fools rush in? The institutional context of industry creation. *Academy of Management Review, 19*, 645–670.

Aldrich, H. E., & Kenworthy, A. (1998). The accidental entrepreneur: Campbellian antinomies and organizational foundings. In J. A. C. Baum & B. McKelvey (Eds.), *Variations in organization science: In honor of Donald T. Campbell* (pp. 19–33). Newbury Park, CA: Sage.

Amabile, T. M. (1988). A model of creativity and innovation in organizations. *Research in Organizational Behavior, 10*, 123–167.

Barnett, W. P., & Hansen, M. T. (1996). The red queen in organizational evolution. *Strategic Management Journal, 17*, 139–157.

Bhave, M. P. (1994). A process model of entrepreneurial venture creation. *Journal of Business Venturing, 9*(3), 223–246.

Campbell, D. T. (1960). Blind variation and selective retention in creative thought as in other knowledge processes. *Psychological Review, 67*, 380–400.

Chakravarthy, B. S., & Doz, Y. (1992). Strategy process research: Focusing on corporate self-renewal. *Strategic Management Journal, 13*(5), 5–16.

Christensen, C. M. (1997). *The innovator's dilemma: When new technologies cause great firms to fail.* Boston, MA: Harvard Business School Press.

Csikszentmihalyi, M. (1990). The domain of creativity. In M. A. Runco & R. S. Albert (Eds.), *Theories of creativity* (pp. 190–212). Newbury Park, CA: Sage.

Cyert, R. M., & March, J. G. (1963). *A behavioral theory of the firm.* Englewood Cliffs, NJ: Prentice-Hall.

Dougherty, D., & Heller, T. (1994). The illegitimacy of successful product innovation in established firms. *Organization Science, 5*, 200–218.

Drazen, R., Glynn, M. A., & Kazanjian, R. K. (1999). Multilevel theorizing about creativity in organizations: A sensemaking perspective. *Academy of Management Review, 24*, 286–307.

Eckhardt, J. T., & Shane, S. A. (2003). Opportunities and entrepreneurship. *Journal of Management, 29*(3), 333–349.

Ford, C. M. (1996). A theory of individual creative action in multiple social domains. *Academy of Management Review, 21*, 1112–1142.

Ford, C. M., & Gioia, D. A. (2000). Factors influencing creativity in the domain of managerial decision making. *Journal of Management, 26*, 705–732.

Gardner, H. (1993). *Creating minds: An anatomy of creativity seen through the lives of Freud, Einstein, Picasso, Stravinsky, Eliot, Graham and Ghandi.* New York: Basic Books.

Greve, H. R. (2003). A behavioral theory of R&D expenditures and innovations: Evidence from shipbuilding. *The Academy of Management Journal, 46*(6), 685–703.

Greve, H. R., & Taylor, A. (2000). Innovations as catalysts for organizational change: Shifts in organizational cognition and search. *Administrative Science Quarterly, 45*, 54–80.

Hargadon, A. B., & Sutton, R. I. (1997). Technology brokering and innovation in a product development firm. *Science Quarterly, 42*, 716–749.

Hargadon, A. B., & Sutton, R. I. (2000, May–June). Building an innovation factory. *Harvard Business Review*, pp. 157–166.

Huff, J. O., Huff, A. S., & Thomas, H. (1992). Strategic renewal and the interaction of cumulative stress and inertia. *Strategic Management Journal, 13*(5), 55–81.

Leifer, R., McDermott, C. M., O'Connor, G. C., Peters, L. S., Rice, M., & Veryzer, R. W. (2000). *Radical innovation: How mature companies can outsmart upstarts.* Boston, MA: Harvard Business School Press.

Levinthal, D. A., & March, J. G. (1993). The myopia of learning [Special Issue]. *Strategic Management Journal, 14*, 95–112.

Levitt, B., & Nass, C. (1989). The lid on the garbage can: Institutional constraints on decision-making in the technical core of college-text publishers. *Administrative Science Quarterly, 34,* 190–207.

Lewin, A. Y., Long, C. P., & Carroll, T. N. (1999). The co-evolution of new organizational forms. *Organization Science, 10,* 535–550.

March, J. G., & Simon, H. A. (1958). *Organizations.* New York: Wiley.

Mednick, S. (1962). The associative basis of the creative process. *Psychological Review, 69,* 220–232.

Miles, G., Snow, C. C., & Sharfman, M. P. (1993). Industry variety and performance. *Strategic Management Journal, 14*(3), 163–177.

Perry-Smith, J. E., & Shalley, C. E. (2003). The social side of creativity: A static and dynamic social network perspective. *Academy of Management Journal, 29*(1), 89–106.

Porter, M. E. (1996, Nov.–Dec.). What is strategy? *Harvard Business Review,* pp. 61–79.

Schrage, M. (2000). *Serious play: How the world's best companies simulate to innovate.* Cambridge, MA: Harvard Business School Press.

Shane, S. (2000). Prior knowledge and the discovery of entrepreneurial opportunities. *Organization Science, 11*(4), 448–469.

Shane, S., & Venkataraman, S. (2000). The promise of entrepreneurship as a field of research. *Academy of Management Review, 25,* 217–226.

Shapira, Z. (1995). *Risk taking: A managerial perspective.* New York: Russell Sage Foundation.

Shook, C. L., Priem, R. L., & McGee, J. E. (2003). Venture creation and the enterprising individual: A review and synthesis. *Journal of Management, 29*(3), 379–400.

Simonton, D. K. (1999). Creativity as blind variation and selective retention: Is the creative process Darwinian? *Psychological Inquiry, 10*(4), 309–328.

Singh, R. P., Hills, G. E., Hybels, R. C., & Lumpkin, G. T. (1999). Opportunity recognition through social network characteristics of entrepreneurs. In P. D. Reynolds (Ed.), *Frontiers of entrepreneurship research* (pp. 228–241). Wellesley, MA: Babson College.

Venkataraman, S. (1997). The distinctive domain of entrepreneurship research: An editor's perspective. *Advances in Entrepreneurship, Firm Emergence and Growth, 3,* 119–138.

Verona, G. (1999). A resource-based view of product development. *Academy of Management Review, 24*(1), 132–142.

Ward, T. B. (1995). *The creative cognition approach.* Cambridge, MA: MIT Press.

Ward, T. B., Smith, S. M., & Finke, R. A. (1999). Creative cognition. In R. J. Sternberg (Ed.), *Handbook of creativity* (pp. 189–212). New York: Cambridge University Press.

Weick, K. E. (1979). *The social psychology of organizing.* Reading, MA: Addison-Wesley.

Winter, S. G., & Szulanski, G. (2001). Replication as strategy. *Organization Science, 12*(6), 730–744.

Author Index

235

240

W

Waber, B., *381*
Ward, L., 318, *381*
Warner, G., 96, *381*
Warner Brothers Studio, *381*
Wattenberg, W., 340, 341, *379*
Weaver, C., 152, *381*
Wells, D., 124, 131, *372*
Wells, G., 264, *381*
Wells, R., 246, 310, *382*
West, T., 90, *382*
Westall, R., 69, *382*
Western Regional Environmental Education Council, 35, *382*
White, E. B., 3, 11, 21, 39, 202, *382*
Whitman, P., 22, *370*
Wigfield, A., 54, *382*
Wilder, L., 24, 25, 27, 98, *382*
Wilkinson, I., 55, 73, *369*

Wilson, P., 74, *372*
Winograd, P., 149, *382*
Winship, M., 296, *382*
Witman, P., 22, *370*

Y

Yaden, D., 226, *381*
Yep, L., 256, *382*
Yolen, J., 86, 169, 288, *382*
Young, E., 318, *382*

Z

Zelinsky, P., 55, *378*
Zemelman, S., 79, 105, *382*
Zhensun, Z., 324, *382*
Zimmerman, B., 237, 264, *382*

Subject Index

Audience
  author's chair in writer's workshop, 217
  brochures on military base closings, 279
  Friday Afternoon Sharing Time experi-
    ences, 261
  individual reading conferences, 165
  interests and reading aloud, 47–48
  listening/speaking activities, 256–257
  puppet theater, 252, 253
  sense
    mini-lessons, 143–144
    teacher forms/guidelines, 363
  writing to create meaning, 199
Audio stimuli, 6
Australia, 353
Australian Children's Book of the Year
    Award, 353
Author's chair, 203–205, 216
Authors, 6, 142
Autobiographies, 80, 81
Autonomy, increasing, 172
Autumn Street, 81
Awards, 350–353

B

Babe the Gallant Pig, 201–202
Babysitter Club, The, 97
Background building, 22
Bare Bear Facts, The, 286
Basal reading program, 150, 181
Basal textbooks, 128–129, *see also* Text-
    books
Bear theme unit, 286–287
Bear's House, The, 317
Bearstone, 142, 143
Because of Winn Dixie, 87
Before We Were Free, 351
Behavior, disruptive, 340, 344
Benet's Reader's Encyclopedia, 167
Best bets review, 67–68
Best Books for Children, 65, 132
Best Practices, 79–80, 105
Bibliography, 61
*Big Book of Picture-Book Authors & Illustra-
    tors, The*, 184
Big Books, *see also* Picture books; Wordless
    books
  kindergarten
    guided reading, 107–111, 119, 123–124

  language/literature learning, 9
  preparation of literature base, 85
Big Mama Makes the World, 351
Binders, three-ring, 208
Biographical writing, 358
Biographies
  importance of expression through art,
    324
  language/literature learning, 18
  preparation of literature base, 88–89
  research about literature in content ar-
    eas, 306
  writing to create meaning, 197, 201
Birthdays, 4
Black Beauty, 96
Blitzcat, 69
Blueberries for Sal, 286
Bobbsey Twins, The, 96
Bonding, teacher–student, 181, *see also*
    Reading conferences
Book Buddy program
  guided reading, 114, 127
  independent reading, 60, 62
  individual reading conferences, 166, 179
  listening/speaking activities, 244, 252
  partnership building and reading aloud,
    52
Book clubs, 82–83, 94–95, 97
Book format, 121, *see also* Guided reading
Book Links, 65
Book previews, 245–246, 276
Book selection literature, 346–349
Book talks, 68
Booklist, 348
Bookmarks, 11, 59, 117
Books
  high-quality and literature evaluation, 98
  independent reading, 60, 67
  literature base preparation, 84–91
  reading aloud, 45
  theme activities, 292
  writing to create meaning, 198, 201
Books on tape/CD, 122
Bookstores, 324
Borrower books, 237
Borrowers, The, 237
Boston Globe–Horn Book Awards for Ex-
    cellence in Children's Literature,
    350–351
Boston Jane Series, 246
Boxcar Children, The, 96
Brain, 37

N

254